MO Publishing.

Life in the Faz Lane

by Michael O'Rourke

Cover and graphics by **2cheeseburgers**

©**2cheeseburgers 2018**

* * * *

Also by Michael O'Rourke:

Black Eyes and Blue Blood - The Amazing Life and Times of Gangster Norman 'Scouse' Johnson.

Arguably the most unusual gangster story ever told... *Black Eyes and Blue Blood* combines violence and humour with an exotic twist of romance. It also offers a fascinating insight into the underworld on both sides of the Atlantic as Johnson mixed with some of the world's best-known gangsters, sportsmen and showbiz personalities....

Mainstream Publishing, 2008.

Contents

LIFE IN THE FAZ LANE

by Michael O'Rourke

Keep silent unless what you are going to say is more important than silence.

Salvator Rosa

Italian painter, poet, printmaker.

(1615 – 1673)

Foreword

It would be churlish of me to say I was born too early, but as a son of the 1950s, I just missed out on the big pay days. Stan Bowles, Frank Worthington and Alan Hudson are others that spring to mind as players that would earn multi-millions in today's game. We still had tremendous fun and camaraderie back then and I can confirm that most of us would have played for nothing, unlike a lot of the modern mercenaries. But good luck to them, far from being bitter, I count myself as blessed.

The old right knee decided to call time when I was only 27. I'd earned less in my career than most top professional footballers bank in a month, but the memories can never be erased. Glory days for Ipswich Town and my beloved England are forever etched into my psyche. It's still an absolute pleasure to sign autographs or have a 'selfie' taken with the fans. Thankfully they never forget.

After the phone stopped ringing with offers or opportunities, Faisal Madani gave me work and friendship beyond the call of duty. I'll always be grateful to him, a real footballers' man, a lifelong friend and definitely one of the good guys. I wish him all the luck in the world with his amazing new book - *Life In The Faz Lane* - a story of hope for all the lovers of our great game.

Kevin Beattie
England defender and superstar.

INTRODUCTION

LIFE IN THE FAZ LANE

Madani is the name - Faisal Madani.

To my friends, I'm known as Faz. Business associates who need something call me *Mr. Fix-it.* Conceived in the Middle East, but hand-reared and educated in England, I've experienced the diversity of three continents: Asia, North America and Europe, settling up as an Anglophile, brought up on the finest British traditions, sport and heritage. I am proud to reside here, not only is it a hell of a country, but it's the place I contentedly call home.

Chain-smoking allied with acute diabetes, I have developed a chronic pancreas and dodgy ticker. I have been married four times, culminating in three divorces. Although my numerous heart attacks have, to my knowledge, no connection to early marital strife.

I have travelled the journey of life, from East to West, experiencing joyful highs and tragic lows, some which were occasionally too hard to swallow - the worst being the death of my father involved in a billion-to-one incident. Needless to say, the sheer exhilaration of ducking, diving, beating the system and coming through on my own terms, more than made up for any regrets.

Along the way, I've been a debonair man about town, businessman, trader, smuggler, secret agent, prolific gambler, TV maverick, forger, fraudster, prisoner and close friend and confidante to many of England's top footballers. I have encountered incredible greed, selfishness, corruption and sheer stupidity from household names: men who should have known better. Now is the time to open up Pandora's Box and reveal the harsh truth about the great, the good and the downright mediocre.

This revealing account of my life pulls no punches or asks for any quarter. It hurtles rip-roaringly into a fully-fledged, fun-filled adventure, with serious repercussions often thrown in. I tell it straight from the heart, with nothing invented, nothing exaggerated, and certainly nothing omitted.

Climb aboard the camel train, grab your red fez, fill your water bottles with hooch, this is a rocking journey not to be missed.

So... could I have your attention please? Strap yourself in, for shortly we will be leaving the safety of the oasis - destination unknown - but heading full-tilt for...

Life in the Faz Lane!

* * * *

CHAPTER 1

GENESIS TO EXODUS

Arabic saying: A sinking man will try to catch any rope

And so, verily it came to pass, that the Vizier's daughter, Scheherazade married the Caliph, Lord of Lords, King of Kings and master of all he surveyed. Holding him spellbound with a thousand and one wondrous stories, tales of love, tragedy and stupendous adventure. Genies, flying carpets, monsters, magic lanterns and giant birds were the fabulous favourites of that ancient era.

The Caliph never, ever doubted a word she uttered, for he loved his young wife dearly, but he was a man who possessed a short and fiery temper and previous wives had been put to death for vexing the great one.

Scheherazade understood that her tales of Arabian Nights, would secure her position as the Caliph's most beloved one, as long as they held her fearsome husband's attention.

One stormy, humid evening, she slept fitfully. A vision permeated her troubled mind which transformed into a strange portent for the future. A small man from a South Persian village would rock establishments, both East and West. A dream so fantastic, she realised that it could never be related back to the Caliph, for fear of her being cast into a lunatic asylum.

The prophesy was never revealed to any living soul. Scheherazade would take it with her to the grave, and for the rest of her life, each morning, the tantalising, cool, soft, zephyr breeze would whisper down to her, 'Madani, Madani, Madani'.

1964 was a leap year, Beatlemania had gripped the USA, where 7-1 underdog Cassius Clay astounded the boxing world by stopping Sonny Liston. On the political front, Jack Ruby had been found guilty of murdering Lee Harvey Oswald, who had, the previous year, shot President Kennedy in Dallas.

Back in Blighty, we had our own big story: The trial and sentencing of the Great Train Robbers. There must have been political intervention after the way the judge Edmund Davis nonchalantly handed out 30-year sentences, like he was doling out speeding fines. The establishment had sent out a stern message, anyone attempting to relieve the Royal Mail of its hard-earned wonga, could expect to go to the big house for a very long time. The criminal fraternity duly took note.

On the crowded Summer seafronts of Margate and Brighton, gangs of Mods and Rockers were beating seven bells out of each other. The more affable British public, tuned into the most-watched TV show, the first episode of a new series of Steptoe and Son, which pulled in 26 million viewers. He was a popular horse, that Hercules.

On the sporting front, the giants of English football, Liverpool and Manchester United, had gone tooth and nail for league glory. The men from Merseyside, finally pipping the Red Devils to win the title for the sixth time.

Asia was as unstable as ever as the Vietnam war was descending into chaos, misery and disaster. That summer the Tokyo Olympics would restore a semblance of goodwill and sanity, only for China to explode its first atomic bomb. Something was in the air... mosquitoes mainly, pesky varmints.

Against all this backdrop of madness and mayhem, events were unfolding in a little known sector, Bandar Lengeh in Hormozgan Province on Iran's Southern coast. Family and friends welcomed in a new arrival as little Faisal Madani - yours truly - came kicking and screaming into the equally troubled and turbulent Middle East.

Chronologically, I was third oldest of four brothers. My parents, Abdullah and Mryam Madani, had married at the ages of fourteen and thirteen respectively, a very common occurrence in our part of the world. Three of the offspring turned out just fine, pious, religious, well-behaved and balanced. The other bounder, quickly became the black sheep of the family and only false modesty prevents disclosure of this culprit. Older brothers Mohammid and Ibrahim grew up to become respected businessmen and by the time our youngest sibling, Mansour was born, I was off and away and on the loose in England's green and pleasant land.

Originating from Iran, I've noticed that Western governments have developed a veneer of subtlety and diplomacy as Middle Eastern oil reserves have become the prime commodity in international trading. Saudi Arabia, in particular, always gets an easy ride from the West, owing much to its vast wealth and seemingly inexhaustible oil wells.

Europeans and Arabs haven't always seen eye to eye, as different cultures, religion and politics have proved insurmountable in the past. If you recall the crusades in the year 1099, when the Christians captured Jerusalem, they slaughtered every last man, woman and child. Less than 100 years later, when

Saladin recaptured the city, every living soul was spared. I'm not saying all Arabs are good people, we've had our fair share of cruel and despotic leaders, but which empire hasn't had their own megalomaniac torch bearer over the centuries.

T.E. Lawrence (Lawrence of Arabia) was treated like royalty by the Arabs and they would have followed him to Hell and back as they pounded the infidel Turkish army in World War I. The mighty Ottoman Empire has long since disappeared and feuding warlike European states hopefully are a fading memory of history, for the new modern arenas for international combat are football stadia.

Galatasaray or Fenerbache away in the Champions League can be a bit lively, the vociferous locals get more than a tad excitable. Leeds, Chelsea and Manchester United can all attest to that.

Football: the game Britain gave the world, in addition to cricket, rugby, golf and tennis if you like, was being constantly upgraded and improved in the 19th century, with the constant implementation of new rules and regulations, which have become the rubrics of today.

Preston North End won the inaugural league and FA Cup double in the 1888-89 campaign, going down in history as 'The Invincibles', having gone undefeated all season. Just how good would they have been, if the South End had got a game as well.

All was well with Victoriana, the industrial revolution put the Brits light years ahead of the opposition. Railways criss-crossed the country, and the stars were the new steam engines, like Stephenson's Rocket and Puffing Billy right up to Edwardian times, with the genius of Sir Nigel Gresley - South Derbyshire's finest son - designing speed world record holders, *The Flying Scotsman*, and the beautiful Pacific Class locomotive *Mallard*.

The golden age of steam was emulated on the seven seas, by genius Isambard Kingdom Brunel, his sensational steamships *Great Western, Great Eastern* and *Great Britain* ruled the waves. The British navy, even at the commencement of the 20th century, was larger than the rest of the world's put together.

The Victorian armed forces were the finest fighting machine ever seen and Britain made its indelible mark - those redcoats rampaging all over the world. The sun never set on the British Empire, and an Irish wag expanded on it, 'Even God wouldn't trust the British in the dark'.

Unfortunately the world and universe are forever in a constant state of flux, and change was soon to be a certainty. The twentieth century was the tipping point. America wanted top billing, and so the baton had to be passed over. After World War II, on the ship's bridge and in the officers' mess, it was - by jingo - regarded as a dashed poor show! Britain's star was definitely on the wane. Back in Iran, this historical period of Britain's demise was known as 'The age when the lion lost its fur'.

Today, modern international sport is played against countries which have long memories of their ancestry - bloody long ones! The lily-white shirt of England, appears like a red rag to a bull to many, and teams regularly raise their game when facing the once all-conquering England.

This was never more finely elaborated than in the 1981 World Cup qualifier in Oslo, between Norway and England. Bjorge Lillelien was the radio commentator that day. England had stunk the place out, losing by a shock score of 2-1. Lillelien ensured the result would reverberate round the world, as he declared in an enthusiastic, breathless Nordic accent: *'Lord Nelson! Lord Beaverbrook... Sir Winston Churchill... Sir Anthony Eden... Clement Attlee... Henry Cooper... Lady Diana... Maggie Thatcher – can you hear me Maggie Thatcher? Your boys took one hell of a beating! Your boys took one hell of a beating!'*.

You wouldn't mind but, Norway was one of a handful of countries that England hadn't actually invaded. I do recall though, Viking longboats, brim-full of men with beards and horned helmets crossing the North Sea. Still, if you dish it out, you've got to take the odd reverse haymaker back on the chin. Brits have developed a lot of resolve, just like myself.

I was always destined to come over here, it was written in the stars... I'll kill that Russell Grant.

*   *   *   *

CHAPTER 2

EAST OF SUEZ TO EAST ANGLIA

Arabic saying: Ask the experienced, rather than the learned

Abdullah Madani, my father, was the person who had the most profound effect on my life. An amazing man, who had achieved so much before I left Iran at the age of twelve. At home we had a privileged upbringing and he wanted me to have the best scholarly learning possible. He informed me a few months before I became a member of the teen club that I was about to further my fledgling education in a mysterious, misty, green land situated on the edge of Western Europe. A little diamond of a country, warmly caressed by the Gulf Stream, nestling on the mighty Atlantic Ocean - England. Geography wasn't my strong suit though, he might well have been sending me to the dark side of the Moon.

Back home in the sun, my father had useful and influential connections. Being a close friend of his, the Shah of Iran was one - a man who was an extremely powerful, omnipotent ruler. After the Shah was deposed in the revolution in 1979, Abdullah got on famously with Ali Rafsanjani, the new President of Iran.

We all resided, happy as sandboys, on the coast of Southern Iran, surrounded by the mighty Persian Gulf, adjacent to the Straits of Hormuz, an important strategic and sensitive part of the world. Britain and Portugal had been at loggerheads for centuries over the area and had frequently come to blows. In modern times, America saw the absolute necessity to be an important player around that sea lane, as oil was vital for Uncle Sam, and he was a avaricious son of a gun, so a clear passage was the least that was acceptable.

A large percentage of all the world's oil travelled through it on massive supertankers. As a small boy, I would often watch spellbound as those gigantic, heavily-laden hulks glided to the horizon, slowly changing into dots in the distance.

The sea was core to my father's businesses, and he regarded it as his mistress and lifeblood, owing a huge gratitude to the waterways. And because of it, the family lived in good style, if not opulence. Abdullah made a lucrative career exporting vast amounts of pistachio nuts around the world. Locally, we oversaw a ship building yard constructing dhows, employing some of the best craftsmen in the area. We also sold building materials and timber to the local populace, thus having fingers in many pies - it was a *pukka* life.

Being a religious man, my father would often be observed praying, but that didn't stop the old fox piloting the sea lanes from nearby Dubai to Calcutta, smuggling gold across the Indian Ocean. (I was definitely a chip off the old block. Daddy was probably praying for an event-free passage anyway) The ocean was the catalyst for my father's happiness. He once told me, 'If a person loves the sea, his vision is limitless'.

My mother Mryam, never, ever got involved in the family business affairs, but in keeping with my father, found solace and joy in her faith, possibly more so. She led a happy but uneventful life and wasn't exactly a material girl, but she never lacked for home comforts. Her world revolved around her four children. She was a wonderful wife and mother.

Around that time, as she was eight months pregnant with the *enfant terrible*, she experienced a strange and vivid dream. Bizarrely, and for no good reason, she was in the company of King Faisal of Saudi Arabia, who inadvertently leant over and off slipped his golden crown. Before the jewelled artifact hit the floor, my mother caught it in mid-air. Only Sigmund Freud could explain the rationale, but the upshot was two months later, the bouncing baby was named Faisal - a very rare name in Iran, the equivalent of a *Rupert* in China.

Mohamed Al-Fayed was a business associate of dad's. He was another well-known friend of the family, and when he occasionally visited, I was introduced to him at the age of nine. A little crackerjack, full of vim and energy, he was destined to become a household name, and the future (and now former) owner of Harrod's didn't disappoint.

At school, Al-Fayed was already making money, selling home-made lemonade to class mates. This stood him in good stead for the rigours of serious business later in his career. As a young man, he set up a shipping company, operating in both the Mediterranean and Red Sea with roll-on, roll-off ferries. In the mid sixties, Dubai was an up-and-coming city, so guess who was at the front of the queue to procure the best building contracts? You guessed it!

Al-Fayed also had the enormous World Trade Centre, Hilton Hotel and Dubai International Airport to construct.

My father had integrated locally and established himself as a businessman and the 'go-to man' in Dubai, supplying a lot of building materials to Al-Fayed's rapidly growing portfolio. Dubai was on an unstoppable forward march, and Abdullah and the family would find themselves spending more and more time in the new desert super state.

Al-Fayed later married Samira Khashoggi, sister of billionaire arms dealer Adnan, thus creating a powerful dynasty. He turned up one day in London, where he purchased a convenience store and an underachieving football club. They didn't do too badly under his tutelage did they? As they've now been offloaded, Al Fayed's ended up sitting on a pretty pile.

Never afraid to speak his mind, he's rubbed up both the government and monarchy. He once described the top serving parliamentarians as 'the Cabinet of Shit' - not a bad assessment! Despite paying millions in tax and raising millions more for charity, he's not been rewarded with a British passport, something an Albanian gangster would automatically get - because we wouldn't want to upset his human rights, now would we? *(There, there, Genti.)*

A lasting memory of Al-Fayed - here was a man who mixed with all races and creeds, could fill a room with laughter and endear himself to the common man. A great man for Britain. May he prosper onwards and upwards. Strange how the Duke of Edinburgh never did get that Harrod's Xmas Hamper.

Good advice from your elders should always be noted. Abdullah lived his life by one such gem: 'There are three bodies one should never confer with about all your business matters - your wife, your bank manager and the government'. I liked that so much, I've adhered to it, right up to the present day. What someone doesn't know about, never hurts them.

I had no inkling at the time, but years later my beloved father would be embroiled in an international incident involving suffering, death and destruction. Lies, political buck-passing and outrageous whitewashing would emerge from the mealy mouths of the so-called great democracies, their murderous hands indelibly stained with the blood of innocents.

All it meant to me though, was that my wonderful father was gone, killed in a billion-to-one miscarriage of justice, where political machinations would twist and contort the truth to its own corrupt satisfaction. If the future spelt trouble, the present wasn't exactly a bowl of cherries. And my own young life would be going through its own massive upheavals.

Copford College, Colchester was where I enrolled. This would be where my first formal school days would unfold. Twelve years old, wet behind the ears and extremely naïve, I would have made Tom Brown look like a head prefect. God, I was slow. I was probably viewed by most as a half-wit. Benny from Crossroads became a role model for me.

Ninety percent of the students at the college were from overseas, so we were all in the same boat... weren't we? No, I was profusely sweating like a bilge rat in a leaking, rusty old bum boat, whilst the others were being served iced cocktails lying on luxury loungers up on the sun deck of the liner Queen Mary.

Most of the kids were sons of bankers, government ministers and barristers, all academically brilliant, light years ahead of the school plodder: thicky Faisal.

As I approached my teens, I picked up half a yard of momentum, improvement was gradually surfacing and by the time I turned thirteen, my initial shyness and single figure test marks were a fast-fading distant memory.

A big advantage for myself was that I looked a lot older than my real age, and I was even starting to excel in one subject, English language. I seemed to have a knack for it. The trouble was, the other subjects: history, physics, geography, chemistry, etc, were all a mystery, wrapped in a riddle, covered by a conundrum and tied up tight in a fucking huge unbreakable enigma. (No, not enema!)

I was still probably the worst student in the college and during a holiday break back in Dubai - the family had recently bought a second home there - I copped an earful. My father, who had just received my latest academic report, roared, 'Two thousand pounds a term, that's what I'm paying for your education... you went away a retard, you've come back a total idiot!'.

I couldn't really disagree, but I vowed to pull out all the stops, saying I'd just found my second wind and certain things were falling into place, and that a marked improvement was only just around the corner. That seemed to do the trick, but I knew if I didn't buck up, I'd be living on borrowed time.

Back in Britain, studying wasn't quite at the top of my agenda. I'd discovered a winning treble - betting, football and the girlies. The first two I'd taken to, like a ferret down a trouser leg, but the female form, was pulling my adolescent hormones, every which way.

Each Friday night was the noted college disco, local girls invited. I moved in on a fifteen-year-old, I'll never forget her name - Emily Lancaster. There she was sitting all alone, resplendent under the flashing strobe lights. Sensually, sipping orangeade through a straw, my lustful leering didn't take into account her teeth braces, lazy eye and acne - but to me she was Raquel Welch and Marilyn Monroe, rolled into one. Wow - she was a babe... nay, a mega babe.

I was smitten, and a couple of slow, smoochy dances later I was madly in love, and strange, unexplained movements were occurring in my trouser area. Next day, she promptly dumped me, minutes after I declared my undying love for her. She had poured icy water on my burgeoning ardour. It took me ages to get over it. Thank God salvation and redemption were just round the corner - it was time for football to enter my life. It would become my new lover and this time, by Jove, there would be no rebuff.

*   *   *   *

CHAPTER 3

CREDIT CRUNCH, NOT CARROT CRUNCH

Arabic saying: Believe what you see and put aside what you hear

Residing close to the Suffolk border in Colchester, the team that attracted my attention were Ipswich Town. I didn't know it then, but this team was about to soar to the pinnacle of English football and graduate into one of the finest sides in Europe. Being in the right place at the right time meant I could sit back, relax and witness a period of greatness for Ipswich Town and the entertainment was sublime.

Ipswich Town was known as a family club. I can never recall much trouble or hooliganism. The chairman was a local legend, John Cobbold, who was born into a brewing dynasty. Here was a man not averse to drinking the company profits. He liked a tipple - who doesn't? - there was no crime in that, but it was his expertise that put Ipswich on the map.

In 1948 at the age of 21, he had the distinction of becoming football's youngest director. Eight years later he was chairman. Cobbold was partly responsible for giving the legendary Alf Ramsey his first start in management and was rewarded with the league championship in 1961 - an amazing feat for a provincial club. I was going to suggest, bordering on the impossible now, with the money and power, emanating from Manchester, Merseyside and London. And I, like millions of others, didn't see the Leicester miracle coming. I think Nostradamus missed it as well - bloody amateur!

Cobbold's best transaction was without doubt the acquisition of Bobby Robson as manager in 1969. Robbo won the FA Cup and EUFA Cup, before going tantalisingly close in the league. During the time I supported Ipswich, I became a lifelong friend of Bobby's and will spread light and happiness about the great man later on in my story.

A lifelong Tory, Cobbold fancied a dabble in politics and stood three times in Ipswich as a Conservative candidate, although he was a true blue, the town's policies always remained red. Undeterred, he maintained his commitment to his beloved football club. He is often best remembered for the remark, 'There is no crisis at Ipswich until the white wine runs out in the boardroom'.

They say the good die young and John Cobbold's untimely death in 1983 at the age of 56 was a dark day for the club. He was a pioneer, a gentleman and a scholar. If there is a heaven, he's probably up there looking down, glass in hand. Cheers John, thank you and God bless.

Even though the top footballers in the 1970s were big stars, they were much more accessible than they are now. A typical player of this modern era who is at the top of the food chain will earn millions, topped up with advertising and commercial contracts. The man in the stand has absolutely nothing in common with today's bright young things. The jury is still out on whether these pampered, but superhumanly-conditioned prima donnas are better than their earlier counter-parts from the 70s and 80s. A lot of fun, skill and laughter have disappeared from the game, replaced by money, work rate, money, sackings and more money.

Football cannot be called the working man's game any more and, sadly, those days won't be returning any time soon. The transformation is called progress, and for a nostalgic yearning for the past, don't hold your breath me old son. One could definitely grow old waiting. Grounds and facilities have all improved though, as has the safety aspect, and the omnipresent surveillance cameras have been a Godsend, so heads you win, tails you lose - but profit is the driving force.

I'm coming down from my high horse with a hump, they call it a camel back home. What prevailed in the 1970s was a drinking culture - and a bloody large one too! (mine's a rum and coke) I know the odd contemporary player, who occasionally has a blowout, but it's a lot less common these days. Players are monitored and weighed daily. It's a different world.

Ipswich Town could sink more than a few. Forget about the old Arsenal drinking culture club and the 1970s shandy drinkers from the King's Road. The Suffolk boys took no prisoners. They could be tracked down all hours round the clock in the fashionable clubs and bars. Some of the sessions were gargantuan, and parties with the local lassies became a source of legend.

Beattie, Brazil, Wark, Butcher, Osman and Mariner, all had the taste for it. Every man Jack of them an international and consummate professional, it never affected any of them on the football pitch. They were the calibre of men you'd want right by your side in the trenches.

Players often popped into the Andromeda Nightclub in Colchester, which was the hot spot at the time. This is where I first met Kevin Beattie - a leviathan, a behemoth, a colossus of a player. I'd like to talk about Beattie for a moment. Born and chiselled from Cumbrian granite in wild and windy Carlisle in 1953. Here was a man dogged by injuries, especially serious knee problems. He once even burned himself badly on a home-made bonfire. The persistent injuries limited him to a pathetic, paltry, nine international caps. But who could ever forget his headed goal in the 5-1 rout of Scotland at Wembley, where his head was higher than the crossbar.

Kevin Beattie, in his prime, was the best defender bar none in the First Division, and acclaimed as the new Bobby Moore or even better than Duncan Edwards. Bobby Robson went further than that and called Beattie, 'the best English player, ever'. And Bobby was a good judge of a footballer. Lightning fast, unbeatable in the air and with a cultured left foot, Beattie was an absolute joy to watch - if he played in present day, and was in his prime, he'd be worth 60 million.

He played in the 1978 FA Cup Final win against Arsenal, but missed the EUFA Cup Final victory against AZ Alkmaar. One highly-anticipated European night at Portman Road proved Beattie's undoubted prowess. Barcelona were in town and Beattie was marking Johan Cruyff, the Dutch magician, and the best player in the world at that time. The Flying Dutchman never got a kick. Beattie had him in his pocket all night. I had previously arranged to meet Kevin after the game. I ambled round the corner down to the players entrance, happening upon the surreal sight of Kevin Beattie, cigarette in mouth, lighting up Johan Cruyff's puffer. Two gladiators winding down with the utmost respect for each other.

It's not widely known that Kevin Beattie was in the tremendous 1981 football film classic *Escape to Victory*. If you can't recall seeing him, it's because he was hired as Michael Caine's body double in the football action scenes. Paul Cooper, the Ipswich keeper, was also brought in to do the same job for the hapless Sylvester Stallone.

Stallone was playing, 'Hatch' the goalie, and even with blatant editing, one could tell that Sly wouldn't ever make a lower league Sunday morning keeper - he hadn't got a Scooby.

That didn't stop him making an audacious challenge to Pele though, who was playing Portuguese forward 'Luis Fernandez'. He wanted to wager money, claiming he could save at least one penalty from five attempts. Pele duly fired all five into the net, and Stallone didn't get close to any of them and silently skulked off in embarrassment back to his trailer.

The following day Stallone was full of it, informing the listening crew and extras that soccer wasn't really his barrow - 'I'm a world class exponent of arm wrestling'. He would later go on to play the character of 'Lincoln Hawk' in the 1987 arm wrestling movie *Over the Top*. Kevin Beattie challenged him - and this is gospel - beat him both right-handed and left-handed. Stallone rapidly did one. He needed the sanctuary of his trailer, the cheers and jeers still ringing in his ears as he retreated again. He must have had a good cry in front of his mirror, because he never spoke to, or even acknowledged Beattie on the film set again. Or maybe he just didn't like the score: Ipswich 2 - Hollywood 0.

Ipswich Town had quite a few players in the film: Laurie Sivell (German goalie), John Wark, Kevin O' Callaghan, Robin Turner and Russell Osman, who for me, has the most poignant line in the film, as the allied team are planning to escape through the base of the fractured team bath at half time, he senses hesitation and pleads with the players to stay, imploring 'we can win it!' - super stuff.

Mike Summerbee was playing the part of Sid 'Buzzer' Harmor, years later we became great buddies after I moved to Manchester. Mike also clicked on -set with Michael Caine. They became mates as well, notwithstanding being a City great, Mike's also one of the good guys.

Just as a postscript, a few years later John Wark confided in me that early on in the film he discovered that Caine and Stallone were earning massive six figure sums. Bobby Robson had negotiated for all the football players to collect £1,500 each, a figure Wark regarded as insulting and derisory. A meeting was convened with the all other players and he was unanimously nominated to see if he could chivvy up new improved terms for the boys. He flounced confidently into the director's office, sat opposite him with a steely resolve and put across the players' demands. The director was pensive, deep in thought. He came across as a reasonable man however, and after a long pause Wark got his answer: 'Anybody who doesn't like the terms, can just fuck off and vacate the film set'. So that was that, Wark was speechless. Negotiations were over before they started, he was outplayed in contractual midfield prenups, he never stood a chance.

Kevin Beattie didn't play a lot of football after the release of the film, the cruel recurring injuries were beginning to take their toll, a heartbreaking scenario for any great player. Bobby Robson had always called Beattie 'The Diamond', a lovely tribute, but there were millions of sparklers in the world, as he was the best around, I just simply referred to him as 'God'.

Let's go back four years again - I know this book has more flashbacks than Tarantino's film *Reservoir Dogs* - but instead of Mr Blonde, Mr White and Mr Pink, I was starting to be known as 'Mr Fix-It', although to be fair, I still liked being called 'Faz'.

When I first made Beattie's acquaintance I was fourteen years young, but like previously mentioned, I could pass muster as a twenty year old, this being a golden period in time when pubs and clubs never, ever asked for proof of age or ID.

Just for good measure, around the same time, I'd been approached by British Secret Service - MI5 - who thought I could be of some use to their cause. It had come to their attention that my father was a well-known peripheral figure in the affairs of state in both Dubai and Iran. I know it's hard to believe that a young teen living in a foreign land would have all that pressure thrust upon him, but sometimes truth is stranger than fiction. Wolfgang Amadeus Mozart was proclaimed a child prodigy, (I was a child problem) but tell me this, when did he ever hang about with professional footballers and spies? Twinkle twinkle little star, my arse.

The spying escapades we can put on the back burner, but suffice to say the detritus went all the way up to parliamentary cabinet level, putting the beleaguered government and the establishment cronies on the back foot.

The friendship with Kevin Beattie has survived and has flourished to the present day, back then we would go clubbing or play snooker, sometimes a card school would be organized with other like-minded Ipswich players - blimey it was a tough life for any youngster.

I was experiencing a period of metamorphosis, from callow youth to aspiring sophisticated young buck. The common caterpillar, would one day reveal itself to the world as a beautiful butterfly, so on that reckoning, Madani could, and would stroll confidently out of the Burton's Tailors shop suited and booted. I'd purchased a light grey, pin-striped, double breasted number off the peg. It was slightly oversized, but sod it, I was a growing lad, and in six months it would look just the dog's bollocks.

Beattie and the boys were having a jar, in a town centre hostelry and I strutted in precociously like a young George Raft. Kevin was casually leaning on the jukebox, clocking me, he started turning crimson trying manfully to suppress a fit of laughter. I defended myself stoutly, 'It's the latest style from America, Rod Steiger wears one'.

'He must be a cunt', replied Beattie.

On Saturdays, I would stand on the Churchman End terrace and cheer on my mates. Over the six plus years I was there, the great Bobby Robson had moulded together a Suffolk super squad. Nobody fancied coming to Portman Road and that was just the way we liked it.

Highlights for me and others over that period, apart from the two final victories, were thumping Manchester United six-nil, despite Gary Bailey saving three penalties, plus a EUFA Cup Quarter Final win against talented French outfit AS Saint-Étienne by four goals to one, Platini *et al*.

Outstanding players were as abundant as stars in the night sky. We were spoilt for choice. England international centre-halves Russell Osman and Terry Butcher were two. Who could ever forget, 'Big Butch', playing for England, head bandaged with stitches re-opened, face and shirt covered with claret - a real hero. Add super 'Three Lions' striker Paul Mariner, and a man who could twist and turn in the Dalglish mould, Geordie Eric 'Lazenby' Gates (nice middle name).

There was also a sensational Scottish trio consisting of right-back George Burley, midfielder John Wark and striker Alan Brazil. Burley would progress to become both Ipswich and Scotland manager. Wark scored for fun from midfield and specialised in hat tricks, while ace goal machine Brazil was prolific in front of goal, a trait he later perfected... alongside drinking and horse racing.

Now a celebrated early morning presenter on Talk Sport 1053, Brazil came up with the greatest quote ever heard on radio. 'Our talking point today is George Best, his liver transplant and the booze culture in football. Don't forget, the best caller wins a crate of John Smiths' - absolutely priceless!

Two lowlanders were Robson's finest signings, the final pieces in the jigsaw: Dutchmen Frans Thijssen, the wizard of dribble and Johannes Hyacinthus 'Arnold' Muhren, (another good middle name) a pass master and superb tactician. These boys were better than 'Regan and Carter' from The Sweeney. They never took any prisoners.

There was once a rumour of contenders when Mike and Bernie Winters split up and Bernie brought in giant dog Schnorbitz for the vanquished Mike, but it never materialised. Laugh? I thought I'd never start.

Has there ever been a better midfield pairing than these Dutch aristocrats? If there has, I've not witnessed it. Other players from that era worth a mention, for valour beyond the call of duty: Mick Mills, Mick Lambert, Clive Woods, Allan Hunter and FA Cup Final goal scorer Roger Osborne.

'The Tractor Boys' always had two grudge matches a season and that was the East Anglian derby. Known locally as the battle of the carrot crunchers, it was against 'The Canaries' - the damned Norwich City, the so called Pride of Norfolk. Reputations and careers could be won or lost in these battles, and for local pride and ascendancy was everything. Defeat would be a bitter pill to swallow, until the attempted reversal next time round. A poor season could always be conveniently excused with two victories against the old enemy.

I attended every one of those matches between 1977 and 1983. The results went as follows;

	Portman Road	**Carrow Road**
1977	*5-0*	*0-1*
1978	*4-0*	*1-0*
1979	*1-1*	*0-1*
1980	*4-2*	*3-3*
1981	*2-0*	*1-0*
1982	*2-3*	*0-0*
1983	*0-1*	*0-0*

Results: Ipswich wins - 6   Norwich wins - 4   Draws 4

So Ipswich held the edge during my tenure, but it was noticeable to see that in the latter seasons, results were tailing off, a bit like my own results at Copford College.

The beginning of the end was in 1982 when Bobby Robson was offered the England job. It was an offer he couldn't refuse. Assistant Bobby Ferguson took over the reins - he knew the players and the system, far better than anyone else. Trouble was, all the best players were being transferred or retiring from the game. The team were on a downward, out of control trajectory, which plummeted into a death spiral. It was so sad to see, but we had punched above our weight for a long, long time. I desperately hoped this was just going to be a period of transition, but we had all enjoyed and dined out on the halcyon days, and it was now somebody else's turn. Little did any of us know, Ipswich wouldn't rise to those rarefied, heady heights again.

I was heartbroken. Ipswich's demise had coincided with my own poor performances at college, and if there had been a record for ineptness, I'd have been a world champ. Blow me sidewards and call me auntie Agnes, if I didn't fail fourteen consecutive maths exams and ended up staying at Copford until I was nineteen - another record surely in the bag.

The gambling gremlins were beginning to hook me in. All lifelong punters will tell you this fact - it's fatal to pull off a large win early on in your betting career, because for the rest of your days you are always chasing 'the lumpy one'.

That fateful day for me was in the summer of 1982. The venue: Gijon in sunny Espana, featuring the World Cup group game between Germany and Algeria. I had a score on Algeria to win 2-1, at the odds of 100-1. The fat sweaty balding bookie smirked, as I tentatively handed the bet over the counter. He wasn't laughing two hours later when he had to push £2,000 back the other way to a seventeen year old jammy little bastard. Walking out, I was going to rub it in - turn round and tell him I was under age, but wisely, I didn't push my luck.

I was smitten - I still am. Casino roulette is how I roll these days, but at the time I would bet on greyhounds, horses, anything - even the University Boat Race. Funny how the same two teams get to the final every year.

In fact, I'd bet on Elvis Presley dressed as Bo Peep, riding into Cleethorpes on Shergar if the odds were right. 1983 would definitely be a big year for me. A move to London was on the cards. Would there be some gambling action in the metropolis? You bet - Had I got the bottle though?

Does Steve Evans like a McDonalds supersize?

Did Fergie like a big watch?

Does Sepp like a backhander?

Did Delia like a lets be 'aving you?

Did Robin Friday give a fuck? (Robin who?)

I certainly had the minerals... boy, it was going to be a hedonistic paradise, but I still look back on my Copford College days with a fond regard - I'd spent seven great years there. A decade later I heard on the grapevine, Mr Green, the former owner, a self-made man who ran around in a Silver Cloud Roller and kept an ocean-going yacht at Lymington Marina, had a reversal of fortune. He had molested two Nigerian first year students which culminated in his arrest, conviction, and sentence of five big ones, courtesy of Her Majesty's pleasure, at Wormwood Scrubs.

The African students had come in for personal, extra curriculum training, casually entering his study room, only to find him stark bollock-naked, todger in one hand, quarter pound of marge in the other. Greeny would have put it down to good old British eccentricity, but I think the courts nailed it to sodomy, though I never got to the bottom of it. (Sorry) The college is now an old folks home. When institutions such as this are gone, it's just like they never existed, but it was a rewarding and important part of my life.

London was fervently calling, and I was soon on the move again heading for 'The Smoke' - the greatest city in the world. Madani was homing in, like a rampant carrier pigeon, fully fledged... the boy had become a man.

*   *   *   *

CHAPTER 4

METROPOLITAN AND COSMOPOLITAN

Arabic saying: Only the tent pitched by your own hand will stand

The sun was radiant, resembling a large orange beach ball in the cloudless, azure sky. Such a perfect day to arrive at my new dwelling, a 'des res' - a second floor apartment in Tufnell Park, North London. I gazed up excitedly. Not bad, not bad at all! I danced a little victory jig and rocketed up the stairs with my suitcases. Situated just off the Holloway Road, straddling the busy borough of Islington, it was typically metro, definitely cosmo, and just a little bit suburbo. Aussie Clive James had spent a large part of his early formative years here. That would do for me cocker. Jamesey wouldn't have slummed it, would he?

Slowly turning the key, adolescent independence was beckoning. I'd finally found my own covert corner, a first bijou address, acquired at the age of nineteen. 1983 was going to be my year. The streets of London were fabled to be paved with gold. I'd earlier spotted and walked right past a ten pound note fluttering on the pavement. Fuck it, I'd start tomorrow morning.

My overwhelming optimism was bordering on hubris, but I was young, ambitious and flushed with an undoubted feeling of invincibility. I was going to become either a millionaire or an international stud - but hey, why not both? What could stop me!? That crazy folly of youth - oh, to be that age again - before the establishment and mundane life kicks the shit out of you.

The David Bowie song *Width of a Circle* proclaimed: 'For I realise, God's a young man too'. Very deep lyrics, eternal youth always has the edge over riches.

Since time immemorial, the aged and experienced have always held the power and the money, but the young have had their ambition and youthfulness. Only when it's long gone do we realise what we once had. How many ninety-year-old billionaires wouldn't give away every last coin to become a young buck again? Queen Elizabeth I, implored on her death bed, 'All my possessions for one moment in time'. I now try to live every day as if it's my last one, because the hands of the clock seem to accelerate as you slow down. As folk physically age something in the brain definitely changes too, whether it be loss of creativity or even an inspirational blockage.

People like the Rolling Stones, or even Michael Jackson, wrote all their great hits when they were young men. Decades later, the actual performance of those classics hasn't diminished, but Jagger and Richards will never again write songs as superlative as, *Brown Sugar* and *Honky Tonk Woman*. Jackson, until his untimely death, hadn't written a good song for years. *Thriller* was consigned to history. Even Dylan, the angry, rebellious mouthpiece of disillusioned young America, has lost his spark. The wonderful and profound lyrics gone, never to return.

Most footballers know when to call time on a fading professional career, that fateful day when the boots are thrown in the locker for the last time. Tick-tock, tick-tock, a decade flown by in the blink of an eye. Blimey, where did that go?! That, me old lad, was your sporting life... what are you going to do now? There's an old adage amongst retired footballers: 'Play as long as you can'. I've seen some players break down and cry when the glamour and the prestige are gone. Some go into football management, others become media pundits, but a lot are lost to the game. Most survive and prosper, but a percentage hit the bottle or even turn to crime, with drug dealing becoming a new way of trying to make big money.

My great friend George Best had the tragic curse of alcoholism, suffering a chronic drink dependency all through his adult years, but he had no regrets about his shortened life and career. I truly miss the old maestro, he turns up at various times in my life, documented in later chapters. A coy, gentle, generous man - what's the worst that could be said about him - a suspicion of unreliability, yes, but when you were as talented as he was, bad timekeeping wasn't too bad a vice was it? The man was fated, he had no chance, but he lived life to the full.

Some sportsmen never realise when it's time to go. How many times have you heard it said of a boxer, 'He had one fight too many'. That said, Athlete Linford Christie actually ran faster after he passed his thirtieth birthday. Make your own mind up, I'm saying nothing about it, but I think the secret was hidden in his lunchbox.

The one man who does confound all the odds without any outside influences is dart thrower Phil Taylor. He's the wrong side of fifty, but his darts average is the right side of one hundred plus. Expect to see the pride of The Potteries, playing the television tournaments for at least another decade still. He's not yet on the slippery slope, even though he's edging towards the oche of the grim reaper.

It's a toss-up for who is Port Vale FC's most famous fan - (not a huge selection) Taylor, or the modest, shy and retiring, Robbie Williams. I know the

Burslem outfit would like a few more bodies through the turnstiles, but they never visited me, when I was bad.

I sometimes worry for Robbie's sanity. All he's done since moving to Beverley Hills is bask by a swimming pool, surrounded by a posse of busty, tanned young ladies, with bikinis made of dental floss. Why would he prefer Los Angeles to Stoke? It's a mystery to all. But a bracing, rain-sodden Division Two match against Dagenham would surely tempt him back. How much longer can the lad take the ordeal of sun, surf and sex on a plate before he sees the error of his ways... don't hold your breath.

Some footballers know that the game is up, but choose to drop down the leagues and play at an inferior standard, even if it means playing in the National League or lower. Who's to say they are wrong though? Some need to play on for financial reasons, others love the game so much, they eke out every last minute of playing time, knowing once they've finished there's no more banter and team camaraderie. Life after football will offer a duller experience. Nothing will ever again compare to the thrill of running out to a packed stadium, but wicked Father Time will always scythe down the very best of them.

My apartment was only a gnat's knacker away from Highbury, home to the mighty Arsenal. It had quantified my move to Tufnell Park. Especially as one of my football Gods, Paul Mariner, had been transferred from Ipswich. Cowabun-ga, it was happy days again - I could now watch him in action sporting the famous red and white shirt of The Gunners.

Ipswich Town were still imploding, and all the great players were leaving and going their own separate ways. Alan Brazil turned up down the road at White Hart Lane, Eric Gates went back to his native North East, signing for Sunderland, while Osman and Mills headed for the South coast to play for Southampton. Even the jolly Dutchmen split up - Thyssen decided to try his luck in the North American league. A criminal waste of talent, as he was still at the top of his game. His good pal, Arnie Muhren, got a dream move to Manchester United. His silky passing skills would stand him in good stead at Old Trafford.

Goalie Paul Cooper followed him up to Cottonopolis, but across the city, to stand between the sticks at Maine Road. Last but not least, big Terry Butcher got the call from Glasgow Rangers, and he headed North of the border, and by God, the massed Ibrox terraces would have a new hero to worship. Butch wouldn't let anyone down.

Ipswich Town were in deep financial trouble and even with all the transfer fund money from numerous transactions, they couldn't keep the wolf from the door. The Tractor Boys were in meltdown and relegation was inevitable. I was gutted for the town and the team, but the times were a-changing (thank you Mr. Zimmerman). I'd detected a new wind blowing away the cobwebs of all that had gone before in the English leagues. Ipswich Town, a team situated in the sticks, had a squad comprising of Anglo-Saxon English, with a healthy sprinkling of Celts, especially Scots and two outstanding Dutch players who were something of a novelty.

Through the late seventies, home-grown black players were beginning to make the grade, appearing on the team sheets of the big city teams. They were the indigenous sons of trailblazing, immigrant workers from all over the Commonwealth, who had, from the 1950s, travelled to Mother England for the opportunity of a better lifestyle.

Modern Premier League football teams, have a large percentage of players from foreign climes, black and white - and the game is all the better for it, but thirty years ago, it wasn't easy to be born a different colour, and a lot of black players endured a rough ride.

Believe it or not, England's first professional black player was way back in 1889 - one Arthur Wharton, who signed for Preston North End as a goalie. A supreme athlete, he broke the world record for the 100 yards sprint that year. It's only conjecture that racism wasn't an issue, but he was never considered good enough to play for England. And this milestone wouldn't be reached for another ninety years.

Over the earlier decades of the 20th century black players have turned up spasmodically: Tony Whelan for Manchester United and Albert Johansson for Leeds United, were prime, but rare examples in the 1960s.

Other top teams were slower to act. Arsenal giving Brendon Batson a game in 1971, but it would take Liverpool until 1980, with Howard Gayle and Chelsea, even longer with Paul Canoville in 1982.

Stamford Bridge at the time was a hotbed for National Front supporters. Every Saturday the Shed End was a sea of white faces, many of them skinheads and Neo-Nazis. Outside on Fulham Broadway newspaper vendors would be distributing right wing propaganda. It was a very intimidating arena for anyone slightly different. Wearing that famous royal blue shirt, was going to be a nightmare for the first black player at Chelsea. This new forward thinking ideology went right against the grain for the hardcore working class supporters who were indoctrinated to hate. A gasket had to blow and all of the red hot bile was directed at P.C.

Canoville was about to become as popular as a pork pie salesman in Tel Aviv. His debut match was away from home, a tasty London derby against the Stripey Nigels of Crystal Palace. As soon as he ran on to the pitch, the racist heckling started. It was very heavy. Canoville remarked to another Chelsea player that the Palace fans were right out of order. His new team mate soon put him right, 'They ain't Palace, mate, they're our lot'.

Chelsea seemed to be imploding. They were struggling on and off the football field, and they only just avoided relegation to the beckoning Third

Division on the last day of the season.

Canoville, a tricky left-sided wing man, turned the tide over the ensuing five seasons, scoring some important goals, and he was also scoring in his personal life, fathering eleven children with ten different women. He was obviously a man for all seasons.

Desailly, Drogba and Makelele and other players of that stature, are now classed as all-time Chelsea greats. The crowds are also much more understanding - bananas once thrown onto the pitch, have been replaced by celery, a much cheaper alternative in these austere times.

1978 was the year the floodgates opened for black players. The tall, gangly Nottingham Forest right back Viv Anderson was selected by Ron Greenwood for a full international cap against Czechoslovakia. Many other black players would follow in his footsteps, right bang up to the present day, but it wasn't all wine and roses.

An amazing game took place in 1984. The setting was the wonderful Maracana Stadium in Rio. A twenty-year-old Watford left winger would be thrust onto the world stage after a dazzling virtuoso performance. John Barnes received the ball standing out on the left wing, just yards inside the half way line. He cut inside, leaving five defenders trailing in his wake. On and on he drove, deep into the heart of the penalty box. He calmly drew the keeper, feinted past him and coolly stroked the ball into an empty net. A goal so good, that if Roy of the Rovers had scored it, readers would have complained that it was too far-fetched.

Can you just imagine it...

Dear Sir,

I can accept Roy Race has an ongoing football career spanning over thirty years and now looks younger than when he first pulled on the Melchester Rovers jersey in 1954. I can even swallow that he scores over ten hat tricks a season, culminating in at least 70 goals, but what I can't resign myself to, is what he is purported to have done in this week's latest issue.

He waltzes past half the Brazilian team on their own pitch, where they haven't tasted defeat in two decades, and without breaking sweat, he walks the ball into a gaping net. This time you've gone too far - fantasy football I like, science fiction, I do not. In future, if you cannot get your act together, I shall be cancelling my subscription and moving it forthwith to Hustler.

Good day sir,

Yours Indignantly

Jimmy Hill.

It was a career-defining moment for Barnes, his growing reputation back home was enhanced enormously, with the goal thrusting him into the stratosphere of a world class superstar. England eventually won 2-0 in the red-hot cauldron of the Maracana, where Brazil hadn't been beaten since the 1960's, one of the biggest shocks in their illustrious football history.

On the plane flight home, National Front supporters were confronting the travelling press corps, insisting that England had only won 1-0, Barnes's goal didn't count - because he was black. What can you say about people with that point of view? All I say is: Life's too short to harbour hate, especially if it's about skin colour.

Barnes could never live up to his early hype, nobody could have done. The goal came too early in his football life - he was barely out of his teens. In later years he would be booed and jeered at Wembley after becoming an England scapegoat. Maybe it was because he had a languid playing style which could often come across as uncaring or apathetic.

He was one of England's most skilful wingers and proved at Liverpool what an excellent player he was, scoring goals for fun. Maybe the goal in Brazil that day hung round his neck like an albatross, but he will still go down in history as an all-time England great.

The same however can't be said of Carlton Palmer. I'm afraid if Barnes was a thoroughbred, then Palmer was an honest plodder. Don't get me wrong, he was a good, hard-working, box-to-box midfielder in the league, but he was never international class in a million years. How on earth did he win 18 caps for England? He even scored against San Marino. I wouldn't have backed him to score against Dan Marino... Many pundits regard the current national team as mediocre, how wretched was it back then.

Frank Worthington and Matthew Le Tissier both won eight caps, and poor old Alan Hudson only earned a couple. Marvellous isn't it - three players blessed with football genius and they couldn't muster enough caps between them to overtake Palmer.

They say life's not fair, but it certainly was to long-legged Palmer. Ali G always used a defence mechanism when ever he was criticised: he would retort back with, 'Is it 'cos I is black?' Well, if Palmer ever used the same tactic, I would counter, 'No Carlton, it's cos you is crap'. If you ever saw him in an England shirt, you'd know what I was talking about. But you can't keep a good man down though, and years later Carlton appeared in a Paddy Power advert. He emerges surreally from under the water in a bath tub, and hands the bather some money. It's not an Oscar-winning performance, because I still think he's playing second best to 'Flipper' the dolphin, but if he plays his cards right, he could become the new legend that was 'Eric the Eel'.

Today in the Premier League, black and mixed-race players abound and the league is a better place for it. Supporters no longer tolerate racist bigotry and I believe we've come a long way. There's still work to be done, but as the Birmingham City fans sing, 'Keep right on to the end of the road'. We are bound to come across the odd red neck or moron, but it's a rarity. Since Viv Anderson's debut for England, this would be my best ever black or mixed-race England team, in the 4-4-2 formation.

David James

Viv Anderson   Rio Ferdinand   Des Walker   Ashley Cole

David Rocastle   Paul Ince   Michael Thomas   John Barnes

Ian Wright   Cyrille Regis

That side wouldn't lose too many.

    Personally, I was encountering no problems at all regarding the race question. London must be the most cosmopolitan capital in the world. I was meeting people from every country, creed and religion. The only geezers I hadn't come across were quintessential Londoners - as seen on film and TV. The 'bowler hat brigade': pin stripe suit, umbrella, brief case and Daily Mail tucked under an arm, walking across the bridge past the Houses of Parliament.

    One profound reason for not encountering the Hooray Henrys was my body clock, I'd developed into a night hawk, never rising before dinner time, and sometimes a lot later. Throughout the evenings and into the early hours, I indulged in my favourite hobby - gambling on the roulette table at the casino. I was a member of Crockfords, Maxims, Playboy, Brent-Walker and Barracuda, amongst many others.

    My daytime duties should have been attending the North London Tutorial College on the Seven Sisters Road, but if I said I went once it would be an exaggeration. I even persuaded my father to send over another thousand pounds a month, due to supposed higher fees from the college. A man could have too much education, nobody likes a know-it-all.

    On the rare occasions that I was up around midday, I would make a beeline for the bookies, where a healthy punt on the horses or greyhounds would set me up for an early evening session at the casino. I had developed golden bollocks for that first month. It was that or jaundice... but as all gamblers know, one cannot sit on one's laurels, because a losing run is always just around the next corner. And that's as true as death and taxes.

    Casinos are great places for meeting the opposite sex and I don't mean

Sad Doris the Rottweiler with the wig from the King's Head snug. I can heartily recommend them, they are full of very attractive young ladies, much better than night clubs. You can actually hear what they're saying. If you want to pull a cracker, join a gambling club, there's many a time I returned home, awash with cash and a beautiful woman on my arm. Strangely though, when I lost heavily, the only things escorting me home were empty pockets and a heavy heart.

David Sullivan, the diminutive future owner of Birmingham City and West Ham United, used to lend money to rich young Arabs. The London casinos attracted clientele from all over the world - film stars, sportsmen, businessmen and royalty, would all sit round the green baize, staking astronomical amounts of money.

Crown Prince Jaffri of Brunei had a few bob, he was a legendary big hitter, but when he came a cropper, it was for huge wads of cash. Back home in Brunei, it was reported that the Sultan owned one hundred and twenty two Rolls Royces, giving a whole new meaning to the term, 'bus-pass'. These fantastic sums were wagered by sheikhs, sultans and emirs, most of them oil-rich, pushing out thousand pound chips like Monopoly money.

King Fahd of Saudi Arabia was 'The Daddy', the biggest gambler of them all. He was a big boy in stature and in wealth. The casinos even constructed a special reinforced chair for him and I used to watch, transfixed as he played two tables simultaneously, betting an amount equal to the gross national product of Belgium. And both balls had to spin at exactly the same time.

The oil moguls were often eclipsed by Aussie big fish, Kerry Packer: a man partial to a big punt. He only ever played with large denomination chips. Kerry often worked up an appetite, and his usual fare was French fries, cheeseburger and Coke. One night it was served up to him on an antique sterling silver salver, and he went berserk and fired the lot up the wallpaper. He hadn't lost the common touch! You can do that sort of thing when you are a billionaire.

Robert Maxwell also liked a gamble. (he couldn't lose, he was playing with the pension money) A favourite haunt of his was Maxim's. I found him to be boorish, prickly and arrogant, especially after he had imbibed brandy. An alcohol ban was enforced at the tables... that was unless your name was Captain Bob. He nonchalantly carried around a large carafe. When he lost, he would curse and scream abuse at the croupiers, demanding they be stood down.

Nobody would sit next to him because of his obnoxious manner, but I didn't mind and more often than not, I would be up close and personal. I always did enjoy good cabaret. Maxwell played a system called *Tier*, which consisted of numbers 27, 13, 36, 11, 30, 8, 23, 10, 5, 24, 16 and 33. Subsequently I took up this particular system, and I still know the numbers off by heart, playing Maxwell's favoured Tier up to the present day. I only hope I don't end up where he did.

During my early forays into London's casinos, I would occasionally give blackjack a whirl, especially if the roulette table wasn't playing ball. One late afternoon in Crockfords, I was shilly-shallying over a few hands of cards, when a certain roulette table seemed to be calling me over. The clock was showing a quarter past five. I placed a few hesitant chips on some random numbers, and by half-past eight, I had a mountainous pile of them in front of me totalling some £365,000. It was a fortune for a teenager and Crockfords couldn't be more delighted to hand the cheque over - they must have known it was coming back to them, one way or another.

It was in Cromwells Casino that I made the acquaintance of the legendary George Best, a classy individual, for whom nothing was too much trouble, he'd sign autographs all night and chat good-humouredly to all and sundry. George couldn't remember, but I'd met him when I was a youngster back in Dubai 1977. Manchester United were playing in the British Super Cup, a competition organised by the Dubaian government against local hotshots Al Nasar. Best, Law and Crerand were amongst the main protagonists and I was introduced to them by my father, who got them to sign autographs for me, not a bad start to any collection.

George recalled that Paddy Crerand, although a Scottish international, was of Southern Irish descent and had big problems at the airport, because everyone bar the British needed a visa for Dubai, Paddy was in danger of being detained and missing his flight home, but it was all eventually sorted out and an embarrassing diplomatic problem was avoided.

At that time, the British navy were the only fleet allowed to dock in Dubai, even the other Arab states couldn't weigh anchor, full respect to all involved.

Back home, London was awash with money. Lovely lucre in Lambeth, wonderful wonga in Westminster and super spondulicks in Stepney. Most of it was legal, but funny money was always sploshing about just beneath the veneer of respectability. By fair means or foul, I was determined to get my mitts on a large percentage of it. I had membership of twenty casinos, each of which allowed you to cash in three cheques. On top of that, I had five cheque books, plus numerous cheque guarantee cards for £250. If I encountered a bad run of luck, I would somehow have to connive to get the money back in the banks before the cheques hit.

There were a few close shaves, (bollocks to you Victor Kiam) but if the shit was ever going to hit the fan, I had a *Plan B* which I would put into operation. My dad had an overseas account in a London branch of Nat-West. The bank manager there, who shall remain nameless, was a man I could persuade to appreciate my point of view. I regally wined and dined him at the best casinos, gave him money to bet with and manoeuvred a few stunners into his flight path. It wasn't difficult obtaining a blank cheque book in my father's name, so, say if a financial Armageddon was looming I'd just sign a cheque with dad's signature - simples! Of course one couldn't do that now, the banking industry is immaculately clean. Our honourable politicians tell us that all the dishonesty in the city is long gone.

Ladbrokes had for years harboured an interest in casinos and they were primed to make their move. They aggressively entered the fray, opening up several establishments, but they certainly weren't the new paragons of gambling, they were bending more rules than Uri Geller had teaspoons. Extremely attractive young ladies were recruited to entice punters from other casinos into their own. It was so blatant that it was only a matter of time before the powers that be started asking questions - they were spilling for a grilling.

The giant bookmakers were rewarded with their day in a court - and it wasn't ladies day at Wimbledon either. Standing in front of the beak, their nefarious tactics were exposed and punished, stopping their little gallop dead in its tracks. I had been propositioned half a dozen times myself on various nights. What a sex god I was! Back to my flat then sweetheart? No, you only want to go to Ladbrokes Casino? How many times did I hear that? On one of those missions, dirty Ladbrokes should have left me well alone, I hammered them for fifty thousand, and afterwards, the girl did come back to my flat. All in a night's work, I suppose.

My confidence had risen so much since I left Copford that life in the casinos was eye-opening and educational, and I was learning so much more than I ever would at day college. London was a magic metropolis for a young man with means, but I also realised, if someone was potless, it could be a cold, heartless, nightmare existence for them.

I became a gambling buddy of arms dealer Adnan Khashoggi. We would chat into the early hours at the Ritz Casino. He was a man of the world who liked to wind down by playing the roulette table. Over one period of time he experienced a disastrous run of bad luck, and he was not best pleased to say the least. Whenever my own luck turned sour, I just used to picture a T-Rex trying to masturbate - now that really was bad luck! Khashoggi presented Ritz with a stellar cheque, it was rumoured to be eight million pounds, but it bounced higher than the BT Tower. Ritz pursued him through the newspapers and courts, but I don't think they ever saw a bean.

The United Nations building in New York should be converted into a casino: Jews, Muslims, Arabs, Indians, Pakistanis, Chinese, English, Irish and Americans, happy as pigs in shit, all mixing and congregating as brothers in arms. As an Iranian man in London, I can safely say I've experienced no racism. The English people are fair and tolerant. My heart is here - and they do say that home is where the heart is.

I do have a theory on snooker though. A game invented in the army mess at Jubbulpore in 1875 by Colonel Neville Chamberlain. It was to combat the long tedious nights whilst stationed in India during The British Raj years. First you pot all the redskins, then you take out all the colours, culminating with just two balls left, the black is always ceremoniously dispatched last, leaving the white ball on an expanse of green. If the politically correct brigade ever cotton on, snooker clubs the length and breadth of the country will disappear.

There will always be bigots on race and religion, but it makes me laugh when the god-botherers of the established faiths, Judaism, Islam and Christianity, unite and all condemn homosexuality. A poor showing in this modern era to be preaching medieval doctrine - divide and segregate. It's now a brave new world, and churches are turned into bingo halls and auction houses. We've lost a lot of our spirituality, but winning the snowball or copping for a cheap leather three piece suite has perhaps been adequate compensation for the rejection of eternal salvation.

Back in 1969, the group Blue Mink made a great record entitled *Melting Pot* that was decades ahead of its time;

Take a pinch of white man,
Wrap him up in black skins,
Add a touch of blue blood,
And a little bitty bit of Red Indian blood,
And turn out coffee coloured people by the score.

Was it an unwitting portent for this country's future? Enoch Powell had controversially embellished on it with his game-changing 'Rivers of blood' speech. A massive amount has certainly altered in a short period of time. Fourteen years of Labour's open door policy for a multi-cultural society has changed the face of Britain forever, and there is no turning back. Some are pessimistic, some confident, a lot are indifferent. Brexit has proved that. I believe we can go from strength to strength if we all stick together, not as Little Englanders or as Europeans, but as decent human beings. The British are the finest people in the world, so let history judge former Prime Ministers Blair and Brown, along with svengali Alastair Campbell. Smugness and arrogance are never a template for greatness.

At this point in my life I was happy and contented, and living the *dolce vita*, but fate always gives long odds for sustained uninterrupted bliss, and it was only a matter of time before the waves broke over the levee. Unbeknown to me big daddy had other devious plans for his demon sperm, and unilaterally had decided that the United States of America was to be my next illuminating port of call. Another huge culture shock was on the horizon, and, like a silent fart in an elevator, I never knew it was coming.

Uncle Sam was hailing me through his megaphone, but for all I cared, he could stick it right up his Grand Canyon. No more football, no more bookies, no more London - it would all be a huge bind. How long would it be before I heard the dulcet tones of Max Bygraves again?

It just didn't bear thinking about...

*　　*　　*　　*

CHAPTER 5

CALIFORNIA GIRLS

Arabic saying: Patience is beautiful

Boom, boom... The screech of rubber tyres assaulting then caressing the hot asphalt runway heralded my touchdown in the United States of America: Home of the brave, land of the free - and locale of a lot of bullshit. Sacramento, the state capital of California was to be my new Yankee Doodle Dandy watering hole. Dear father had enrolled me at Sacramento State University, a massive labyrinthian complex covering over 300 acres. The campus had a hornet as site mascot. Somebody with a warped sense of humour must have been impressed by Watford's black and yellow kit. Sacramento was a beautiful city with stunning architecture, so really it was fuck-all like Watford, despite the big wasp connection.

Since 1967 Ronnie Reagan, Maggie Thatcher's number one supporter, had resided there as the Governor of California. The ex-Hollywood actor had once starred in a movie called 'Bedtime for Bonzo', featuring a trained chimpanzee who had been allocated the title role, and which proceeded to out-act 'Big Dutch' and steal every scene in the film. Politics was the only way up for Reagan after that. The Californian electorate certainly loved an actor, and Arnold Schwarzenegger got the same gig years later. The comic equivalent in England would be my favourites *Del Boy* as Mayor of London, and *Boycie* as Chancellor of the Exchequer. They would definitely have had the edge.

In 1849 at nearby John Sutter's fort, a substance was discovered that sent people crazy and irrational - and it wasn't cannabis. Gold (everybody's favourite Spandau Ballet record) was reported to be as abundant as the grains of sand on Santa Monica beach. That year heralded the great gold rush. Wagon trains of washer-women from Washington, bus loads of brick layers from Boston, and numerous night watchmen from New York accompanied one virgin from Vermont to move steadily due West across the massive open prairies.
Now you know why the San Francisco Gridiron football team are called

The 49ers. It was the year huge migration, when dreamers, gamblers and optimists all packed their worldly possessions to ply for the golden dream. Most returned home potless. The people who made the big money were crafty, astute merchants, who provided basic essentials such as tents, spades, picks, salt, meat, and even blue jeans, which were all needed for the long haul.

Sacramento's population was doubling every few months. In 1848, a year before the madness, there was a stable level of 7,000. By late boom year the number had swelled to over 300,000. Today the population has reached a respectable half a million, thus making Sacramento California's seventh largest city. The state capital, compared to L.A. or San Francisco, has very low crime figures and is regarded as the most racially diverse and integrated city in America.

The city's most famous son, Rodney King - infamous more like - must have wished he was back home on the night members of the Los Angeles Police Department stopped him in 1981. Suspected of drink-driving, King was told to vacate his motor and was then manhandled to the floor. LAPD officers then tried to handcuff him as he was lying on his stomach. King lashed out, and received what they would call in Britain 'a bloody good hiding'. He was Tasered numerous times, and received 56 baton blows from the officers' night sticks. And just for good measure suffered a few well-aimed kicks to various parts of his anatomy. He put Mick McManus and Kendo Nagasaki to shame... the plonker kept getting up. How he never got a contract with the WWF is baffling by anyone's standards. What L.A.'s finest didn't realise was that a curious bystander was filming the whole debacle. Watch the video on YouTube as King breaks three national records: namely America's toughest man, America's most stupid man and most pain-numbing drugs ever ingested before getting a good thumping.

The incident went to court the following year (1982) and the four most bellicose officers were acquitted on the grounds they had used reasonable force. It was par for the course. Justice had been served in the courthouse, but outside on the mean streets of lower Los Angeles, they went berserk at the verdict. The locals were not happy. 7,000 fires and 3,000 businesses wrecked with a billion dollars lost in damages. For three days the police, US army, Marines and National Guard tried to quell the riots, but not before the casualties numbered 53 dead and nearly 2,500 seriously injured. In the Watts district of Los Angeles, police knew that the usual suspects were partial to a riot. They'd had a few explosive incidents before, but this time the law machine was declared a corrupt entity. People had had enough of rank prejudice and unfairness. The four acquitted officers were sent for retrial, with two receiving small prison sentences.

This was the backdrop for my arrival, though while I was there, calmness was the norm, but I soon realised that simmering racial tension was always just bubbling under the surface in the melting pot of the big two tier American cities.

So here I was, miles from home, different customs, eccentric people... Mind you, they all had great teeth, but this was California. You could sunbathe, swim in the ocean, and ski in the mountains - all in the same day. That would be bloody tiring, but it had the edge on ferreting in Barrow-in-Furness. They all bloody drove on the wrong side of the road too... sorry, freeway. I figured it would be rude not to follow suit, and could even be dangerous. I was also determined to adapt and pick the lingo up as I went along. I even turned up at Sacramento University. Had I seen the light? Well, there were thousands of pretty young girls enrolled there pursuing further education. I might even be able to share some of my unique knowledge with one or two... or thirty.

Strolling aimlessly down the faculty corridors, confidently chilling while trying to find my bearings, Cupid's golden arrow struck. There she was at the drinks fountain, small in stature, but with an ample frontage and a J-Lo derriere - a gorgeous Latin-American brunette. I made discreet inquiries and discovered her name was Brandi Ramirez, and that her family had moved from Chihuahua, Mexico, for a new life in the States.

She was studying science, thank God - it wasn't philosophy, but that would ding dang do for me. I fancied becoming a budding Michael Faraday. On enrolling into her class, I found myself situated at a desk miles behind Brandi; I could just about make her out. Binoculars were not practical, so I gave a spotty Herbert 50 dollars to swap places. That put me in prime position just to her left. I was now ready to make my move. Over the first month we got chatting and I was making her laugh, which was a good sign and I was still behaving like a perfect gentleman.

On the scientific front, I was completely out of my depth, the lecturer, Mr. Donald, a man who spoke like W.C. Fields would bluster, 'Faisal, my boy, I'll wear a monkey's ass for a hat if you graduate from this class'. I told him it would suit him! He'd laugh and clap me on the back. God bless America. I was there for one reason, and one reason alone, to deflower the fragrant, ravishing Miss Ramirez.

One Friday afternoon, walking out onto the parking lot, I spotted my darling angel and made a beeline approach. Two large dark forms emerged from the shadows. It was her two older brothers, Ramon and Raoul. I extended a friendly hand out to shake, Ramon spat on it. I reasoned that this must be an old Mexican custom. Raoul brusquely intervened, *'If you so much as glance at our leetle seester, we will cut off your tiny pecker'*. Surely he hadn't seen me in the showers?! Grassed I'd been, a month's courting up the Swanee.

I returned home downcast, but still fully intact. I valued my pecker. I hadn't made any American buddies, but had befriended a chirpy cockney, Dave

34

Anderson from Bromley, a good looking, affable chappie in his mid twenties. He was over on extended holiday, staying with relatives, after recently taking a decent redundancy deal back home.

The following Saturday morning we drove into downtown Sacramento. Dave had a very tidy, poser blue Ford Thunderbird. Destination: the huge shopping mall. He needed some new Adidas trainers, prior to sampling a Bud or two. Strolling through the mall, I overheard a sibilant whisper of 'Faz, Faz', coming from over my left shoulder. Swivelling round, I caught sight of Brandi in a figure-hugging, strapless red dress. She was enjoying a coffee at the Plaza Café with her best mate, a tall willowy blonde, Ingrid Gunderson. Dave and I swaggered over like Steve McQueen and Paul Newman. (stop it)

Brandi fluttered her ample eyelashes, rolling her huge almond cow eyes like a little girl lost, 'Faz... Myself and Ingrid have no-one to take us to Disco Diva's tonight'.

'Too bad treacle', butted in Dave trying to sound cool, his slabbering tongue hanging out over his chin like a rabid Alsatian, putting Gene Simmons to shame. A swift forceful kick by me to his shins sorted it, 'Myself and young David here, have no prior engagements, can we be of service?'

Ingrid trilled 'Oh, I love this English etiquette!'. Dave was starting to hyperventilate badly, so I told the girls that we would be back in two ticks after we had got him his new trainers.

The crown prince of Bromley was being fitted up in the sports shop, 'Bloody hell mate, they're two babes, gagging for it!'. No shit Sherlock, things were looking up, 'Nonchalance is the key David', I advised.

'Do what Faz?', he quizzed blankly.

'Forget it mate', I concluded.

We swiftly got back over to find the girls being mithered by two local dudes, both baseball-capped. One hadn't missed many dinners, whilst the other one definitely knew where all the Burger King franchises were situated.

There was a survey done, and it said that a third of all Americans are classed as obese. So why it is that everyone on Baywatch looks a million dollars? That Hoff's full of crap. I still watched it every week though... just shows you what bad scripts and teeny swimwear can achieve.

'Who's ate all the pies!?' shouts Dave, doing his bit for the US-England 'Special Relationship'. Porker Minimus came back lamely with 'I've only had a pizza, man'. Dave followed it up with, 'You two are definitely taking the piss'. Porker Maximus was indignant, 'Look buddy, we haven't been to the john'. It was at that moment, I realised, England and America were two different nations divided by the same language (and thankfully, the fucking Atlantic Ocean). With that, the two yanks departed...struggling manfully through the café door, after becoming wedged the first time.

Brandi was straight to the point, 'Would you boys like to escort us to the dance?'

'Not many, sweetheart', replied Dave.

'Excuse me?', Ingrid interjected.

'Of course we do!', I assured her, restoring the voice of reason to the situation.

While Ingrid gave Dave her address and phone number, (both girls were staying at Ingrid's) I warily took Brandi aside, 'What about your two brothers, remember?', I said, pointing to my crotch. She giggled, 'Don't worry about them, sweetie. They have gone to a mariachi concert in San Diego. Besides, I think Raoul likes you, when anyone ever besmirches the family honour, he usually threatens to kill them. No one will touch your pecker... bar me'. At that moment, all my ducks were in a row. Faisal, you lucky, lucky bastard... and I could even end up having Pancho Villa for a brother in law. Long live the revolution.

Returning home I needed some well earned shut-eye, it was going to be a long hazy, crazy night, within minutes I began falling in and out of consciousness, as parts of Americana were disturbing my fragile equilibrium, and with that, sleep became my master. America really is fifty countries in one union, no state is similar to another. California is nothing like Alabama or Montana. One in eight Americans live in California and it became the first state to achieve a trillion dollar economy. Barbie, blue jeans, the pill, wet suits and the computer mouse were all conceived in the golden state.

Americans are strange birds, a quarter of the population has appeared on TV, while the same number deny there was a moon landing. A quarter of American adults don't understand that the earth orbits the sun yearly. Only a fifth of them own a passport. Not great travellers, a high number have never been out of their own state or even seen the ocean. Of course it's a country of paradoxes - massive wealth, abject poverty, skyscrapers and shanty towns. Britain has its sink council estates, and chavs with Dobermanns or Staffordshire Bulldogs, America its trailer parks with uneducated trashy underclass.

Despite its brilliance as self-proclaimed leader, the policeman of the world and a powerhouse economy, the USA gets a lot of bad press. The American motto of 'Big is best' gets short shrift from countries abroad. Forward thinking, the USA was building skyscrapers in the 1930s, afterwards six lane freeways and huge building projects like dams and bridges would follow. Their debatable foreign policy has made the country unpopular around the world, especially in the Middle and Far East, but closer to home there is a love-hate relationship with northern neighbours Canada, a touch like England and Scotland.

This is a true transcript of an actual radio conversation of a US naval ship contacting Canadian authorities off the coast of Newfoundland in Oct 1995, showing bully-boy methods don't always pay.

Americans: *Please divert your course 15 degrees to the north to avoid a collision.*

Canadians: *We recommend you divert your course 15 degrees to the south to avoid a collision.*

Americans: *This is the captain of a US navy ship, I say again, divert your course.*

Canadians: *No, I say again you divert your course.*

Americans: *This is the aircraft carrier USS Lincoln, second largest ship of the Atlantic fleet, accompanied by three destroyers, three cruisers and numerous support vessels, I demand you change course or measures will be undertaken.*

Canadians: *This is a lighthouse... your call!*

That shows the stupidity of some people at the top of their profession, but stupidity isn't confined to Americans. The Beatles were knocked back by ten recording studios. J.K. Rowling spent seven years and 35 rejections trying to get Harry Potter published. Benny Hill had his contract cancelled by Thames television in 1989. At the time, *The Benny Hill Show* was being watched by over twenty million people. No more Hill's Angels, a disgraceful decision.

There are still executives dining out on 'I told John Lennon, guitar groups are dead, ha-ha!', or 'Miss Rowling, this is pretentious nonsense', or 'Thanks for twenty glorious years, Benny, but your shows are smutty and in the words of the immortal Harold Steptoe, you are a dirty old man, so grab your grubby mac and fuck off!'.

Listen to this one, Pacific Airlines ran an advert: *You're scared of flying? So's our pilot!* They went bankrupt two months later, the execs probably got a golden handshake.

George Bernard Shaw had a high opinion of Americans: he said 'The hundred per cent American is ninety nine per cent idiot'. Praise indeed. So now we know how Regan and Bush reached the top. Even Napoleon Bonaparte had them sussed. He remarked, 'In politics, stupidity is not a handicap'. Which takes us to George W. Bush. Incredibly he graduated from Yale University and Harvard business school - they've gone down in my estimation. Bush was governor of

Texas before becoming president. The Lone Star State led the league tables for administering the death penalty, and Bush never once pardoned a felon on death row. So when he hit the White House with his ultra right-wing, Christian policies, I thought we were in for a nuclear winter. Thank God someone else was pulling the strings. What he gave us though, was gaffe after gaffe. At the G8 summit he once shouted over to the Italian prime minister, Silvio Berlusconi, 'Amigo, amigo'. Brilliant, not even the same language. It's on a par with your average Brit abroad on holiday. You know the one: bloated with peeling lobster skin and obligatory union jack shorts, sitting at the one star hotel poolside table with his new single mother girlfriend from Wolverhampton and a couple of pals of the same persuasion. He tries to attract the attention of the wine waiter, shouting across, 'Hey cunto, cuatro San Miguels, pronto bastardo'. His girlfriend looks up adoringly at him, 'Gary, I didn't know you were bi-lingual!'. He now mistakingly thinks that she's just insulted him, 'Shut the fuck up, Brittney, don't mug me off in front of my mates'. With that she bursts into tears and runs off into the hotel lobby to cop off that night with the understanding, but amorous Pepe on reception.

Believe it or not, that was verbatim, word for word the very first scene from the ill-fated, short-lived, BBC flagship soap opera, 'El Dorado'. With a script as good as that, how could they have ditched it.

If, like me, it brought a tear to your eye, please picket the BBC studios, Shepherds Bush (placards acceptable) and demand the return of this great drama which would once again put our young actors and actresses in the shop window for the world's media. If successful, they can proudly walk down Hollywood Boulevard, or, on a lesser night, Hull Boulevard... the choice is yours.

Back to Bush. What a role model he was. When asked about education he commented, 'Rarely is the question asked - "Is our children learning?" '. So enough said, but we shouldn't be so smug. We let John Prescott go all the way - then again he did have a good left jab.

Where America ventures, we usually follow. Blair was known as Bush's poodle but I think of him more as a Labrador trying to messily hump your trouser leg. Thank God we didn't go into Vietnam, because they did want us there. America's finest hour must have been 1983 when they invaded the smallest independent country in the western hemisphere: the island of Grenada in the Caribbean. There was a rumour of Cubans on the island; revolution was afoot, and damn commies threatening the security of the homeland. Send the boys in. 7,500 troops obliged and blew up two fruit stalls. There was mango excrement everywhere. Back home for tea, a ticker tape parade, medals for the ships' cooks and cigars all round. A New York Times pressman summed up the nation's mood succinctly, 'A lovely little war!'. So it was, and so it is today.

I awoke from my slumbers. I'd teamed up with Marlon Brando in *Apocalypse Now*. It must have been a dream, as all my medals were gone. Why was I in bed at seven o'clock? It came back in a flash, Dave was coming round at eight, so just time for a shit, shave and shower followed by liberal drenching of Kouros, all over my erogenous zones. Miss Ramirez, please surrender now, you have no defence.

Dave turned up in a battered, rusty old Nissan Bluebird. I screamed, 'Where's the bleeding Thunderbird?'.

'Valves gone. This is my uncle's motor. You're not disappointed are you?', said Dave.

'No, I'm over the fucking moon, we're picking up two of California's hottest totty, driving this total pile of shit'.

I had to think fast. Leaving nothing to chance, I came up with a brilliant plan. We drove over to Ingrid's. They both came out wearing micro satin hot pants. Dave gasped, 'I love this country, Faz'. I was in no mood for small talk, but he did have a point.

'Shut the fuck up Dave, keep your hands on the wheel, your eyes on the road and let me do all the talking'.

I could see the girls were genuinely underwhelmed, but I had more cheek than Kim Kardashian's bigger sister. I went into bullshit overdrive, 'Dave's had to come straight from work, we didn't want to be late'. They liked that. It showed we had a caring nature. Now for the killer move... It had been remarked on more than one occasion that I had a passing resemblance to a young Omar Sharif. It . was time to play my trump card and it had nothing to do with Donald.

'I'm going up to Hollywood next month, did I ever mention that I'm also an actor and stunt man? Would you young ladies like to accompany me to Columbia Film Studios? I'm contracted to Omar Sharif's new feature film - as his body double'.

The screams nearly burst my eardrums. They were bouncing up and down, the car was rocking, and I was on a roll.

'Did you ever see Lawrence of Arabia?'. Sighs and yesses, nods and more sighs.

'Well, that was me on the lead camel, charging into Damascus. David Lean came over after I dismounted and shook my hand for that'. Brandi excitedly exclaimed that first thing tomorrow, she was going out to buy the video. The film was made two years before I was born, but both the girls took it as gospel.

We parked up at *Disco Divas*. 'Faz, you're a genius', said Dave.

'I know', I replied modestly.

Inside, Brandi was living up to her name. She certainly liked a drink, and by ten thirty she was rat-arsed. The last straw came when she stumbled head first over a table laden with beer bottles and glasses. The occupants, four French-Canadian lumberjacks, didn't look overly impressed as all the drinks shattered on the tiled floor. I was given an ultimatum by the smallest lumberjack, six-foot, six-inch tall Louis. 'Get the beers in Abdul, unless you fancy a trip to the dentist'.

I've still got all my gnashers and the tree fellers never did go thirsty, but it was a timely reminder for a tactical retreat. I phoned for a taxi cab, bade farewell to Dave and Ingrid, before eventually loading Brandi onto the back seat. The driver was a kindly soul, 'If she fucking honks up man, it'll cost youse a 100 dollars'. I assured him that there was more chance of Joe Pesci turning out for the Boston Celtics. 'Fucking limey', he muttered under his breath.

We coasted into the cool moonlit night, I cupped the back of the half comatose Brandi's head in my gentle hands. What a looker she was. It took a supreme effort to keep my eyes on the taxi meter.

Then, without warning, a rumbling gurgling sound was fermenting from deep inside her. It didn't sound that favourable. Brandi lurched forward, spewing out a hot discharge with all the force of Krakatoa, depositing a Technicolor yawn all over my lap. Three Miller Lites, a bag of pretzels, four Bloody Marys, a chilli dog, six pina coladas and one Drambuie shandy, pebble-dashed my beige suit trousers and the once pristine taxi upholstery. I smiled sheepishly at the driver, 'I think she's had one cocktail too many'.

'That's a fucking hundred man', riposted the cabbie.

Thank you, thank you very much. I'd wanted to swap bodily fluids with Brandi, but not like this. There was no option but to drop her off at Ingrid's. I carried her right up the garden path, then desperately tried to ring the door bell. A light went on, Ingrid's mother sidled up to the scene, 'Hurry up she's heavy!'.

The door opened, and I stepped forward and slumped Brandi into the passageway. 'Hey, where's my Ingrid?', inquired Mrs Gunderson. I wasn't in the mood for gay banter, 'She's still out, but in safe hands... nighty night!'

And with that, I left the two women, one astonished, one unconscious. Weighed down by three litres of sick, I'd managed to attract a local street dog with the unbelievable stench emanating from round my bollocks.

Even in adversity I had magnetism...

'The meter's still running, buddy'. The driver was a laugh a minute, but at least he stepped on the gas. I was just relieved to get home. The cabbie was straight on my case, 'With the collateral damage, that's one hundred and forty nine dollars and fifty cents'.

'At least Dick Turpin wore a mask', I countered

'Dick who?', he growled, nonplussed.

'Forget it and please keep the change',offering 150 bucks.

'Tightass!', he muttered, and sped off, but not before giving me a one-fingered salute through the side window.

That was me done with Brandi, tacos, cacti, sombreros, tequila... and Aztec Camera. Just for good luck, Sacramento University was going on the back burner as well. Was it all kismet or destiny? No, it was sheer bloody stupidity and I badly needed redemption. America itself was giving me the pip more than ever, and even their very best washing powders couldn't remove the reek of Brandi's toxic assault on the suit. It went in the garbage can - beige was so last year anyway. I had to make a life-affirming decision - babes or bets. Both could be very expensive, but it was now perfect timing for me to hit the green baize. I'd been a good boy on the gambling front, but I needed that buzz again before I got withdrawal symptoms.

My dear father, please forgive me, but could you look away now, some of your inheritance might just be heading for *32 red*.

* * * *

CHAPTER 6

SCOTLAND THE BRAVE

Arabic saying: A friend advises in his interest, not yours

I was utterly, butterly over Brandi, thank God. I couldn't afford the bar bill, but out of the blue, I took another blow to the solar plexus. Dave was heading back to Blighty, he'd run out of wonga, and besides he was desperately homesick. I'd offered to avail him of more of my dad's money, but he was adamant (ridicule is nothing to be scared of, sorry). So I reluctantly saw him off at the airport'. Just think Faz, this coming Wednesday, I'll be watching Bromley FC, and at the weekend, a run down to Selhurst Park, Palace v Burnley'. I joked that I was glad to be staying.

That's when it struck me like a juggernaut shunting a lame, partially sighted traffic warden up in the air. I was fucked. Here I was, in a country of three hundred million and I had nothing in common with any of them. It was the only nation in the world at that time that totally shunned football.

I gave Dave a long man hug, 'Go, and don't look back, brave Lochinvar'. He shuffled to the ticket booth and looked devastated. We were like kindred spirits. All we needed was James Blunt to strike up with 'Good Bye My Lover'. Daft really, we weren't lovers and the song wouldn't be recorded for many years.

Then he was gone.

I've never felt so isolated as I was at that moment - miles from home, and my beloved football, a forlorn distant memory. What I needed was an adrenaline boost, and there it was on the airport wall. The advert trumpeted, *Come to Lake Tahoe, for fun, frolics and entertainment*. What really caught my eye was a roulette table in the bottom left corner. Lake Tahoe is the largest alpine lake in North America, situated bang on the California-Nevada border, 6,000 feet above sea level, and standing in an area of stunning natural beauty, surrounded by the enigmatic Sierra Nevada Mountains. Faz, you're thinking, why are you telling us this shit, you wouldn't know a chipmunk from a groundhog.

I shall continue. Noted for the clarity of the water, it's truly a popular tourist attraction for the skiing community. Since the 1950s there have been large casinos constructed on the Nevada side of the lake (Hallelujah, it was beginning to sound like a Judith Chalmers travelogue).

So there it was, manna from heaven. I booked my ticket. I thought, tomorrow afternoon, I would be inhaling the glorious mountain air, taking in the aroma of the spruce forests, but only on the short run from the airport to Cal-Ne-va Casino. You don't want too many healthy options.

On returning home, I flicked through the TV sports channels; baseball, basketball, ice-hockey and gridiron were the only options. How optimistic would you be, trying to sell Test Cricket to an American sports executive?

'So just go through it again... You play for five days, have five dinners, five teas and on the last day you can still draw - are you jerking me off, buddy?'.

What chance had football got. It was the number one game everywhere else, but here it wasn't even on the radar. It was *the* world game and I was feeling nostalgic about the World Cup. The first one I'd watched was in 1978, hosted by Argentina. England wasn't there, but it was still a spectacle.

As earlier mentioned, America has a very strong rivalry with Canada, and back home in '78 it was anyone's to win, bar 'The Jocks', or as my cockney compatriots would fondly describe them, 'the sweaty socks'. Scotland were regarded by the English as having a self-destruct button and it wasn't a question of if, but when it would be pushed.

It had all started so promisingly. In 1977 the Scottish FA appointed club manager Ally Macleod as the new supremo. A shy and retiring type, he announced himself to the world with the statement, 'I'm Ally Macleod and I am a winner!'.

To be fair, Scotland qualified well and even got to number six in the hit parade with *Allys Tartan Army*. A banal dirge that wasn't a patch on England's *World in Motion* - surely the finest football song of all time. Yes I know, *Three Lions* was great... leave it out.

Macleod had convinced everyone north of the border that the World Cup was in the bag. Naïve confidence turned to outright boasting, and they even had a tartan army victory parade, attracting 25,000 fans to Hampden Park a few days before they left for the Argentine Republic. At Prestwick Airport a young reporter, wistfully asked Macleod, 'What do you plan to do after winning the World Cup Ally?'. He came back with a classic, 'Retain it laddie, retain it!'

This was just too good to miss. He thought Scotland could win back-to-back World Cups. There was more chance of Blakey from *On the Buses* procuring the romantic lead in the new West End production of *Grease*. All England sat back, beer in hand and waited for the carnage. And it wasn't long in coming. The beginning of the end was at Cordoba, a provincial town in the foothills of the Sierra Chicas. June 3rd 1978 was the date and it was a night I'll never, ever forget. Minutes prior to the big match, I was sampling a couple or three, in an Ipswich backstreet pub. In strides William 'Jock' Reynolds wearing a garish kilt. I'd never seen it before, apparently it only came out if Scotland reached the World Cup finals or if he bought a round of drinks, so it didn't see the light of day very often.

Jock was a man on a mission, here to watch Scotland v Peru. 'Brace yourself, Faisal, we are going all the way', declared Jock, all but knocking me over with his whiskeyed, halitotic, paint-stripper breath.

I shrugged my shoulders. 'This is our time boy'. Jock was another poor, gullible sod, who'd had been taken in by Macleod, the great pretender. 'Mines a double Glenfiddich, Faisal... I'm going to relieve myself', and off he trotted to the toilet.

'Are you sure you don't want the ladies door darling?', someone called out to a round of cheers. Jock was from the land of Rabbie Burns and Sir Walter Scott, he'd have a rapier riposte for that frivolous remark, 'Fuck off, you English wanker!', followed by two fingers and more cheers. This was brilliant. We all settled down to watch the match and it hurts me to say it, but Scotland had a very strong team: Rough in goal, with a back four of Buchan, Kennedy, Forsyth and Burns. In midfield, Rioch, Masson, Hartford and Willie Johnson, and up front Joe Jordan and Kenny Dalglish. At that time, you were only allowed two subs, and Scotland had Archie Gemmill and Lou Macari. Not even making it on the bench were players of the calibre of John Robertson, Graham Souness - and Derek Johnston, a man who had scored 40 goals for Glasgow Rangers that season. They didn't even bother taking Andy Gray and he'd bagged 29 goals in the English First Division. So what could go wrong? I had an opinion on Alan Rough the goalie, who I regarded as dodgy, but I would keep it under my Tam o'Shanter.

Scotland started the better, and Joe Jordan put them ahead after 14 mins. Jock was out of his seat like an Apollo rocket. He attempted a paraplegic highland fling, which turned into a combination of a demented Moon Walk and a Gay Gordon.

'Dynamite moves, Jock,' I commented, 'move your arse to the bar laddie, it's celebration time!', he countered. The rest of the half was nip and tuck, but on the stroke of half time disaster struck and Cueto scored for Peru. A cheer went up that shook the rafters. The English were behind Peru to a man. Jock must have felt like the last Scotsman at the battle of Culloden, where William Duke of Cumberland massacred the Scottish Jacobites. In England the flower 'Sweet William' was named in honour of the duke, but over the border, to this day, it's known as 'Stinking Billy'. Nice.

Second half, more Glenfiddichs. Jock was a man possessed, then on the hour, penalty! Jock was hugging and kissing me, it was the worst sexual encounter of my life. Up stepped Don Masson. Big mistake. Masson was having a stinker, and every pass he made had gone to a white shirt. He loped up, and sent a pathetic penalty kick to the goalie's left. A shot your arthritic granny in the hospice would have saved, and it was palmed away to safety. I saw Jock visibly shrink. It was cruel really, but I had to laugh on his blind side, it was starting to resemble a bull fight. The end was coming, but who was going to enforce the *coup de grace*. Cometh the hour, up stepped the man: Teofilo Cubillas, a player who would be one of the stars of the tournament. On 72 mins, Peru got a free kick just outside the box, Cubillas struck the ball with the outside of his right boot. Rough leapt like a salmon! The trouble was, it was a tin of condemned John West salmon... and the ball sailed past him into the net. Jock glanced over at me, 'Rough by name, Rough by nature'. Quite a beautiful quote really and I couldn't disagree. Five minutes later Cubillas hit a scorcher, five yards further back than the previous free kick, the wretched Rough never smelt it.

Jock was a broken man. His hunched body departed through the bar door into the unforgiving twilight. Later on, someone saw him in the town centre, threatening an inanimate concrete lamp post. A true warrior. Later on, as I walked home that evening, I passed his house. His front garden overgrown with thistles. What a patriot the man was. Let's hope the clans never rise again.

It got worse after the match. Willie Johnson failed a drugs test and was sent home. It was rumoured at the airport that he was so high that he didn't bother with the plane.

All was not lost though. Scotland's next match was against the football Galacticos of Iran. Even the Jocks couldn't fuck that up... could they? It was a banker, one to lump your wages on, just what the doctor ordered. The match had Argentina spell bound. All of 8,000 turned up to watch it. The crowds at the 1978 world cup produced a strange phenomenon, they all seemed to be middle aged men in sheep skin coats. Watch some old videos, its amazing. Scotland went ahead again, courtesy of an Iranian own goal, only to be pegged back when Danaifar, that Persian household name, netted the equaliser. I'm from Iran and I've never heard of him. Scotland held out for a fighting one-one draw. The Shah was happy, I was happy, England was ecstatic. You could hear the wails emanating from north of Hadrian's Wall.

It was now backs against the wall time. Macleod had visibly aged 10 years, and he looked close to a nervous breakdown, but if Scotland could beat a strong Dutch side by three clear goals, they could still pull it out the fire and qualify.

Souness came in for his first game. A good man for a battle, and how come he wasn't used before, I'll never understand. It looked a better balanced Scottish side, and they nearly got off to a perfect start, Dalglish having a goal disallowed. Robbie Rensenbrink, then twisted the knife in and scored the 1,000th goal in World Cup history from the penalty spot. Scotland now needed four. Dalglish got one back, then wee Archie Gemmill got a second with another penalty. Greatness and immortality were looming up for Archie. Twenty minutes later, picking up the ball outside the penalty area, Gemmill took the ball past Jansen, then Krol and then jinked past the despairing lunge of Poortvliet, before casually lifting the ball left footed, past the advancing Dutch keeper.

It plays a noteworthy part in the film *Trainspotting*, and I wish I had a pound for every time that's been shown in Scotland. It made Gemmill a folk hero. The tiny man had the body of a Skoda, but the engine of a Rolls Royce. Scotland were now 3-1 up. They only needed one more, but a late Johnny Rep goal for Holland spoiled the party. Scotland had won the match, but lost the battle, it must be ingrained in their soul and psyche.

Before they flew home, Macleod, who must have been dreading stepping off the plane at the other end, was sitting alone contemplating what might have been, when a small Jack Russell dog came waddling over to him. 'Ma only wee friend in the world', he uttered, smiling for the first time in days. He bent down to stroke the dog and it bit him on the finger. What a fine hound the little nipper was. The Scottish charabanc had careered into the dark tunnel of elimination, headlong into the inevitable collision with underachievement, and after it came, there were few survivors.

It was a wonderful World Cup though, the ticker tape ovation each time Argentina played was magnificent, and they rewarded the home fans with victory in the final against gallant Holland. Who could ever forget the graceful goal machine, Mario Kempes, the pampas bull, Leopolde Luque, a young vibrant Ossie Ardiles and rock-hard captain Daniel Passarella. Memories I'll always treasure. And you know what, in some strange and perverse way, I felt sorry for all Americans, for they would never understand the sentiment and the beauty of the people's game.

* * * *

'Have a good day sir', said the beaming stewardess, 'I'll try', I replied pathetically, whilst dropping down the steps onto the South Lake Tahoe apron. Thank god I was out of California. Nevada had a much more liberal attitude to gambling and I was going to take full advantage of it. Strangely, Californian cities like Los Angeles are riddled with gang wars, multiple homicides, drug racketeering, bank heists and serious crime, yet if you wanted to place a bet, the response of the police would be, 'Not on our beat, weirdo'.

I decided to stay at the Cal-Neva Casino, it was probably the best known gaming house at Lake Tahoe, because Frank Sinatra had once owned it in the

1960s. What a stunning part of the world. Charles Bronson, Sammy Davis Jr., Cher and Lisa Minnelli had all lived on the lake's shore at one time or another.

It had become more commercialised in the 1970s. Two Mississippi paddle steamers (don't ask) were performing pleasure cruises around the lake. Of course Las Vegas was the Nevada kingpin, but casinos were sprouting up around Lake Tahoe. I played in all of them, with differing degrees of success. Hyatt Regency, Biltmore, Lakeside, Harrah's, Harvey's and Horizon all enjoyed my patronage.

The American roulette wheel is harder to win on, because as well as the zero, there is a double zero... robbing bastards. It really gives the house a big edge, but beating the casino is what really rocked my dhow.

I checked into the hotel suite. A few hours rest and recuperation wouldn't go amiss before I hit the tables. My room had a panoramic view of the lake that took your breath away. I'm a typical concrete jungle, city boy, but if you liked country pursuits, boating, yachting, hunting, rambling and skiing, you were in your element. Hollywood hadn't been slow in using Lake Tahoe as a backdrop, and had filmed *Indian Love Call* there in the 1920s (with Nelson Eddy and Jeanette McDonald)... 'When I'm calling you-hoo-hoo-hoo-hoo-hoo-hoo' (There was a rumour of a fifth Beatle)

Ask your mum and dad about the film... then give it a swerve.

Later movies shot there included, *The Bodyguard*, *Smokin'Aces*, and *City of Angels*. My favourite though was *The Godfather II*. The sumptuous house and grounds were up on Lake Tahoe. Do you remember the film's final minutes? The useless Fredo Corleone goes fishing with Al Pacino's hit man and gets one in the back of the nut. That's typically Italian, but way too sad. My preferred finish would have been Michael Corleone waiting anxiously on the jetty, the hit man guiding the boat in after bottling it, with Fredo standing triumphantly on the prow holding a 20 pound rainbow trout, then calling out, 'Mikey, get the sauce on, this mother wont fit in the pan'.

Francis Ford Coppola still regrets not going with it.

The TV series *Bonanza* was shot above Lake Tahoe. 'The Ponderosa' ranch stretched from the north shore of Lake Tahoe, all the was up to Carson City. Lorne Greene, who played Big Ben Cartwright, appeared in all 430 episodes from 1959 to 1973. That the series rolled for 15 years is a fitting tribute. Bonanza must have been very good, but all I can recall about it were the opening credits burning away, and the theme music. I have a conspiracy theory: I can't remember any of the scripts, did I just imagine it? Then again I thought Steve McClaren did a better job than Mike Bassett, England Manager. Controversial I know, but just my belief.

I played the tables at the Cal-Neva for the first two nights and I was up about a cheeky 500 dollars, even so, I decided on a change of venue as that might bring more success. I booked a taxi at reception. I'd give 'Harvey's' a whirl. I recalled, Harvey had been the name of a giant white rabbit in a Hollywood film of the same name. Every time James Stewart had one sherbet too many, the bumper bunny would appear and start talking to him. Maybe Harvey had made enough royalties from the flick and ploughed them into the casino.

The taxi pulled up. The driver even opened the rear passenger door, that was definitely a first. Up to that point, I'd rated American cabbies somewhere between unrefined faeces and a Jim Davidson audience. He was a gentleman of oriental persuasion, I had a quick gander at his lapel badge to confirm - 'Sung-Joo Choi'. I guessed Korean or Vietnamese. We drove for two miles and the silence was deafening - courteous he was, garrulous not. I decided to break the ice with a quip, 'You're a long way from Pearl Harbor'. Not a titter. A silent hiatus and then, 'I'm from Bussan'.

'Is that near Tunbridge Wells?'

'No, South Korea'. I persevered, 'You'll be home late tonight then'. He burst out laughing, 'You are a funny man!' I'd got him. All the way to Harvey's, it was non stop chatter. He was on duty all through the night, passing back his courtesy card to me, he insisted, 'You ask for Mr. Choi'. I paid the fare with a generous tip. I'd enjoyed his company, he could come back in the early hours.

The front facade of the illuminated Harvey's was impressive, but there was absolutely no evidence of a giant rabbit. I was welcomed by the large commissionaire doorman, who sported a thick, luxuriant brown moustache - a beauty, he resembled a friendly walrus. He would be known as Craig, in honour of Stadler, the rotund golfer.

I hit a tremendous winning streak at Harvey's. It had been a fortuitous move. As I counted my profits, I got chatting to the head floorwalker, Bart, a man born and bred in the Montana badlands who moved to New Jersey as a teenager. He had degenerated into a compulsive gambler around his mid to late twenties, losing his wife, kids and property, courtesy of roulette and slots in the cruel casinos of Atlantic City, on the Eastern Seaboard. He'd moved to Huntington Beach, California to get away and forget, but decided to confront all his demons, by moving to Lake Tahoe, gaining employment at the Biltmore Casino, starting at the bottom of the pile. He worked his way up and was head-hunted by Harvey's.

'Faz, I haven't struck a bet for over thirty years. If I put so much as a dime in a slot, I'll fall off the precipice'.

It was a sobering story alright. Britain and the States are littered with men who have gambled away their happiness, fortune and ultimately their family life. Bart turned raconteur and told me about an incident at Harvey's four years previously in 1980. John Birges, an inveterate gambler who claimed to have lost over one million dollars at the tables, was not a happy man.

In the early morning of August 6th, three men in white jump suits entered Harvey's Casino wheeling in a IBM copier. However, this was no copier. It was a thousand-pound rolling bomb, fitted with automatic timers and trigger mechanisms which would make it impossible to deactivate without complex instructions. John Birges contacted Harvey's, demanding a three million dollar ransom for information on making the bomb safe.

Harvey's immediately contacted the FBI, who evacuated the building. They then decided to detonate the bomb, as the uniqueness of it, would render deactivating it too dangerous. A remote-controlled detonation caused a five storey crater in the front on the building. Toilets and TV sets were dangling from pipes and electric cords, but at least nobody was injured. Birges never got his ransom money. The plot was cack-handed, with no chance of success. He was arrested with his two sons after the bomb delivery van's number plate was traced back to him. Birges was sentenced to life imprisonment and died in jail. His two sons, after co-operating with the authorities, got suspended sentences. John Birges had played his last roll of the dice and lost. He had ultimately taken things to unhealthy extremes.

Bart continued, 'Faz, can I ask you a pertinent question?'. We were in the land where all men had the right to bear arms. 'Shoot, fire away Bart.', I said.

'How do you compensate when you've lost more money than you can afford to? You've had a great night, but don't tell me you win all the time, because there's only one person who never loses and that's God Almighty.'

I came clean. 'I go cap in hand to my father'. Bart chugged on like a benevolent uncle. 'Son, one day you're gonna have to stand on your own two feet, your daddy ain't gonna be there forever, believe me, that time will come, as sure as eggs is eggs'. They were profound words, notwithstanding the bad grammar. It struck me like a thunderbolt from Valhalla, a cataclysmic eureka moment, I was nearly 21 years old, with no qualifications of any magnitude, and frittering my inheritance away on the green baize. I'd experienced multiple emotions on three continents with my exploits and escapades, but now, I vowed, this was the time to make a difference and accentuate the positive. 'Thank you Bart, could you call me a cab please? Mr. Choi would be first on my shortlist'.

On leaving Harvey's, I came across the Walrus and Mr. Choi both grappling with the rear passenger door handle. It was East vs West in a titanic supremacy struggle. The nimble Mr. Choi resembled Bruce Lee in *The Green Hornet*. Whilst the Walrus had the advantage of extra poundage, it could all have escalated into Pork Chop Hill. Being a pacifist, I wasn't going to get in between them, so I simply wafted a ten dollar bill under the nose of the heavier man. 'Here you are Craig, treat yourself to some fish fingers'. He was made up, and a quick bow from Mr. Choi and we were speeding off into the last remnants of the morning gloaming.

By the time we got back to the Cal-Neva, Mr. Choi's life story was indelibly implanted. He had left Korea as a teenager and moved in with relatives in San Francisco, met and married a local girl of Korean descent who had blessed him with three young children. He decided to move the family to Nevada to avoid the kids getting sucked into the gang culture that prevailed for young Hispanic and Asian offspring in that city.

I gave him a 200 dollar tip, telling him to buy something nice for his wife and kids. After that I was a friend for life.

My body clock was suffering. I was tossing and turning in my hotel bedroom. Bart's words kept reverberating through my mind. Had I really under-achieved?

A God-like vision recalled two years earlier that my all-time favourite football team, Brazil, were expected to win the world cup in Spain and emulate the dynamic 1970 side.

The manager, Telly Santana, wanted the team to put on a performance every match with attacking football, and bookies were running scared as the money piled in for them. What a team they were! Zico, an attacking maestro, Falcao, a midfield dynamo, known as the 'King of Rome' from his time in Italy, and Socrates, the thinking man's footballer. They had Cerezzo who was perpetual motion, the flying left winger Eder, and world class artisans, Junior and Oscar. The keeper, Vadir Peres, didn't inspire much confidence, but he wasn't going to be overworked was he? Brazil beat a decent Soviet Union side 2-1. Then, next up, were the Scottish. Where was Ally when you needed him?! The Caledonians were 1-0 up with a great goal, but that just upset the Samba boys, and four goals later, Scotland were bowed and beaten. Another easy victory, 4-0 against the football minnows, New Zealand, set Brazil up for a grudge match against the old enemy Argentina.

The boys from the Pampas couldn't live with Brazil and went down 3-1; it was all too much for a very youthful Diego Maradona, he was sent off near the end for violent conduct. His time would come, genius can never be held back. Brazil were like a Japanese bullet train: anyone or anything on the tracks were buffeted into oblivion. Brazil versus Italy in the 1982 World Cup was one of the all-time great matches - the masters of defence against a superstar attack. Brazil were on top, but forgot to defend against a red-hot striker, the lethal Paolo Rossi. Twice Rossi scored, and each time Brazil pulled it back, but the Italian eventually converted a hat-trick to scupper Brazil.

The Samba side joined Hungary in 1954, and Holland in 1974 as the greatest sides not to win the world crown. No one would taint Puskas, Cryuff or

Zico as being failures, so I was feeling a lot better about myself. I was still young enough to turn things around. On future flights out to Lake Tahoe, I would stay at the Choi household - he absolutely insisted - and I learnt to love Korean cuisine. Bart became a close friend and we would spend many an hour sharing a Sioux City Sarsaparilla putting the world to rights. I was in my element in Nevada, but California was still dragging me down. I'd had my fill of Ken and Barbie, cheerleaders, Oompah bands, skateboards and bodybuilders.

Enough was enough. My studies were up shit creek without a paddle. I had less friends than a leper, and was itching to start up a business career back home in Dubai. 'Dad, I want to come home', and my father could hear the desperation in my voice as I phoned long distance. After a short pause, I heard the second sweetest words after 'Not guilty'.

'Why not!'.

It was like the weight of the world had lifted from my shoulders. I prepared my tactical withdrawal - one last trip to Lake Tahoe, gifts for Bart and the Chois, a few tears and a few porkies that I'd be back. I wasn't coming this way again. Regrets, I had none. It was like regressing back to the kids' boating lake, with the attendant shouting out. 'Come in number 16, your time is up!', only for him to shout a minute later, 'Are you in trouble number 91?!'

And if that gag went over your head, it coincided with where boat 91 was...

Goodbye America, I wouldn't miss you, and if you thought, I might just harbour a soft spot for The States... well I did, but it was in the middle of a swamp. Columbus had a lot to answer for, the poor deluded boy. I was charging back East, renaissance time was at hand, glory was beckoning, it was now time to earn my corn.

*   *   *   *

CHAPTER 7

DUBAI OR NOT TO BUY

Arabic saying: Ask thy purse what thou should buy

What a relief to be back in Dubai City amongst family, friends and like-minded people. The USA was an ocean and two continents away, and I could thank providence for that. I returned home largely unscathed, apart from a few superficial mental scars. The Star-Spangled Banner resembled a tarnished rag to me - the only red, white and blue flag for me was the Union Jack. Conversely, notwithstanding the criticism people have for America, no one could ever deny their status as the world's greatest economy. And as a consumer nation they have no equal, and I intended to aggressively export across the Herring Pond to both East and West coasts in pursuit of the mighty Yankee Dollar.

Younger brother Mansour had quickly grown upwards and outwards like a bamboo forest bereft of pandas. Whilst back in California I'd frittered away many a happy hour watching *Top Cat*, *Happy Days* with 'The Fonz', and my own personal favourite, *The Flintstones*, which seemed to be on every day. The question was, were Fred and Wilma household viewing in Dubai? Mansour quipped, 'They don't show them here, but Abu Dhabi do'.

And I thought I was the only joker in the family. It was a shame, Dubaians had everything really, but did anybody here own a baby brontosaurus as a house dog? I don't think so.

It was now *Faz time*. A man for the time and place, I had come back to sell, and sell I would, proving that I was no nine-day wonder. All the Madanis were traders, it was in our DNA. Transactions started to rock and roll, second nature. I was becoming a *whiz at biz* - they say salesmen are born, not taught and with a little training and mentoring, I was exceeding all the family expectations.

If Alan Sugar could manipulate his Amstrad tower music system into 20 million homes - an apparatus about which he proclaimed was 'A mug's eyeful' (a 'crock of shit' was nearer the mark), then I could certainly move quality stock to the world's bourgeoisie and proletariat. I could and would cross the class divide, with all the smoothness of a classic single malt.

Jeweller Gerald Ratner made a fatal business mistake when he was asked how the devil could he sell merchandise so cheaply in his shops. He cockily orated that it was because it was all crap. But that frivolous statement knocked hundreds of millions of pounds off the value of the company, culminating in Ratner getting the heave-ho from his own company.

I hoped to emulate Sugar, and unlike Ratner, never would I describe my goods as substandard, even if they turned out to be just that. Business has no boundaries. Anyone with determination, an idea, and planning, can succeed. Looks don't hold you back. Bill Gates looked every inch the archetypal school swot, whilst Donald Trump has the dodgiest barnet in North America, a sort of very posh Arthur Scargill, but neither let their appearances get in the way of legitimate profit. The world was my oyster and I didn't need specs or a syrup. I was an up-and-comer, the parvenu, an uber-salesman destined to go all the way. When people bend down to shake hands with Bernie Ecclestone, they shouldn't feel overawed, though I did hear he once intimidated Jeanette Krankie. Each morning, after waking up, I would stand in front of a full length mirror, repeating my daily mantra, 'Faisal, you are the finest salesman in the world, sell, sell, sell!'

Men who exclusively trade in monster deals, regard themselves as having big cahoonas - or 'bollocks' as they are known to your average working man - but I wasn't interested in that machismo guff. If I was, I'd put on six stone, shave my head and talk with a lisp like Tony Soprano. (Rest in peace, the genius that was James Gandolfini) All I was bothered about was the bottom line. The dividend was the juice for me, and by Jiminy, did I love a deal.

It was the middle of a turbulent decade. 1985 was fraught with chaos as crisis followed crisis. The colossal Soviet Union was starting to break up, Iran was struggling under a strict embargo, which coincided with fighting a costly and bitter war against the old enemy, Iraq. One might think this was a time for keeping your head down.

Not bloody likely!

Dubai City was growing. They say timing is everything, and I was in the right place at the right time. It was great to be there. I had a good feeling that a raging profit was in the offing, and I didn't need Mystic Meg to confirm it. The Chinese dictionary translates the word *crisis* as meaning 'opportunity'. They have been unstoppable since the great world recession.

The initial commodity I got involved with was the good old staple favourite, pistachio nuts. Since 1979, the United States had led the world for stringent sanctions against Iran. And that being the case, I would just move the goalposts and tiptoe round the embargo.

The first procedure was to smuggle the nuts into Dubai, courtesy of my father's dhows, all the pistachios being packaged into unmarked hessian sacks.

I would then store them inside a dockyard warehouse until a Dubaian certificate of authorisation arrived, then 5,000 tons would set sail for California. The U.S. customs office fell for it hook, line and sinker. We had a mark up after expenses of 400%, as Arthur Daley would say, 'A nice little earner'. I knew it couldn't go on for ever though, and it was only a matter of time before someone would blow the whistle. Unbelievably, the dodge flourished for over a year. In 1986 our lucrative line came to an end, when the newly-appointed head customs officer in the Port of San Diego realised that pistachios were not a natural product of Dubai, which is 95% desert.

Through the nuts, I went nuts. The family had made over five million quid, and I was due a little treat, and it came in the shape of my first owned property back in England bought entirely with my own hard-earned money. I had been flitting to and fro back to the old country for football, gambling and womanising. (I know I'm shallow, but it's good fun)

In late 1986, I paid 220 grand - cash - for a two bed flat in Knightsbridge overlooking Harrods. The experience was like dying and going to heaven. Within a ten minute walk, were my favourite escort agency, numerous casinos and a plethora of top restaurants. If I come across as a flash bastard, I wasn't. However, I was 22 years old, single, with wads of cash hanging out my pockets, a burning libido and a lust for life. What would you want me to do in London, visit the British Museum?

The Bank of Credit and Commerce International (BCCI) of Mayfair were the custodians of my filthy lucre, and depending on how I fared on my nightly jaunts to the roulette tables, 20 to 50k could be deposited the following day. Needless to say, I always got a side plate of chocolate digestives with my coffee when I visited the branch manager.

Girlfriends were flying in from the Philippines, Malaysia and Brazil. You see, I was doing my bit for the poorer countries of the world, spreading the wealth, so no one could say I was disregarding my philanthropic duties.

Money was piling in, I made a decision to buy a second property as an investment. Ealing Broadway looked an area to get involved with and I purchased a five-bedroomed, detached house for £310,000. It was two doors away from Tory heavyweight politician Ken Clarke. In the two months I stayed in Ealing renovating and refurbishing, I bumped into Ken three or four times. One night in the local Indian restaurant he came over for a chat. He was always accompanied by his burly bodyguard. I found him, down to earth and approachable. A man who enjoyed an honest pint. We discussed football and he mentioned that he followed 'The Spireites' - Chesterfield FC. Well, somebody has to. He was a good guy, with no airs or pretensions.

Rental was agreed on my new home with a Japanese businessman, a top executive with the Fuji Camera company. He had plenty of yen, and he needed it - at £3,000 a month. I was happy. They were model tenants - him, his wife and seven little samurai. (There's a film title there somewhere) I could now get back to Knightsbridge, and from there I would resume my shuttle service between London and Dubai, seeking out the next big deal.

And it wasn't long in coming. Every time Ronald Reagan popped up on TV, bashing Iran with another sanction, the cartel of crooked dealers like myself celebrated with a 'high five'. Another moneymaker was on the way. It invariably became manna from heaven for most Dubaian businessmen, the only people suffering were the poor of Iran, especially the children. I wouldn't pay any politician or councillor of any party persuasion in washers, they are all corrupt and useless.

Iran was suffering from a chronic shortage of tyres. Surely it was in my remit, with a glorious sense of patriotic duty, to remedy the situation? I turned my napper East, towards South Korea, and homed in on a rags-to-riches company *Kumho tyres* - who were only founded in 1960. Kumho, whose name literally translates into 'bright lake', started off making 20 tyres a day. Now this international company makes and sells millions to all corners of the globe. I made it my mission to swot up and learn everything I could about this extremely ambitious outfit. It got to the stage where I could have named every worker on the Monday night shift - and what was in their lunch boxes! Kumho, who later in 2007 became platinum partners with Manchester United, were firmly in my sights. Through my extensive network of informants I discovered that the Chairman of Kumho was flying back to South Korea from Singapore at the end of the week. A few greased palms later and the chairman found himself sitting on the airliner next to Faisal Madani, Rajah of the Radial, Count of the Cross-ply, Baron of the Bullshit. What a coincidence! Somehow, fate has thrown us both together. Never in doubt was it. I introduced myself with some friendly chit-chat and gay banter. He was warming to me, when I innocently mentioned tyres were my consuming passion and livelihood back in Dubai.

A look of amazement, puzzlement and delight simultaneously beamed across his face, I can still picture it today. 'Me too!', he excitedly exclaimed. Then he proceeded to bore me shitless, pontificating about tyre technology for the rest of the flight. If I ever get an invitation to go on Mastermind, my specialist subject would be 'Vulcanization: advanced level'. Anyhow, I now had my opening. Tomorrow, he would send over the Kumho head of sales to the Seoul Hilton to discuss terms for future business.

I had booked myself into the Presidential Suite, which had cost an arm and a leg. I was leaving nothing to chance, as first impressions always count. Next day, the Kumho executive and his personal assistant entered the suite.

They were blown away. I wish I knew the Korean translation for 'Bloody Nora!'. After amiable low key discussions, I invited them to an upper class restaurant, the deal was in the bag.

The initial transaction was for five container loads of assorted tyres. I arranged a letter of credit and that concluded all the business. It was now time to have some fun. I headed for the Sheraton Grande Walkerhill, at the time the only establishment in Seoul with a gaming licence for roulette. There was a small army of American GIs playing the tables and also attracting the attention of the local ladies. Indiscreetly, I ordered two magnums of the dearest champagne. It had the effect of an invisible magnet. Within five minutes I was surrounded by a throng of ardent females, some as pure as the driven slush, and I made my move to the nearest green baize table, the accumulating fan club in tow.

A gasp went up when I placed my first monster bet, putting the soldiers stakes to shame. I turned to the girls and modestly declared, 'I like to start cautiously'. A black GI sitting close by looked at my chips, shook his head, whispered, 'Motherfucker', then burst out laughing. He could have some of my champers.

I definitely drank too much Dom Pérignon, but win followed win. I was throwing in chips with reckless abandon, and in my drunken stupor I roughly calculated that I'd won well over a million. I had, but it was South Korean Won, the local currency. After I cashed in the chips, there was just £2,500 profit. The English Pound was equivalent to 1,750 Won. Still, a win was a win. I put a monkey behind the bar for the ladies, but not before inviting two belters back to the Presidential Suite for a nightcap. A good night was had by all. Discretion stops me giving out any details, but suffice to say, no roulette was played. As I lay under the luxuriant silk sheets, a naked Oriental beauty snuggled up to me on either side, I looked out through the huge panoramic windows into the Korean night, a full moon and thousands of stars sparkled back. It probably wouldn't ever get better than this, still it wouldn't hurt to try, you could never have too much of a good thing.

I got back home to Dubai just in time for the arrival of the tyre containers. They were safely stowed into my warehouse, from where we delivered the tyres by dhow to our home base in Bander Lengeh, before smuggling them into all parts of Iran via backhanders. In the next 30 months we operated at warp factor eight supplying Iran with a vital commodity. It's something of which I was very proud. The half-million we made was the cherry on the iced bun, but the country of Iran was the biggest winner.

In 1986, Ayatollah Khomeni decreed that any soldier killed in the war would go straight to heaven. Iranians believed that Khomeni was a messenger of

God and that you could see his face in the full moon. I came up with a plastic key which sold in its millions. It was given the grand sounding title, 'The Key to Heaven', and went out to the soldiers in the field. The Iranian Revolutionary Guard kicked it all off with an order for 200,000. It soon became a must-have item for the troops, who religiously wore it around their necks, giving them hope for the afterlife if they were gloriously slain in battle.

My father had only met Khomeni once, but knew all the military leading lights, so even with all the restrictions, the army knew the Madanis could come up with everything they wanted. I started to imagine I was James Garner in the Great Escape, Hendley, the 'go-to guy' when something was desperately needed. I was rock-and-rolling. Another best seller that fell on my lap was a one band radio from Taiwan. I couldn't get enough of them, but the only programme the troops got was twenty four hour propaganda from the ruling ayatollahs. At least the poor sods didn't have to listen to 'Diddy' David Hamilton, or the drivel from Tony Blackburn.

I then received a request to supply donkeys to the Iranian Army. I scoured Cyprus, Somalia and the Sudan for these beasts of burden. And somehow I managed to amass a thousand braying mokes on Dubai's seafront in the port. They were fed and watered in a large corral. There was donkey crap everywhere. The word spread about the free show, workers would knock off early and mothers would bring their kids down for a gander. Hundreds of people were up for a spectacle and by Jingo, we gave them one. I became known locally as King of the Donkeys. I'd been called worse, but apart from eating, drinking and crapping, some of the donkeys became amorous. They started mating. No Viagra needed! And some bandit donkeys who couldn't find a mate, started bumming other male donkeys. It was a surreal sight.

In the middle of all this Bacchanalia, a group of about a dozen donkeys broke out of the corral. They were being led by a large grey animal, who had a big brown patch around his left eye, which gave him the appearance of a pirate. He reminded me of Errol Flynn, who played Captain Blood in the swashbuckling film of the same name. On looking down at his undercarriage, his member was nearly scraping on the floor...

Yes, he was definitely an Errol!

There were large, erect members everywhere. It was putting 'Debbie Does Dallas' to shame. Women were fainting, crowds of kids were crying their eyes out - we had to get the donkeys on the dhow as quick as possible. Luckily for us, Errol and his boys had misread the streets and had run down a cul-de-sac, been retrieved and tethered back into the corral. The captain of the 500 ton dhow was very skilful and adept at getting the donkeys on board safely. There is an art to placing live animals on a dhow and the skipper made sure his ship wouldn't capsize. The last thing we wanted was a donkey Titanic in the Persian Gulf.

Over the next six months, donkeys became very scarce, their price rocketed through the roof, they became dearer than thoroughbred racehorses. The story went global, Paul McCartney and Wings, even had a number one with *Mule of Qatar*. I naively presumed the animals were for carrying supplies and transport, but an Iranian friend reported back me that they were being sent into minefields laid by Saddam Hussein, resulting in most of them being blown to smithereens.

They didn't even have a Key to Heaven.

That was it for me. In some people's eyes, a donkey killed is better than a human being, but a life is still a life. No more donkeys were going to Iran on my watch, at whatever price. Donkeys are for Blackpool beach not a war zone. I pray old Errol came out of it safely. If there is a donkey heaven, I hope he's up there, crunching carrots.

I still think about him fondly.

Postscript:

A while later I would be embroiled in accusations and recriminations about working for MI6 concerning spying, espionage and the smuggling of machinery parts into Iran. A little matter that went all the way up to 10 Downing Street, another pain in the backside, but at least it beat clocking on 9 to 5. Let's lighten up, and next meet the quartet of brave ladies who were at some period in my life, Mrs Madani.

*   *   *   *

CHAPTER 8

FOUR BETTER OR FOUR WORSE

Arabic saying: Many are the roads that do not lead to the heart

It was a God-given truth that I enjoyed the company of the fairer sex. If my parents had known the half of it, I would have been disinherited, but I was a gentleman, and what went on under the sheets, stayed under them. Both older brothers had married young and settled down, courtesy of local girls chosen by my parents. Arranged marriages had been a way of life from time immemorial in the Middle East. It was in the Spring of 1985, I was approached by my father as I relaxed after dinner, 'It is time my son'. I didn't like the sound of that. 'Time for what, father?', I pawed back in puzzlement. I should have known what was coming. Both mother and father wanted me to settle down. The die was set, cast and delivered. 'Your future wife comes from a prosperous and religious local family, the union will uphold the Madani dynasty. She is known as Leila'.

'I'm not marrying any Eric Clapton cast-offs!', I jested, trying to bring some levity to the situation. My father's face was like thunder, 'Enough Faisal! Have some respect'. Point taken.

So that was that, over the coming weeks, I spoke to Leila many times on the telephone, and she sounded fantastic. I wouldn't meet up with her until the wedding night, but both my brothers' two wives were truly wonderful women. I'm sure my parents had worked diligently behind the scenes to come up with a stunning bride of the same excellence. I started to accept the situation, in fact I was quite looking forward to becoming a married man, it would help me become more responsible. More importantly, it would make my parents proud. I would do anything for them, especially my father, and as I had put him through a lot of stress over the years, now was the moment to give a little back. So, I sat back and waited for the wedding day. Would it all go to plan? With my track record, it was just too much to ask.

In Dubai, if one isn't married by the age of twenty, you are considered to have gay tendencies. I wasn't having that, I was all red-blooded male. The local custom stipulated that the groom didn't meet his betrothed until the wedding night, and that particualr tradition made me extremely nervous, especially as there was a massive reception of 1,400 people invited. I descended the stairs from my hotel room in trepidation. Tennyson's Charge of the Light Brigade, reverberated inside my head: *Into the valley of death, rode Faisal Madani.*

On entering the huge reception room, I immediately relaxed. Some wag had dialled up an agency for a 'blobbogram'. It was brilliant: she was hideous, an absolute rotter, 20 stones, hairier than me - and I'm very hirsute - and with more chins than the Shanghai phone directory. I bounced over to where my family were sitting... *come on, let's get the show on the road.* There were beautiful women everywhere. They were coming out the rafters. I asked my father which one was Leila. I was buzzing, he pointed over to where Two Ton Tessie was. Oh no! It suddenly dawned on me. The blood steadily drained out of my face, and at that moment I realised there was no way out. I couldn't even have a few stiff drinks, alcohol might just carry me through, but Arabic weddings never have drinking and dancing. It had been a stitch-up. I was a doomed man.

She waddled over, snooker table legs holding up the biggest backside in Dubai. In the Arab world a large behind is most desired, but Leila's cheeks had different post codes. If she had broke wind, I'd have been blown back to London. I glared at my mother. She had insisted before the wedding that Leila resembled Grace Kelly - well, it must have been after the car crash. Younger brother Mansour quipped that if her knicker elastic ever snapped, it would take down three palm trees. I was now a quivering wreck, the marriage ceremony came and elapsed in a nanosecond, I remember absolutely nothing about it, being in a state of shock and paralysis.

I had to make my move, and it wasn't upstairs to the honeymoon suite. Her family would be expecting the marriage to be consummated that night. Horror of horrors, what if she demanded oral sex?! I'd have to go down to the midnight bazaar for a snorkel, goggles and a bullock's tongue. I just didn't have the equipment to satisfy her.

If the chance for escape came, I would have to take it. There was a slight lull in proceedings... now was the time for a swerve! I darted out into the crowded corridor. Freedom was calling, so don't look back, and stampede for the front doors, they were only twenty yards away. I'd only taken two paces, before somebody had grabbed my arm, it was father. He demanded to know where I was going. I bluffed it on the hoof, saying I felt a tad queasy, might even have a touch of diarrhoea, that I needed the toilet, badly.

I was in and out of the gents in a jiffy, and I surveyed left and right, the coast was clear, I had to get far away. I left Dubai. I left the Middle East. I left Asia. I left the Northern Hemisphere. I left the Earth. I left the Milky Way. I left the Universe... Ok, well I didn't go quite that far, but I tend to exaggerate when I'm under pressure. I hailed a cab to the airport, and bought a ticket for the next available flight to Singapore, I'd lie low at a lady friend's flat, I'd had a very lucky escape.

The in-flight movie was *Return of the Jedi*. Jabba the Hutt had never looked so damned attractive.

The next day, I rang my dad up, and he said, 'That must have been the longest crap in history. Don't even think about coming back for six months. Her family want to kill you. Her father has vowed to cut off your wedding tackle and stuff it down your throat'. They obviously hadn't taken it well, but the in-law's promise was just plain unhygienic. My own father was disappointed, but surprisingly cool about the situation. Mother was obviously devastated, so I'd just have to make amends when I eventually got back home.

After a fortnight in Singapore, I'd recuperated enough to take a flight back to London. It had been a traumatic ordeal, but hey-ho, I still had my health and a few vital organs - I was fond of my genitalia. The family negotiated a generous dowry with Leila's lynch mob and true to form, over time the rumpus all died down. I still wouldn't have wanted to meet her father down a dark alley, but as far as I could ascertain, cordiality had prevailed.

You just can't beat a good bung - it's the universal sweetener.

It had proved a costly divorce, but at least I could return to Dubai without fear of having a scimitar blade thrust forcefully between my shoulder blades. Less than a year had passed, I was now quite proud of holding two unofficial Dubaian records: The shortest ever marriage (30 minutes), and the longest dump under pressure.

It wasn't long before my mother was at it again. She wanted me to do the decent thing. The younger brother Mansour was itching to get married, and family tradition decreed that the sons of Madani got hitched in chronological order. Fair enough, it was my turn. So for the second time I was to tie the knot. I recalled an old East Anglian adage, 'One should try to experience everything in life at least once, except incest and clog dancing'. Wise words indeed. I'd give good old matrimony another shot.

My father put a different twist on it, he reckoned it would be a good economic move. I'd now spend less money than I would have done on call girls. I gave him a slantendicular look, 'What you talking about Willis? You mean I can't see them any more?!'.

He burst out laughing... all was well with the family. I was ready for my second marriage.

In Iran they say 'Drink a pint of camel's milk, get an erection'. Very catchy. I've never tried it myself, never needed to, but if ever Viagara was in short supply, it would be a blindingly cheap alternative. TV and radio channels are awash with erectile dysfunction adverts, so it must be a prevalent problem. My advice: buy a camel, keep it in the back garden, it will keep your grass down and put a smile on the wife's face. Double bubble, every ones a winner!

Naturally my second foray was another arranged marriage, but this time I laid down a few caveats. I insisted on a small ceremony and reception, with just a few friends and family - I couldn't go through all that embarrassment again. Plus a butchers hook at the future bride, that was non-negotiable, although a photo would suffice nicely. Although it went against all the customs, my father arranged everything that I wanted, he knew it made sense.

Her name was Fatima, 18 years-old, short, petite and very pretty, she definitely would fit the bill. It went without saying that she was also a virgin - most teenage girls in Iran are. She seemed a perfect choice, and I had a good feeling about this one. My parents were delighted when the wedding and reception, all went off swimmingly.

We retired up to the honeymoon suite and I was right up for it. Literally - you know the saying, different strokes for different folks. Well, in Iran, the in-laws, wait outside the bedroom, until the deed is done. Sure enough, we arrived to find Fatima's mother and father sitting outside in the corridor. As we approached, her father passed me the obligatory white handkerchief. He hadn't surrendered, it was all just part of the ritual.

It was my very first time with an Arab girl, and definitely my first with a virgin. She had layer upon layer of clothing on. It was going to be a long night, but I found it strangely alluring, much more enticing than if she was scantily dressed. She put up a good fight, but after a near-submission with my Boston Crab, I eventually won on points and the inevitable happened. I staggered over to the bedroom door, passing out the handkerchief. She had passed her personal M.O.T, it was smeared with traces of blood. It wasn't exactly like a Mills and Boon romance, but that was the tradition here. Who's to say it's any worse than all the single mums and abortions back in Britain. Her parents were elated, they were celebrating like lottery winners. I quietly closed the door and they danced off into the night, happy as lottery winners.

Madani was number one son-in-law.

We all lived happily ever after. Actually, did we heck as like. I think my smoking, drinking and gambling shocked her. Fatima had led a sheltered life and wasn't expecting her new husband to be acting like the Spawn of Satan. She was a very sweet girl, religious and moralistic. Butter wouldn't melt in her mouth, though she did love the old rumpy pumpy - what a little minx! She tried desperately to change me, but better folk have tried and failed. My behaviour was making her unhappy, which wasn't fair. I made a decision to do one in Lord Lucan style and flitted back to London. There is a school of thought that says, confront your demons head on, but I never attended that academy, I bolted back to my glory hole in Knightsbridge, after all it had been a week of marriage, a man can only take so much.

Fatima's family swiftly realised, I was not the man for their daughter, and they took her back under their wing, for which they were rewarded handsomely for their travails. It would have never worked, we were both polar opposites. It would be three long years, before the family tried one last time, determined to couple me up with that elusive Arab wife.

The third and final part of my disastrous triptych of wedded mismatches was to another Arab lady named Asha. This one came from a very opulent family of high social ranking. Again, I was prepared to give it one last hurrah, just for the sake of my mother - the things we do for love. A bijou ceremony was planned. Photographs were not needed this time, as their family were regular visitors to our residence, and I had clocked Asha a good half dozen times. Whilst not coming across as a ravishing beauty, she had a good deal of form. What the English term 'fit'. Put it this way, I wouldn't be climbing over her in bed to get to Dot Cotton.

It was a lovely wedding. I was ready to commit myself to a life of fidelity and harmony, but early on, I realised there were going to be big problems. The crux of the matter was, Asha absolutely worshipped me (I know, it's the after-shave). She followed me around like a little puppy dog, wanting to be with me 24 hours a day. If I left to go to work, she would become hysterical. At first, it was nice to feel wanted and I was prepared to put up with it, hoping the possessive behaviour would dissipate into the ether, but if anything, over time, she became even more clingy. I warned her that she would have to back off, but that made it worse. She was becoming neurotic, taking copious amounts of antidepression tablets. I went on a downer myself, the 'black dog' enveloped me and wouldn't let go. We were both popping the antidepressants like Smarties. The bathroom cabinet wouldn't close. It was crammed with pills.

The share price of Glaxo Smith Kline shot through the roof and I got a commendation from Boots the chemist... but seriously, we were both in the slough of despair and a tragedy was imminent. Action had to be taken. One or both of us were about to fall off the precipice. I arranged a grand conclave between the two families. Both sides were horrified at our appearance and the subsequent downward spiral of our life together. It was reluctantly agreed that we should go our own separate ways before too much damage was done. Under Islamic law all it required me to do was utter 'I divorce you' three times. Job's a good 'un.

There was no question of recompense however, as both sides had agreed that a parting of the ways was the only way to go. Anyhow, Asha's family probably had more money than we did, so nobody was going to go hungry. The bottom line was I was a singleton again. I'd been hitched three times in four years, and it evidently didn't agree with me. I was a lone wolf. Marriage was for couples (you don't say, Einstein). I wasn't a team player, but each marriage had lasted longer than the previous one, 30 minutes, a week and a lunar month. I was obviously improving.

At the time, I didn't know it, but in less than three years, I would be going through with it all again, and remarkably, it would be me making all the running.

It was just one of those things that you can't explain. I was pacing around Selfridges Department Store on Oxford Street - if memory serves me correctly. I'd gone in to buy a couple of leather belts. My weight had plummeted, I'd been in ruinous form at the casinos. All the bets I'd staked at the time had paddled right down shit creek. Subsequently, this was the fittest I'd been for years - if only the same could be said for my wallet.

I was passing the perfumery counter when out the corner of my eye a lovely young lady caught my attention. It literally staggered me to a halt. The little devil on my left shoulder gave out instructions, 'Keep walking, you soppy twat, haven't you suffered enough?!'. But that was countered by the mini archangel on the right shoulder, 'Don't let this one get away, she could be the one'. I was in a quandary. I'd purchase the belts and make a decision on my return. I was always confident in female company, but strangely, this time I had the butterflies and my fingers were trembling. It was strange, I hadn't felt like this for many years... way back when David Dickinson was white.

It was a case of *in for penny, in for a pound.*

'Hello my name is Faisal, would you like to come out for dinner?'.

'No thanks, I'm busy'. With that, I bolted out of the department store, tail between my legs. I was losing my touch. That night in bed, I decided the next day I'd give it another stab. After all, what was I, man or mouse?! Stilton was off the menu, I was bloody rampant.

Would you believe it, she only knocked me back a second time. She was 'washing her hair' this time - a fine old chestnut that gave me the bums rush. I'd give it one final thrust on the morrow. I didn't lack for determination and per-sistence, two traits any good sporting or business coach will tell you are better than all the natural talent in the world.

I made my grand entrance. She was smiling - maybe I was a bit camp, or was she pleased to see me?

'Would you like to come out tonight to the casino?'.

She nodded her head. 'Not too late though, I'm on the early shift tomor-row'. She offered out her hand, 'It's Sharon. Sharon Manuel'. I clasped her manicured fingers. That would ding dang do for me. We clicked straight away. Sharon turned out to like a smoke and a bet - music to my ears of course, as a life long puffer and inveterate gambler.

We courted for four months. She definitely didn't want me for my money, the flat in Knightsbridge had long since gone and the proceeds from the sale of the house in Ealing were receding rapidly. I tried to impress her, pretending I had a PhD in international politics and numerous business degrees, but she couldn't have cared less. My recent luck took a turn for the better, and I had a couple of moderate wins on the tables, so I decided to take Sharon out to Singapore - my old stomping ground - for a holiday. I needed to ask her a very important question.

Sharon has always considered me as enigmatic, a man from the mysterious East, but she also felt that I was a lost soul in need of redemption. On the second night of the holiday, after a fantastic meal in a fish restaurant on the sea front, I made my move. Back in our hotel room, I went down on one knee. 'Would you marry me, Sharon?', I implored. She gave me the Man from Del Monte nod of approval and we hugged for what seemed an eternity. I gave her a get out, 'You do realise that with my marital track record and gambling habits, we'll be lucky to last a year?'.

She didn't care, and was still up for it.

You know when you've found the right one. What a wonderful woman, and we are still together after over 22 years. We've had many ups and downs, I've been away for periods, courtesy of HMPS, but our marriage is stronger than ever. I'd improved my personal marital record of a month by two decades.

Now, who says practice doesn't make perfect?!

*　　*　　*　　*

CHAPTER 9

IRAN AIR FLIGHT 655

Arabic saying: Every day of your life is a page of your history

It was a calm, shimmering, sun-baked Middle Eastern summer's morning. Nothing seemingly out of the ordinary. The airport at Bandar Abbas, Southern Iran, my father's local terminal, was teeming with passengers and staff going about their business, scuttling around like worker ants. But this was to be no humdrum day. July 3rd 1988 was to be a moment in time so extraordinary that it would be etched into Iranian consciousness for the next thousand years. Events would change my life forever, and the way I perceived the world, leaving a malevolent, indelible stain on my heart. The perpetrators responsible for the carnage that unfolded, the United States of America, tried everything humanly possible to deflect blame and accusation. The truth though first filtered, and then flooded through the rotten barriers of deceit to maul those who had been dishonest and immoral. Iran's own bloody Sunday would never be forgotten, but in America, that day seems to have been erased and whitewashed from their annals of history. For my father's sake, and the many that perished with him, I must return, revisit, and recall this largely forgotten tragedy, and again remind the world about the wrongdoings, with facts and clarification. So, it is with a heavy heart that I go on record, digging up past demons, regarding the most surreal and darkest of all days.

My father had booked a one-way ticket, business class, for Flight 655 from Bandar Abbas airport to Dubai International Airport, United Arab Emirates. It was a journey he'd flown both ways, many times previously. The short twenty-eight minute trip was, as always, undertaken in Iranian airspace on the usual flight path above the Persian Gulf. The Iraq-Iran War which had ignited in 1980 was coming to an end, and in fact hostilities would cease a month later in August. Throughout all this conflict, the commercial flights never, ever encountered any problems.

Iran Air A300 Airbus Flight 655 was running 27 minutes late. It had flown in from Mehrabad International Airport Tehran. On the final stopover before continuing to Dubai my father boarded the plane with 289 other civilians, which included 38 foreign nationals and 66 children. On this fateful morning the plane took off from Bandar Abbas at 10:17 a.m. Just seven minutes later, while still ascending, it was gone, smashed to smithereens. All 290 passengers and crew, including my beloved father, killed in a flash. It was a pernicious act of incompetence. The debris from the plane was scattered far and wide, plunging into water around Hengham Island. There is documentary film of burning, bloated bodies, including children, grotesquely floating in the calm blood-strewn waters of the gulf. Which savage terrorist organization would come clean and admit responsibility for this act of madness and inhumanity?

The United States begrudgingly held up their bloodied hands, but culpability would take a lot more time, effort and persuasion. Damage limitation was all the Americans were bothered about, and their reputation as 'defenders of the free world' trumped proper dignified remorse regarding civilian deaths. It would take a thorough investigation to fit all the jigsaw pieces together. The U.S. Propaganda machine huffed and puffed, lied, fabricated, blustered and feigned responsibility, and while it prevaricated, we can scrutinise step by step what the American forces were doing in the Persian Gulf that day, and why they did what they did.

The instigator of one of the world's worst aviation disasters was the American Navy in the shape of the USS Vincennes, a state-of-the-art, Ticonderoga-class Aegis guided missile cruiser that had been in service since 1985. Launched in 1984 by Marilyn Quayle, wife of Vice President-to-be Dan Quayle - a man who couldn't spell 'potato' - the ship was named after the Battle of Vincennes, a major skirmish in the War of the American Revolution. She carried lethal guided missiles, rapid fire cannons and two Seahawk helicopters. She'd been deployed in the Persian Gulf a few months earlier, courtesy of navy chiefs requesting an Aegis ship for a dangerous mission.

The frigate Samuel B. Roberts had struck a rogue mine in the Persian Gulf the previous April, and so the mighty Vincennes was sent to stand guard and protect the stricken frigate's hasty exit through the Strait of Hormuz to safety. From thereon she was to cruise the gulf for a six month deployment, protecting merchant shipping, mainly oil tankers that were being threatened by both feuding Iraq and Iran.

The war was in its last knockings, and America was ambiguous over which side she supported. There were the agitated ayatollahs in Iran or the mad, sadistic dictator Saddam Hussein in Iraq. The United States was supposed to be neutral, but the common perception was that there was a slight preference for Iraq. It must have been a close run decision, as Henry Kissinger, off the record, proposed that it was a pity Iran and Iraq couldn't both lose.

Captain Will Rogers III was the man at the helm of the Vincennes, one of only five cruisers with the Aegis Combat System, a billion-dollar computerised integrated battle management system, that could track a hundred targets simultaneously up to 200 kilometres away. A man should know his responsibilities with that much inordinate fire power, but was the captain like Cool Hand Luke, calmness personified or was he like his namesake, Roy Rogers, a man with an itchy Trigger?

Will Rogers's ambition was always to taste combat action in service. He came into the navy late. He had turned 27, but soon made up for lost time. He had a gung-ho attitude and seemed to have impeccable insider naval connections. In 1987 the right people in high places put the wrong person in command of a lethal Aegis cruiser. Rogers, like many peacetime commanders, had never been involved in a battle situation, but it was something he had dreamt and yearned about for many a long year.

Events had started to unravel earlier that same morning. Occurring shortly before flight 655 was airborne, one of the Vincennes' patrolling Seahawk helicopters had come under fire from Iranian local paramilitary forces in high speed patrol boats. These craft were known as Boghammers, highly manoeuvrable busy bees, ideal for militia. They could dart about at 69 knots. They were manufactured in Sweden by Boghammer Marine. Unarmed, they could with improvisation, carry recoilless rifles, mortars and heavy machine guns.

It was Rogers's time - his 'eureka' moment. He went full tilt after the Boghammers. If it was a fight the Iranians wanted, by God he'd give them one. The most expensive ship in the American fleet steamed full tilt into Iranian Territorial waters pursuing half a dozen adapted speedboats. It would hardly be a fair fight, but if you liked to shoot fish in a barrel, it would be just what the doctor ordered. Will Rogers was in his element, and the Vincennes' five-inch guns pounded the wretched Boghammers. His ship, especially constructed to tackle the might and sea power of the Soviet Union, found little patrol boats that disappeared off the radar as they bobbed around in the surf extremely hard to hit. The Vincennes fired off multiple rounds of heavy fire, but in the end, all they had sunk was one Boghammer and half the marine life in the gulf. It was a pathetic effort from a billion-dollar, floating, computerised killing machine.

To be fair to Rogers, he was commanding a young and inexperienced crew, but the buck had to stop with him on his watch. Now he'd got the smell of cordite in his nostrils, he was up for more confrontation. Suddenly he got a call, 'Possible F-14 Iranian fighter plane approaching'. That was all he needed. A warning was sent out to the plane to change direction. Lieutenant commander Scott Lustig, tactical leader for air warfare, asked Rogers, 'What do we do?'. He was going to be a hell of an asset with remarks like that. The incoming plane was only 32 miles away. Rogers decided that the automatic fire control radar would 'paint' any possible hostile plane that got within 30 miles. If it got within 20 miles, the Vincennes would shoot it down. A pensive Rogers was sceptical of it being an enemy plane, for one thing it was flying at 7,000 feet, too high for an attack approach. The Vincennes warned Flight 655 three more times, 'Iranian fighter you are steering into danger, we will take defensive measures'.

Captain Rezaian of Iran Air had heard none of these warnings, his four radio bandwidths were all taken up with air control chatter. On the Vincennes a strange complex situation developed, something psychologists call 'Scenario fulfilment' - that is to say the Navy controllers' training predisposed them to recognize any approaching aircraft as a threat, rather than evaluate or analyse what it actually was.

Simply put, you see and hear what is expected.

Both Petty Officers, Anderson and Leach, were yelling that it was definitely an F-14 and it was descending and picking up speed. Anderson's screen showed the plane travelling at 380 knots and ascending to 12,000 feet, but he was screaming that it was descending at 7,800 feet at 455 knots. It was still Rogers's call. And with the plane now eleven miles away he gave the fateful order to fire two guided missiles. Lieutenant Zocher, was given the green light, but he was so pumped up that he wrongly hit the console keys 23 times, it was left to a veteran Petty Officer to lean over and calmly push the correct ones.

Flight 655 was blown out the sky. On the Vincennes' bridge a shocked lookout cried out, 'Too much wreckage to be an F-14'. Three miles away on the USS Montgomery, they observed with horror as a large wing with engine still attached plunged into the waters of the gulf. Nineteen miles away the USS Sides' top radar man told Captain Carlson, 'In all probability, that was a commercial airliner shot down'. Carlson vomited violently. There was an eerie silence on the Vincennes, the awful enormity of their irresponsible actions was slowly sinking in. The tension was broken by a frantic Rogers ordering the ship South on the double, out of Iranian waters.

My family lost a loving and wonderful man. A tragic loss, he had so much more to give. What words could reason why 66 children were blown to oblivion? An apology proffered by America, however heartfelt, could never be enough. That same afternoon, apologies and eulogies were not even on the table, the great cover-up had started. I didn't know what was worse, the criminal, trigger-happy actions of a bellicose captain, with a crew so inexperienced that to dispatch them to the gulf was a crime in itself, or the lies and half truths from America's top-ranking military and politicos. The anguish was unbearable, the United States' authorities were squirming, and it was painful to behold. The whole world began to realise they were lying. They knew themselves they were lying, but if they kept repeating the same sound bites often enough, could it perhaps all just fade away?

It didn't, and it never would. I don't blame all Americans, but when tragedies like this occur, how can you just forgive and forget? I couldn't, but what came next was sickening.

Back in America that same afternoon, Third Admiral William Crowe, Chairman of the Joint Chiefs of Staff, met with reporters and broadcasters at the Pentagon to brief them on the incident. He just couldn't help himself, he should have auditioned for Jackanory.

LIE: 'The suspect aircraft was outside the prescribed commercial air corridor'

FACT: *The aircraft was flying well within the commercial air corridor.*

LIE: 'More importantly, the aircraft headed directly for Vincennes on a constant high speed bearing of 450 knots'.

FACT: *At the time it was shot down, Flight 655 was actually turning away from the Vincennes, its top speed, a relatively minor point was 385 knots.*

LIE: 'There were electronic indications on the Vincennes that led it to believe that the aircraft was an F-14 fighter'.

FACT: *The only electronic emission from the plane was its correct transponder signal, identifying it as a commercial airliner.*

LIE: 'It was decreasing in altitude as it neared the ship."

FACT: *The aircraft had been steadily climbing since lift-off and was still gaining altitude at the time of the missile impact.*

Even President Ronald Reagan got into the act. He made himself busy the following Monday, July 4th, which was Independence Day. 'The plane began lowering it's altitude'. Reagan might have been told by his advisers to lie or he may have unwittingly been fed incorrect data. There was to be no 'mea culpa'. An all-encompassing whitewash was emanating from the White House.

Over the days and weeks that followed, many claims and counter-claims would be made, but two critical issues were never addressed in public. Well, not truthfully anyway. Where was the Vincennes at the time of the shoot-down and what was she doing there? The official response to those two pertinent questions, vacillated between a tissue of lies, some half-truths and many convenient omissions.

One has to remember that America was in the middle of a presidential campaign during that Summer of 1988. Notwithstanding the home public's ambivalence to anything Iranian, but the shooting down of 290 civilians in a commercial airliner was another matter altogether, an embarrassing political hot potato. The ruling Republican party had only one course of action: to reinforce and reiterate the two points that would get them off the hook and prevent electoral meltdown. Firstly, that the captain of the Vincennes was blameless, and secondly, that this shameful episode was all the fault of the Iranians.

Vice President George Bush Sr. was next to get his penny's worth in. Addressing the United Nations Security Council in New York city, he steadfastly toed the party line. 'This tragic accident occurred against a backdrop of repeated, unjustified, unprovoked and unlawful Iranian attacks against US Merchant shipping and armed forces. It happened in the midst of a naval attack, initiated by Iranian vessels, against a neutral vessel and subsequently against the Vincennes, who came to the aid of the innocent ship in distress'.

As Lincoln once said, 'You can fool some of the people some of the time, but you can't fool all of the people, all of the time'. That address must have fallen on deaf ears in the inner sanctum of the high-ranking Republicans - they *were* attempting to fool everyone. The international community, the American public and the National Congress were all led to believe that what happened that day occurred in international waters and was directly provoked by the Iranians.

The crux of the matter was this: everything rested on the position of the Vincennes at the time of the conflict. For example, Iranian gunboats firing on a US Warship in international waters would be universally regarded as unwarranted aggression, but doing so in their own sovereign territorial waters would be regarded as a different matter entirely.

Will Rogers to this day, against all the evidence, advocates he was in international waters. Talk about being self-delusional - he took it to new levels. Admiral William Crowe would later come clean and admit the Vincennes was in Iran's territorial waters. The Vincennes own navigator was on record, stating the ship had crossed three miles into Iranian waters. The other American warship in the vicinity, the USS Montgomery, was even further inside.

So why was the Reagan-Bush administration hell bent on engaging in a massive cover up? It couldn't have been to save one naval captain's hide, there had to be more than that at stake.

Admiral William Fogarty was given the job of officially investigating the downing of Flight 655 by the Vincennes. An establishment man, Fogarty would only release information that suited his brief, because like his masters, the Navy, Pentagon, State Department and White House, Fogarty was protecting a gigantic cover up. If this entered into the public domain, the game would be up. The full disclosure about the Vincennes incident would blow the conspiracy wide open.

The real reason was a bombshell - America was participating in a super covert military operation - 'The Secret War'.

The catalyst for all this was an incident that happened a year earlier in 1987. The frigate USS Stark was hit by Iraqi missiles. (That's right, Iraqi not Iranian) The bottom line was 37 American crew members were killed in the attack. What followed was a misadventure that had more coils, bends and turns than a giant Amazonian anaconda.

The Reagan administration could not, and would not, tolerate any belligerent incursions against America in the Persian Gulf. Transporting oil in supertankers was vital to their economy, and to protect the national interest a military presence of overwhelming superiority was deployed. The attack against the Stark was a huge shock, and there would have to be repercussions. America had to dissuade copy-cat assaults on the fleet.

At the sailor's memorial, Reagan announced, 'Peace is at stake here, and so too is our nation's security and freedom. For a hostile power ever to dominate this strategic region and its resources, it would become a choke point for ourselves and our allies'.

It was a 'gloves off' warning to the 'hostile power' - don't play with fire, someone will get burnt. Reagan had every right to be outraged after 37 able-bodied souls had died in the Iraqi missile attack. Perversely, the president wasn't directing his diatribe at Iraq. The nation Reagan feared most in that region was Iran. The vital sea lanes of the gulf could never be dictated and controlled by the Ayatollahs. Privately against all the odds, the Stark incident brought the USA and Iraq close together, making them bizarre covert allies against Iran. Truth, it is said, is always stranger than fiction. The 'Secret War' was now up and running.

Iraq started to allow American personnel into the country to share intelligence. US Military officers were permanently stationed in Baghdad to monitor Iraqi fighter planes ensuring the Stark incident wasn't ever repeated. America pledged its support and aided Iraq in conducting long-range strikes against key Iranian sites by using US ships as navigational aids.

The war was starting to go Iraq's way, albeit with American know-how. They were getting well on top in the struggle, and America now regarded Saddam Hussein as 'The Lesser Wolf'.

In early 1987, the USA discovered Iran was planning to invade Kuwait. It would need an escalation in the undeclared naval war with Iran to prevent the invasion taking place. In the Summer of 1987, all Kuwaiti oil tankers would sail under the American flag. This undertaking became known as operation 'Earnest Will'.

All naval commanders had a new set of rules of engagement: fire first, ask questions later. Captain Will Rogers would implement the new rules to the letter with its tragic consequences. 'Operation Earnest Will' got off to a bad start though, when the USS Bridgeton hit a mine laid by Iranian boghammers. To combat the Iranian mine-laying, special operation helicopters were dispatched to the gulf. The choppers always operated at night, they were exceptionally quiet, making them almost invisible. The boghammers had been laying mines previously in the hours of darkness, but it soon became clear to the Iranians, that this was one activity to put on hold as the choppers were taking out most of their boghammers. America was now ruling the gulf at night. Back home the unsuspecting general public were under the impression that the military was still playing a passive role in the Persian Gulf.

On the 14th April 1988, a few months before the Vincennes incident, passiveness was put on the back boiler. A rare, undiscovered newly-laid mine, practically blew the USS Samuel Roberts into two parts. America reacted like only America can - they came back with major retaliation. Operation 'Praying Mantis' was the biggest US Naval engagement since World War II. April 18th saw special forces decimate major Iranian oil platforms, while the US Navy destroyed at least half of Iran's fleet. The action was condemned all round the world as a gross overreaction, and Kuwait and Saudi Arabia showed their disgust by refusing America permission to use their military bases.

So that was the backdrop, in the spring and summer of 1988, culminating in the downing of Flight 655. In the words of the immortal Oliver Hardy, 'Another fine mess'. A blood-ridden one at that, showing American foreign policy at its most retaliatory. Captain Carlson of the USS Sides, one of the few good guys to come out of the debacle with any dignity, quoted 'The problem I've always had with the incident - why the hell was Rogers there, shooting up small boats? It just wasn't a smart thing to do'.

Controversially, Rogers couldn't keep out of the news. In 1989 his wife, Sharon escaped with her life after a pipe bomb attached to his Toyota Minivan, exploded while she was driving. Terrorism was eventually ruled out. 300 police and FBI agents had conducted a major investigation, which unearthed nothing. Pipe bombs in San Diego county were a common occurrence. (over 200 that year) The case was never solved, and the official explanation decreed that it was committed by someone with a grudge against him.

That statement clearly didn't take into account 200 million people in the Middle East.

The year after, President George Bush Senior awarded Captain Will Rogers the Legion of Merit medal for outstanding service as a commanding officer. The downing of Flight 655 was never mentioned, conveniently brushed under the carpet. It's what the Americans do best, plethoras of citations inducing and encouraging patriotic bullshit.

In 1996 America and Iran reached full and final settlement at the International Court of Justice, the United States agreed to pay just under 62 million dollars in compensation to the families of the deceased, my own included. Personally, I regarded it as blood money, because right up to the present day, America has never admitted responsibility or apologised to Iran and its people. I suppose saying 'sorry' would have been construed as showing weakness from the gigantic war machine?

Postscript 1

The USS Vincennes subsequently saw further action across the oceans of the world, until she was decommissioned while berthed at the US naval base of San Diego in 2005. So that was that. The beginning of the end. She was later moved up to Bremerton in Seattle state, where she was mothballed, before the *coup de grace*. November 2011was the glorious month that saw the USS Vincennes completely scrapped at the facility in Brownsville, Texas. I hope to God she was transformed into cheap tins containing dog food. A few ghosts were duly exorcised, but while Will Rogers still arrogantly struts about, the whole incident can't be put to bed. I still class Rogers as a murderer, but he has about as much chance of being prosecuted as a war criminal, as have Blair and Bush for invading Iraq. How do they all sleep at night!?

All I can relate to them is dead men tell no lies, while all their friends and family, never, ever forget.

Postscript 2

The carnage continued. On December 21st 1988, Pan Am Flight 103, Clipper Maid of the Seas, a Boeing 747, left London Heathrow Airport on a transatlantic flight to New York. Flying en route over Scotland, another airborne pilot saw an orange fireball light up the sky, an explosive device had detonated inside the plane. It crashed into a row of houses in the market town of Lockerbie. All 259 crew and passengers were killed, plus 11 residents of Lockerbie.

The incident became the largest murder investigation in British legal history. 15,000 witness statements were taken, but there have been so many conspiracy theories that the whole truth will probably never be known. Could the downing of my father's Iranian Airbus, just a few months earlier, have been the reason for this further travesty? I couldn't say for sure, but it had all the hallmarks of a revenge mission from somebody in the Middle East. The prime suspects were Libya, under the behest of Colonel Gaddafi or a group called 'The Popular Front for the Liberation of Palestine', a terrorist group backed by Iranian money.

Whoever it was, two wrongs don't make a right, and it saddens me to witness man's senseless cruelty to his fellow man. Innocent men, women and children were on both planes, all pawns in the worst sort of political game with dire fatal consequences.

Two Libyans were eventually handed over by Gaddafi: Abdelbaset Al Megrahi, a Libyan intelligence officer and Lamin Fahima an airport manager. They went on trial at the neutral Camp Zeist in the Netherlands. A Scottish panel of three judges with no jury presided over the sombre proceedings. Fahima was acquitted, but Al Megrahi, who had pleaded his innocence right from the start was convicted of murder and in 2001 he was sentenced to 27 years imprisonment. The evidence against Al Megrahi was pitifully scant and the prosecution witnesses were unreliable and contradictory. Someone had to take the big fall, but for me Al Megrahi was just the unlucky patsy, and much bigger fish were off the hook.

It was a sad day for Scotland. The British government were for years under international pressure following the verdict to grant a retrial, but with the United States a powerful ally, Britain couldn't be seen to cave in. That all changed, on the 21st August 2009, when the Scottish government released Al Megrahi on compassionate grounds. A chance for him to return to Libya, as he was suffering from terminal prostate cancer. The Scottish authorities cited he had less than three months life expectancy. This had fallen conveniently onto their lap. It was on the cards Al Megrahi was about to get his retrial and the rumours abounded that new evidence would completely exonerate him. The British government could take advantage of the situation, even coming across to the general public as benevolent souls. Al Megrahi miraculously lived on for another 2 years 9 months, the master physicians who claimed he was at death's door were never named or shamed. Professor Robert Black, a top Scottish law expert, called the Al Megrahi murder conviction, 'The most disgraceful miscarriage of justice in Scotland for a hundred years'. And he wasn't on his own, the reek of dishonesty was overwhelming. Abdelbaset Al Megrahi was the only person ever convicted of the Lockerbie bombing. He served eight and a half long years. Undoubtedly somebody out there knows the true version of events, but they will probably take the secret to the grave.

I couldn't dwell on all the death, lies and tactlessness, I had to move on, my father would want me to carry on regardless, I now had to prosper for the memory of the greatest man in my early life, I would not deviate from my destiny.

*　　*　　*　　*

CHAPTER 10

THE SPYING GAME

Arabic saying: Winds do not always blow as the ships wish

Believe me, British espionage is not anything like it is in the glamour spy films: shot in exotic climes, with world-class marques and ingenious weapons and gadgetry. It's a nasty, grubby environment, where nobody seems to come out smelling of roses. The endgame is all that matters and anyone that is unlucky enough to stand in the way is suitably steamrollered. The British are as ruthless as any nation that people like to tarnish with the epithet, rogue state or corrupt regime.

MI5 and MI6 were very small at first, starting out from an anonymous building in Gower Street, London. MI5 was concerned with internal spying on the homeland, while MI6 was gathering intelligence worldwide.

I was approached in 1978 at the age of 14 by John Trevis, a director of educational consultants, Gabbitas, Truman and Thring. I'd been talent-spotted as a potential future spy and friend for Britain. He started seeing me monthly, asking pertinent questions about Iran and Dubai. I was being groomed with the intention of gaining information for the benefit of the establishment. I felt like James Coburn in the film *Our Man Flint*, but I was never surrounded by a bevy of bikini-clad beauties.

As a callow youth in his mid-teens, I regarded it all as bollocks, but a voice in the back of my head told me: *play the game with a straight bat, these people have influence, give a little, you might get a lot back.* And with that philanthropic thought, I did indeed do my duty.

It was late 1986 when I first met Vice-consul Andrew Balfour in the British Embassy in Dubai. He had the upper hand, being well versed about my past. He probably even knew my inside leg measurement. But what did I know of him? - jack shit, that's what. He'd been briefed by MI6 to get in close and personal, do 'a Donnie Brasco' and become my friend. I knew what he was doing but it didn't matter a jot, we immediately bonded and got on great socially.

MI6 had been watching me like a hawk, they knew I'd been importing food and commodities into Iraq, but they drew the line, when they heard Chinese Silkworm missiles had turned up in Southern Iran via Dubai in 'Madani style'. A prize but no cigar, I'd acquired two crates of rusty old spare parts for Silkworm missiles, been offered top money and much against my better judgement, sent them over. It immediately felt wrong. There were no warheads, but I had made the wrong call, and it just wasn't my style. I didn't need British Intelligence all over me like a septic rash.

I confided in Balfour, admitting I'd made a massive rick, insisting it was absolutely a total one-off and a repeat was not an option. MI6 seemed to back off, and they would turn a blind eye to my trading with Iran so long as weapons were not involved. Providing an offering of a juicy tit bit or one or two snippets of local strategic information would also help. Suited me, the last thing I wanted was to urinate on the leg of the ferocious British Bulldog and suffer badly from the serious repercussions.

Andrew Balfour and myself became great lifelong friends, we talked for hours on end about our consuming passion, football. He would invite me to watch televised matches at the country club in Dubai. They were lovely, lazy days, where we were both in our element, but certain circumstances started to unravel - not for me - but someone behind the scenes was slowly turning the screw on Balfour.

At no stage did Balfour ever ask me to do anything at all, legit or nefarious. He was a man of honesty, very matter-of-fact and truly patriotic. Of course, he was always asking questions about Iran - probably pumping me was nearer the mark, but while he caught the odd tiddler, the great white whale never landed in his keep net. He was extremely popular in Dubai, and all the relevant data and information was going through him instead of the embassy's First Secretary. Someone's nose had been forcefully tweaked. Balfour's career would be going down the plug hole, and it was very sad to watch, being helpless on the sidelines.

Before we come on to Balfour's demise, it's frightening to think that the establishment can ruin a top diplomat like a Vice-consul in a blink of an eyelid - and so easily too. What chance the man in the street? When they come for you, beware the men in bowler hats.

Earlier that Summer, May 1986, three British diplomats were ordered to leave Damascus, Syria. They were Defence Attache Colonel David Maitland-Titterton, First Secretary David Taylor and my pal, Andrew Balfour. They hadn't been naughty boys, it was a tit-for-tat expulsion after the British government ousted three Syrian envoys days earlier. That's how nations play the game, kick one of ours out, you can expect retribution. It's pathetic, really.

Three golden years out in Dubai was to be Balfour's next engagement. The Vice-consul's work was exemplary, when it came out of the blue - a recall to London. I was extremely happy for him. Surely a top promotion was on the cards. I bade him a cheery farewell. We would catch up the next time I was in 'The Smoke'.

It wouldn't take long for his world to fall apart. A few days after he got back he was on his way to work in Whitehall, when he got lifted by the heavy mob - Special Branch. He was detained under the Prevention of Terrorism Act. At the time, it was extremely rare for an Englishman to be taken under what many considered to be an anti-Irish law. While incarcerated, his home in Walton on Thames was 'vigorously' turned over by the police - a euphemistic term for having every room trashed.

Balfour was accused of seeking an advantage for his brother in law's business in exchange for obtaining a visa for an Iranian businessman, a certain Mr. Merhdad Ansari who, it was claimed, was a gun-running terrorist. Perversely, Ansari was also arrested, but quickly released without charge. Makes you proud to be British.

Transcripts from Special Branch imply that Balfour was accepting money - five thousand pounds - off a well-known terrorist, namely, Mr. Ansari. These funds still sit in his relative's printing business account. Balfour has never tried to deny or disguise the fact, maintaining that Ansari asked him to find someone who could help with a printing contract. The irony of all this was that MI6 insisted that Balfour was to befriend Ansari, exactly the same as myself, all in the line of duty. It's a pity they turned their backs on him when the heat was rising, just when he needed them most.

Balfour was actually released without charge, but the stench of a stitch-up was overwhelming, and sure enough, shortly after, in 1990, he was dismissed from the Foreign Office after twenty years untarnished service. He then did what any good honest man would do - he vowed to prove his innocence. But he came up against the Berlin Wall, the Great Wall of China and the Iron Curtain - all surrounding the Houses of Parliament and Lords. What happened next will shock, amaze, but most importantly, really disappoint every seeker of the truth.

His plight went right to the top, landing on the desks of Foreign Secretary Douglas Hurd, and also Home Secretary Kenneth Baker. I've seen the classified paperwork from both ministers and yours truly features in a few paragraphs, but the crux of the matter was that the truth would not be released, even after a lot of the less classified information had been redacted - in other words, blacked out. These people are crazy. No wonder politicians are despised.

He next took his case to an industrial disciplinary hearing, stating MI6 had ordered him to get close to Ansari. A reasonable proposition, as part of his job was to feed local information back. As he had befriended a lot of people in Dubai, this was hardly out of his remit. Men from the ministry countered with

Public Interest Immunity Certificates - that's gagging orders to the man in the street - the truth wasn't coming out any time soon. Why not? Because we say so.

At the time, the highest court of appeal was the House of Lords, home of the Law Lords. There was nowhere else for Andrew Balfour to go. These good and honourable men would surely see him right. In 1994 after taking four years of bullshit, dog shit, horse shit and chicken shit, it was time for absolute redemption. Champagne and cigars would be the order of the day.

On the 28th March, the Law Lords made their decision, but only after listening to an affidavit by Douglas Hurd, stating that there was alarm at Whitehall which would 'put at risk the effective discharge by the security and intelligence services of their current and future operations'. All Andrew Balfour had ever wanted was for the so-called secret documents to come to light. This would prove conclusively that MI6 were right up to their necks, covertly involved with the terrorist Ansari.

He was going to be disappointed - the old boys club decreed that his attempts to force disclosure would fall on stony ground. Where there was a risk of prejudicing national security, it ruled that all relevant documents should be kept secret. A good old chestnut, that when you are as guilty as sin, throw in the national security clause as a 'get out'. That was that. Since then Andrew Balfour has been unable to reclaim his job and his attempts to sue the Foreign Office and the Metropolitan Police haven't raised a bent penny.

A few tried and failed to help. Conservative MP for Torbay, Rupert Allason, took an interest in the miscarriage of justice and tried to bring the case to the attention of parliament, but just as he was gaining momentum, he lost his constituency in the election of 1997. Another untimely body blow to Andrew Balfour. What really went on will have to come out one day. I suspect MI6 fucked up big somewhere and pinned the blame on someone else - a fall guy - the readily disposable civil servant who was a few rungs down the diplomatic ladder. A man who just happened to have the initials AB.

For all you poker players out there, here's the kicker. Whilst a good man is now moping around aimlessly, his career and life in tatters, Merhdad Ansari's family have been given rights of residence in Britain. How did a man with his appalling track record pull that off? Oh, and by the way, he comes to Britain whenever he wants on a visa. It made me think: who can you trust, this was years before the MPs expenses scandal - the lunatics were definitely running the asylum.

I tell you those James Bond scripts are full of it.

*   *   *   *

CHAPTER 11

LAND OF ILLUSION

Arabic saying: What is coming is better than what is gone

The Singapore Airlines Boeing 747 skidded on to the wet, greasy runway at London, Heathrow. It was approaching midnight, both myself and Sharon were absolutely cream-crackered. The weather had been turbulent for most of the long journey back. We carefully descended the passenger stairs. London was in the clutches of an extremely wet pea-souper.

It was early Summer 1992, the new Premier League was just a few months from its inception, a move destined to change the face and finances of English football forever. I couldn't even raise a *yippee-ki-yay*. In fact I couldn't have cared less. I'd gambled away both my London properties on the roulette tables. One had long gone, the other had me holding just 15 grand from the equity, and that was the only collateral between me and Queer Street. The Singapore jaunt had been my prenuptial holiday present to my future wife, Sharon. She was the one and only sunbeam in my life at that moment.

'Where to guv?', enquired the chirpy cockney cabby. 'Gloucester Terrace, Lancaster Gate, please', I wearily replied, careful not to make eye contact. We were residing at my uncle's flat, but only temporarily, and for the first time in my life I felt like a has-been. As the old blues song went: *If it wasn't for bad luck, I wouldn't have no luck at all.* I had to give serious consideration to the way I conducted my affairs, it wouldn't be fair on Sharon to fritter away our future.

The cabby was loquacious, but soon realised he was talking to himself. Sharon was in the Land of Nod and I was cogitating. I was deep in thought about why the fuck was my life experiencing small peaks and monumental troughs. Was it just down to me, was it luck, or could it even be fate? As the hackney cab shunted through the grey London streets, I recalled an amazing Japanese guy back in 1945. You decide if he was lucky or unlucky.

Tsutomu Yamaguchi was visiting Hiroshima for business reasons on August 6th, the day the Americans dropped the atom bomb. He suffered burns and wounds, but decided he was well enough to travel back to his home town the very next day. He hit the road for Nagasaki, AND he even returned to work the day after that. So next time any of you pussies want a day off for man flu or a hangover, remember the little man who had an atomic bomb dropped on him, shrugged his shoulders and clocked on again in the next 48 hours.

Yamaguchi was at work, heavily bandaged on Aug 9th, the day the Americans dropped the second atom bomb - on Nagasaki. I wish I knew the Japanese phrase for 'fuck me, not again!'. A blinding flash pushed all the windows in, but Yamaguchi was a tough old bird, he came through that one as well. The amazing thing was that for both detonations, he was only three kilometres away from each epicentre. He lived on until 2010, finally succumbing to cancer aged 93. Was he the world's unluckiest man, or was he truly blessed ?

'Gloucester Terrace, guv'. We were home. I gave the cabby the fare and a good tip. The taxi ride had put a spring in my step. Everything was going to turn out fine. How did I know? Because there was only one way to go: I would 'do a Yamaguchi'.

The next morning I sat Sharon down. 'How would you like to live in Dubai? We could even get married over there'. She took an age to answer, 'I'd love that, let's do it!'. We kissed and I held her tight. We were both like-minded souls, a new life in the sun was beckoning. I phoned home. My mother was over the moon. It would be great to have the whole family together again. I thought of my father, the four years had flown since we lost him. A tear rolled down my cheek, I was very emotional. I would have given anything for him to see me marry the woman I loved, he would have been so proud.

*   *   *   *

Sharon settled into the Dubaian way of life straight away, becoming close to all the family, especially my mother Mryam. She treated Sharon like her own daughter. My uncle and brothers wanted to put on a big spectacular hot shot wedding with all the great and good from Dubai coming, but I'd been down that avenue of indulgence before and I still bore the mental scars. After discussing it with Sharon, we decided on a low-key event, with just family and a few choice friends. It made sense, Sharon hardly knew anyone in Dubai anyway.

After the wedding we rented a luxury flat in Jumeirah. The family had been very generous with wedding gifts and goodwill money. I realised my playboy days were over... well mostly. I'd put the casinos on the back-burner. There would definitely be no more womanising, but I still hankered after a bet.

A man has to have one vice. My new married responsibilities meant I had to hit the ground running, so with my old connections, the sensible way forward was to attempt import and export again. I'd only been away for four years, but things seemed different. I couldn't put my finger on it, but something in the air told me, it might just be a trifle harder second time round.

We were very happy in Jumeirah, a residential, coastal area of Dubai. A lot of English ex-pats lived there, but something was still bugging me. Maybe the pressure of having to pay the bills and put food on the table was winding me up. Sharon loved Jumeirah, the shore front area had once been called Chicago Beach, named after an engineering company that had operated in the area. Even though I clocked quite a few shady characters down there, Al Capone was never spotted. What I didn't know then was that an influx of recent foreign arrivals in the country would make Big Al look like a minor recidivist.

The ruling family of Dubai - the Maktoums - had brilliantly masterminded a miraculous conversion of the city, transforming Dubai into a state-of-the-art, modern day El Dorado. Even the poor benefited from the gargantuan building project - libraries, parks and amenities would propel the state into the 21st century and beyond. Opportunists from all parts of the world had made a beeline here for the promise of easy money and a route to the top. One didn't need to be Albert Einstein to realise that some of the newbies might bend a rule or two, or even God forbid, break the law.

Sharon had no worries. She loved the family-oriented, easy-going lifestyle. I was working long hours, striving to achieve the past glories of the booming 1980s. That gave her the ideal opportunity to start teaching English Language at a private nursery school. She was always home way before me, so it all worked perfectly well and with two salaries we managed to save a respectable amount of money.

I did have an occasional foray to the casino, but was betting minimal stakes. I lost the odd few hundred, but I needed an occasional blow out from work. Every time I lost money, Sharon was the first to know - I had nothing to hide, but she did get a cob on, putting her foot down one evening when I really fancied a punt. She locked every door and window in the flat, so I did a Harry Houdini, and squeezed through the small toilet window. Madani was out on the loose.

Sharon waited up until 5am. I sidled in and just before the dam burst, I lobbed seventy thousand onto the settee. She was speechless, so I did the talking, 'Fancy a fortnight in the far east? We deserve a break'. We both broke down in laughter, life was definitely for living.

On our return, a bombshell landed on my lap. I had acquired worrying information from high-ranking Dubaians in the know. It brought me right down to earth. Certain people had got the hump over my involvement in the last Iraqi conflict, my collusion with British Intelligence, and the substantial profit I'd banked from my wartime dealings.

The threat was deadly serious. The British Embassy had heard whispers as well, and they advised me to get out of Dubai as soon as possible. Sharon had herself in the meantime become homesick, she was really missing her mother. Maybe it was all for the best. Our adventure in Dubai had lasted just under three years. My mother was going to be devastated again, but I couldn't put Sharon in the line of fire.

Things had changed in Dubai. The age of innocence was long gone. Russian Mafia had infiltrated deep into the heart and infrastructure of the city. And anything they missed was hoovered up by gangs from the Balkans and the Orient. Prostitution, drug dealing and gunrunning were not uncommon. I had smelt the wind of change, the sparkling bouquet of a vintage Bordeaux had soured into a cheap bottle of red biddy... sometimes a tactical retreat can answer all questions.

*   *   *   *

CHAPTER 12

A BANK TOO FAR

Arabic saying: Stretch your legs as far as your blanket extends

The fledgling marriage had come back fit and healthy, the Madanis were back in the land of Magna Carta - not in Runnymede, or London, but Denton, a suburb of East Manchester. The reasons were threefold; close vicinity to Sharon's mother; Lancashire, a proven footballing hotbed; and lastly, a reluctant retreat from London - it was too bloody expensive. Notwithstanding that our exodus from Dubai was accompanied with a blossoming bank balance - we certainly had a substantial nest egg, and that's the way we wanted it to stay. It was good to be back. Garry Glitter had uttered those same words, but he'd been wearing handcuffs.

I knew in my heart that England was the future. Dubai wasn't an option any more. I was born a lot closer to Jerusalem than William Blake, but the man was spot-on with his description; *a green and pleasant land* - though he would have never foreseen the proliferation of Mecca bingo halls. Many ex-pats miss the village green, the cricketing sound of leather on willow, foaming pints of real ale, Colman's Mustard, HP Sauce, Stinking Bishop cheese, Coronation Street and Eric Pickles (not). Even a cool, breezy, rainy day, walking the barker could make any Englishman abroad feel nostalgic, especially in a hot arid country with wall-to-wall sunshine every day, week and month.

I hankered for my English student days again, fun-filled, immature and definitely shallow. 'Pull a pig night' was an old English custom. If we were visiting a posher town, it would be 'take home a truffle-hunter'. The back street dodgy pub which put on the weekly meat raffle, walking home worse for wear with a frozen chicken underarm. Back for the Monday night quiz. First question by the emcee, 'Who the fuck are you looking at?'. Those nights were character-building. Forget about the playing fields of Eton, the empire was built on the Saturday night obligatory punch-up at the Red Lion hostelry.

We had only been back in Denton a week when Sharon, in the process of crossing the road, got knocked over by a van. I let my imagination run away with me, thinking it was a hit squad from Iran, but the assassination vehicle, a clapped-out, twenty-year-old, yellow and rust Bedford panel van, was hardly a killing machine. It was an accident pure and simple. Sharon had to undergo four weeks of recuperation in hospital with ruptured cruciate ligaments in the knee. While she was fighting the good fight, I figured she wouldn't mind me popping over to the Stakis Casino in Stockport. That month, I put two hundred grand into our bank account. Lady luck was back, but most importantly, so was Madani.

Ipswich Town came to Old Trafford in 1995. Manchester United, my hot, new, virile, athletic girlfriend hammered my former ageing, varicose-veined, old flame Ipswich Town nine-zip. Andy Cole went nap, even Cheryl Cole could have scored a couple against that defence. It was the most bitter sweet moment of my life, an oxymoronic moment which made me physically sick. My Suffolk was reluctantly fading into the annals of history. I was watching plenty of Premier League football, meeting players, agents, ex-managers and supporters with clout - in essence, the great and the good of Manchester. I'd have gone to Chicken Town if John Cooper Clark had arranged a football match. I couldn't get enough of the great game.

There was a school of thought in Manchester that Blackburn Rovers bought the league that season. I didn't subscribe to that, it was a great moment for an unfashionable club to win the big one. We all had to take the medicine and come back, better and stronger.

I was alternating weekly between Old Trafford and Maine Road. I was leaning towards United, but I had a lot of friends who were City fans. Christmas came and went, Sharon had made a full recovery, so 1995 hadn't turned into an *annus horribilis*. It wasn't a bad old year considering. In February I watched Manchester City play Newcastle United in a fantastic three-all draw. Georgian playmaking midfielder Georgi Kinkladze was magnificent, displaying cat-like balance and superb dribbling skills. The game had everything, Colombian Tino Asprilla elbowed Keith Curle, and just for good measure, head-butted him as well. That's why the Premier League is the number one, year in, year out. The action and controversy never stop.

Newcastle manager Kevin Keegan later scoffed at suggestions that Asprilla was a nutter who loved playing around with guns. This was the season Manchester United overhauled the large Newcastle United points advantage. Who could ever forget Keegan on Sky TV wishing Sir Alex all the best before the final match at Middlesbrough!

I became close friends with City legend Mike Summerbee. He would often invite me to Maine Road. Peter Barnes was another ex-player I was fond of. There were many influences drawing me to the sky blues, but I just couldn't commit. Maybe it was Stockport County calling - one could do a lot worse than Edgeley Park.

Sharon deserved a break. I'd been coming and going all the hours round the clock. She was used to the way I operated, but another excursion abroad would be just the vicar's knickers for us both. In any given year March in Manchester could have four seasons in one day, and I craved to feel the sun on my back for a couple of weeks, so we flew first class to Las Vegas. Sharon loved the slots and a hand of blackjack, and I'd keep the roulette croupier busy. Probably wouldn't see that much sun, but it was a chance I was willing to take.

Who said only women can multi task? I'd arranged the holiday to 'coincidentally' fall in the same week as the Tyson-Bruno rematch. I wanted to experience the atmosphere of a world title fight at the MGM Grand. Two ringside seats had cost a small fortune, but it was worth it to see Sharon's face. She was thrilled. I had a sneaky feeling that Bruno could take Tyson this time. 'Iron Mike' had recently spent three years in the big house. No athlete could improve in that environment. Of course, I was talking through my patriotic arse as per usual, and the local bookies had Tyson an overwhelming odds-on favourite. Those shrewdies are rarely wrong.

Bert Sugar, the famous American boxing pundit, was sitting to my left. I inquired optimistically, 'Bruno, any chance?'.

He drew on the huge cheroot, contemplated the question in his brain, an organ that contained many decades of boxing knowledge. He exhaled, trapping smoke under his trademark fedora. 'He's got two chances, slim and none. And by the way, slim's just about to leave town on a one-way ticket'.

I got the feeling that Sugar didn't rate Bruno as a fighter. I should have left it at that. But no, like the twat I was, I added, 'Well, I think he's got a puncher's chance'. All credibility was lost at that moment. Sugar looked at me in disbelief and smirked. No more words were needed.

Bruno's entrance to the ring confirmed my worst suspicions. He was sweating profusely. It looked like he had shit himself in the changing rooms. He obviously didn't fancy it. Two rounds and less than a minute later, it was all over. Had no one told him you can punch back? It was a massacre. I grabbed Sharon's arm, 'Come on we're out of here'. I couldn't face Sugar. I bet he dined out on that story. What an absolute embarrassment. Bruno announced his retirement after the fight.

His timing was terrible, he should have retired before it.

The fortnight flew by. I'd like to tell you Las Vegas was the poorer for it, but I'd be fabricating, as every last dollar was gone. I didn't have a bean. No, tell a lie, arriving at Manchester Airport we still had *BFH*. Jim Bowen on 'Bullseye' made it immortal: *Bus Fare Home*. But Sharon was confident I'd get it all back and then some. That made me feel a lot better, but I needed a big lump of spondulicks to bounce back. Needless to say, I went about it totally the wrong way...

It happened entirely by chance. I was dining out in Manchester with friends, putting the world to rights, when the subject of Coutts the bank cropped up. The general consensus was that one needed a million pounds in blood, or belong to aristocracy, to open an account with Her Majesty the Queen's bank. I wasn't having that. Amid roars of laughter, I announced that I would open two different, separate accounts with Coutts. What on earth was wrong with me?! I didn't have a pot to piss in, it could only end in tears.

It took me a couple of months to get the bogus paperwork properly prepared, and just for good luck I created three new identities; with fake passports, driving licences and endorsements. I opened an account in Manchester at Coutts and Co. under the name 'Al Midani'. At the time, a man of that name was on the board at Manchester United. Mancunians would often ask me if was I related. It was something I always encouraged, as it opened doors for me. I was probably the brother he never had... or even knew he had.

The account I opened at Coutts in Manchester was activated so simply and easily that I wondered if checks and procedures hadn't changed since the bank's formation in 1692. It probably was the five million I promised to deposit in the next three months, transferable from banks in Dubai, that clinched it. Time and again, avarice affects the judgement of experienced hard-nosed businessmen. That's how top fraudsters pull off unbelievable coups - the fall guy at the other end is a greedy bastard.

The old reputable gentlemen banks are full of shit. Barings was a younger sibling of Coutts by 70 years. Nick Leeson, a derivatives broker for Barings Bank in Singapore, was regarded as the golden boy. He was making fortunes investing in risky trades on the futures markets and always coming out on top. Barings let their standards and safeguards slip. Why? - because Nick was making millions for the bank. He was given money *carte blanche*. Anything Nick wanted, Nick got. Didn't anyone back home suspect the profits were too good to be true? In 1995 all the chickens came home to roost, and Nick swerved out of Singapore leaving a debt of £827 million. He couldn't manipulate the numbers any more - 233 years of history gone in three years of suicidal gambling. How did it happen? - *greed, greed, greed.*

If a young lad from Watford could shut a bank with bullshit figures from abroad, I might as well chance my arm and open two more accounts with Coutts in London. I only intended to have two accounts, but the ease with which I opened my accounts in Manchester gave me unbridled confidence to try for a royal double down South. It was like taking strawberries off a donkey. Coutts was wide open and I drove a tank through the security checks, two more different names accompanied with the same standard dodgy paperwork. I made small adjustments in the reasons for wanting a Coutts account before dangling the carrot: a promise of massive funds arriving in the near future. I now had accounts at Coutts headquarters, 440 The Strand, and the now closed for business branch in Fleet Street.

Coutts bank very graciously deposited just over 100 grand in credit, spread over the three accounts. Never would the old adage, *bullshit baffles brains,* be so apt. All I had to do was keep winning at the casino to stay one step ahead. Luckily I embarked on another sustained run of God-given fortune. With new money in my pocket, I didn't skimp when in the company of the power players involved in the great game. Champers would always go on to my bill, and a lot of the multi-millionaires were only too happy to accept my largesse.

I developed a reputation for generosity and a penchant for blowing money on the finer things in life. Invitations to matches, events and dinners, would give our postman a right cob-on, as he struggled to get them all through the letter box. I was renting match day boxes at Old Trafford through Cavendish Travel of Leeds, who specialised in hospitality and event planning. My phone would be forever ringing, ex-footballers requesting an invite. Food and drink were gratis in Madani's box. And sometimes there were more stars in the hospitality than on the pitch.

This cornucopia of overindulgence lasted well over a year. But I knew for certain that the day was coming when funds couldn't be replenished. It was only a matter of when. I felt like the condemned man on death row, and it occupied my every waking hour. The irony of it all was that the *coup de grace* would be a blessing. The end came in one night. And it came swiftly. And it mortally wounded me financially. The casino on that personal Black Friday had previously been a lucky hangout. That evening nothing seemed amiss. In fact, I was ahead to the tune of three grand, when, wham, bam! - I couldn't beg a winning number. I lost all discipline. The best and only thing to do when experiencing a long losing run on the night, is to walk out before you lose your shirt. Easy to say, very hard to follow through. The fatal weakness of most gamblers then surfaces - chasing losses with ever increasing wagers. It's the classic *fait accompli,* in which one seldom emerges smelling of roses.

In less than two hours I'd used up all three Coutts cards, emptying each account of thousands of pounds. All bets nullified on the turn of the wheel. My chin was on the floor. And as I slowly trudged home, the night air brought out the enormity of the situation. I could have wept, 'You bloody idiot, what have you done!'. I kept repeating it, but it was no good berating myself. Sharon was sound asleep when I arrived back. I'd have to bottle it all in, well for the time being anyway... the repercussions were going to be serious.

For every action, there is an opposite reaction. Well, that reaction surfaced on the Wednesday afternoon which followed the gambling debacle of the previous Friday. I'd slowly and softly put Sharon in the picture, no melodramas, tantrums or screaming matches. She was brilliant like that, and knowing she was full square behind me meant a lot. I'd expected to get a tug at the weekend, but the fact that the three different cards were all used in the one casino was a situation that probably didn't happen that often at Coutts Bank. Their internal fraud department must have been non-plussed before they smelt a rat, and they contacted the Old Bill.

The doorbell rang at our house in Denton. The chimes were like a dagger through the heart. I knew it wasn't the Mormons. They'd given up on me months ago. Sharon opened the door to WDC Christine Davis, who turned out to be a lovely considerate woman (and Manchester City fan), and DC Paul Walsh. They had me bang to rights. Over numerous interviews I played the stupid card, talking in riddles and telling them everything - yet nothing. The elephant in the room was my spying background. And that would muddy all the legal waters when the circus eventually came to town.

It was early September 1998, and the trial coincided with Rupert Murdoch's abortive attempt to buy Manchester United. The British Government, through the Monopolies and Mergers Commission, had decided Rupert already had enough clout with Sky under his wing, and they weren't going to allow him access to England's premier club as well.

In the real world my upcoming case would be the first fraud trial ever to be heard in camera, and not only that, part of the trial would have no jury, owing to the British Secret Service having to contribute their remit to the court, which amongst other matters, was to protect my family name. I turned up at Manchester Crown Court No.1 and encountered maximum security. There were police everywhere. Never before in the history of fraud cases had such safeguards been on show. The trial would deviate into ten unbelievable days of helter skelter. The only thing missing would be Charles Manson. The judge allocated to preside over the madness, was Michael Henshall, and he gave me the impression straight away that he couldn't stand the sight of me.

That was just dandy - the feeling was reciprocal.

Exact minutes of a trial with no jury can never be disclosed. Even now I can't say a word about it - courtesy of the Official Secrets Act. Notwithstanding the gravitas of the information, whether mundane drivel or earth shattering revelation, it goes to the grave with me, Judge Henshall and The Almighty. I can't say I was too confident at this initial stage, but what I did expect from a British court of law was an impartial, fair judiciary... was that too much to ask for?

The next day the jury were sworn in. Most high profile fraud cases are extremely complicated, and this one was a bobby dazzler. The twelve jurors, on first impressions, looked perceptive and capable. I only wish the same could have been said of the man in the robes and wig. My *not guilty* plea was based on Coutts questionable working practices, information about which I'd gleaned from a couple of the bank managers. Over the previous months, the men looking after my accounts hadn't gone hungry - they were beneficiaries of the Madani *share the wealth under the table fund*. I know that's a posh term for a backhander, but I liked to treat people right. Sometimes, what goes round does come round.

Apparently Coutts had known for months that only one person, namely moi, was controlling three different fraudulent accounts, but as long as the exorbitant interest on the credit was being paid on time, they would just keep racking up the ante. Even on wipe-out night, they could and should have declined the second and third cards, but chose not to. I had that information from the very best insider authority, so even on a technicality, I'd surely have the chance to walk free. Coutts certainly hadn't acted like gentlemen.

Michael Henshall, the supposedly reputable judge, was totally out of his depth. He fucked up numerous rulings and directions, either by incompetence or by covert government intervention. I wasn't actually denying the accusations of three identities - there was plenty of evidence of multiple documents, including a driving licence in the name of Nabina which was the family name on my mother's side. The judge wasn't helped by constant misrepresentation by Coutts aiding the prosecution. At one stage I was accused of holding account 26238460 in the name of Hashemi. When the chance came to rebut the allegation, I told the jury, 'I wish I did have that account, it had 247 million pounds in it!'. That produced a roar of laughter. I half-turned to the judge, but he had a face like thunder. He still wasn't warming to me.

Every item of evidence that supported me, he poo-pooed with disdain, but anything incriminating, however frivolous was backed up to the hilt with his endorsements. The trial was approaching endgame, and surprise, surprise, he directed the jury towards a guilty verdict. Couldn't fault him for consistency; he kicked off hating my guts, by the end, he detested every molecule in my body. It didn't look good. When the jury came back in, I knew I was toast. Hensall had done a hatchet job on me. To be fair, I'd have voted guilty myself if I was on the jury. I had no hard feeling towards them, they were pure and simply pawns in the game.

When the foreman iterated the word *guilty* on all of the charges, it was the only time Michael Henshall smiled throughout all the proceedings - he had me by the balls. My brief requested bail while the comprehensive reports were being prepared, even I smiled at that - there was more chance of Graham Norton playing prop for St Helens Rugby League team. No, I was remanded to the

'Strangeways Hotel' in Cheetham Hill, Manchester. At least it was only up the road, handy for when Sharon visited, and at that stage we were both thankful for any small mercy.

It's never nice adapting to a strange and alien environment, but that first night behind bars on remand was as bad as it ever got. Your imagination plays tricks with the actual reality of the situation. Think bad thoughts and that's probably what will happen. That was not my way. The trial had completely drained me mentally. My head adapted to the contours of the lumpy, government issue pillow, and within seconds I was under the wing of Morpheus - and it wasn't the black dude in The Matrix.

Next morning I gingerly encroached past my open cell door onto the landing, two doors down from mine out strolls Harold Shipman, one of the biggest serial killers in world history. At that moment I was absolutely convinced I was on the English version of The Truman Show - all these incidents couldn't be just coincidences. A lesser man might have cracked there and then.

A month into the remand and Dr. Shipman started coming into my cell. He imagined both of us were kindred spirits. He opined, 'We are both innocent, we shouldn't be here'. Well, I was as guilty as sin, and he was obviously delusional, but I perpetuated the charade.

I didn't want arsenic in my tea.

Let me categorically stress at this juncture, I couldn't stand Shipman. I regarded him as an arrogant, cocky bastard who had a superiority complex. That assessment didn't even take into account the alleged 250 murders of which he was accused, but what a chance it was, at close quarters, to see how he ticked. I would like to think he opened up a lot more to me than to any prison psychiatrist. He trusted me, and in a relaxed atmosphere I gleaned a lot of interesting facts from him.

Shipman regarded the Polish doctor of Strangeways as incompetent, a total blithering idiot. Shipman himself started conducting ailment diagnoses - whether you wanted it or not. Myself, the cons, and even the screws would receive advice about colds and stomach problems. He reminisced to me about the old days back in his native Nottingham, where his beloved mother was dying of terminal cancer. Morphine from the doctors was her only solace from the ravages of the terrible disease, and the more she suffered, the more morphine the doctors administered, which mercifully helped her through the last days. Shipman became mesmerised by the drug of sleep, years later 'Doctor Death' would become a killing machine, ably assisted by his trusty sidekick, morphine.

After his mother died, he never used morphine to deaden his own personal pain, instead he would hit the pavements, and regularly run twenty miles a day.

He was really big into Rugby Union and loved the Six Nations tournament. But football was not on his sporting radar, in fact, he hated the great game with a passion. He was fascinated by Dubai, pumping me for information about the old country, but Malta was his favourite country and destination. He'd spent many happy days there on holiday with his wife Primrose. That name, however, was a misnomer... on prison visits she resembled a giant redwood. She was a big lass. I wouldn't have wanted to upset her, but another one mad as a march hare, she was adamant her husband was innocent.

Primrose wasn't a looker, but Shipman must have had something going for him, for at Christmas he received over 500 cards. You couldn't make it up. What's wrong with you ladies! He was extremely hairy. I could grow a follicle myself, but if we stood next to each other, I resembled Duncan Goodhew. He was like a silverback; chest, arms, legs, back, hands all covered in fine down.

Amazingly, for a doctor, he was very unhygienic - seldom showered and more often than not, stunk like a pole cat. Maybe that was just his way, but it didn't endear him to cons or staff. For good measure, his cell resembled the municipal rubbish tip. They say cleanliness is next to godliness, but I don't think God was ever considering coming down with Imperial Leather and Mr Muscle.

We both happened to be in the hospital ward on the day Princess Anne was making an official visit. Surrounded by her lackeys, she stopped to shake hands with Shipman. But to be fair, she had no idea he was a mass murderer - he looked more like a seedy librarian. I wonder how much would a photograph of that encounter be worth now?

We used to play the quiz game, *Who Wants To Be A Millionaire*. My team was me, a smackhead and a serial burglar against Shipman's mob, which included a bent ex-copper and a crooked accountant. Our side had an eclectic range of knowledge. We knew loads about a little, and fuck-all about a lot. We never won, but Shipman was always in his element. One random question was, how do you spell 'anaesthetic'? Shipman piped up, 'Do you want the English or the American spelling?'.

I shouted over, 'Nobody gives a flying fuck, spell it in Arabic if you like!'.

Oh, what fun we had! The boy from the desert... and the mass murderer from the shires.

Arrogance was still Shipman's forte, and, in his own case, he considered that a *not guilty* verdict was going to be a formality. He reckoned the case wouldn't get past Ashton-under-Lyne Magistrates Court. When it did, he was escorted to Crown Court by a huge police escort. He even applied for bail.

However, the 250 bodies in the morgue might have been a reason for knocking back that request. It would be a long, drawn out and complicated trial, but the one certainty was that Shipman was going to get his day in the spotlight and everything that was coming to him.

There were a lot of strong personalities on the wing; a couple of reputable Manchester hard men for example. Paul Massey, a man who was respected by all, and Paul Doyle, a lovely, humorous individual, who I bonded with straight away. He was a fanatical red, and was once arrested in Turkey after becoming involved in a bloody fracas with Galatasaray fans. He was universally known as 'One Punch Doyle'.

Paul had earned that nickname, because it did exactly what was said on the tin. I used to get the hump with Peter 'One Dart' Manley, as that geezer always carried three on to the stage. Full of crap he was, winning only one tournament throughout his career. If he had been known as 'Five Dart', he might have done a bit better. The Staffordshire darts player Mark Frost has the world's best sporting nickname - 'Frosty the Throwman' - a classic. Talking of darts, a tribute to the late, great Sidney Waddell - 'the voice of darts' - an intelligent, thoughtful Geordie whose unique use of the English language was always entertaining. My personal favourite, 'Jocky Wilson approaches the oche, treble twenty, treble twenty, another treble twenty....what an athlete this man is!'. Magic commentary, but I've also just realised that the anecdote is so old, all the protagonists are now dead.

Back to Paul Doyle... he helped me greatly in prison, supporting me with kindness and positivity, making my time in Strangeways bearable. I want him to know, my door is always open to him, thank you so much.

September came and went, as did October, and it was now turning chilly. November was the month I was destined to return to Manchester Crown Court for sentencing. I can't say I was looking forward to it, and my legal team were pushing for early release with a nightly curfew. Feasible I supposed, but the fly in the ointment was the malevolent Michael Henshall. I couldn't envisage him doing me any favours, I was tensing myself for when the boot came in.

It came in the shape of a size twelve volley in steel toecaps. *Three years' imprisonment.* He smiled again - the man was obviously a sadist. I was tempted to counter with 'Is that all?', just to wipe the grin off his face, but he probably would have added a year or two for contempt of court. I had to take it like a man, stiff upper lip, and back to the big house for lunch. I had one trick left up my sleeve, an appeal. The last refuge of all scoundrels... hope sprang eternal.

The routine of prison life soon becomes second nature. I got my head down. Nobody was giving me grief, but the worst thing was the mind-blowing boredom. Behind the scenes Lord Chief Justice Thomas Bingham was delving into my case. He had the reputation of being scrupulously fair. Now, that would be nice, I hadn't bumped into many of that ilk wearing a peruke.

Seven months were on the back boiler. People regard the number seven as lucky: the seventh son of the seventh son, apparently is considered to be extremely fortunate. I was third of the fourth, so it just didn't have the same ring. The landing screw marched military style into my cell and proclaimed, 'Gather all your kit Madani, you're out of here'. Over the last hundred years, that command has always been succeeded by this question, 'Where am I going boss?'.

The turnkey must have clocked it a thousand times, 'I doubt it's Torremolinos... now move your arse!'.

I was in transit to Stafford Prison. The flat Cheshire Plains gradually changed into the more rugged industrial Staffordshire heartlands. My new home, a pre-Victorian category C establishment, had a reputation for being harder than its moderate given status. Stafford had staged many hangings in the past and was one of the last prisons to desist from using a human treadmill. On arrival the front gates didn't look too ominous, and I thought that perhaps once I'd got settled in, I might enjoy the experience, even make a few good friends.

I was wrong on so many counts.

Back at Strangeways, I'd been in the company of a lot of Lancastrians, men with whom I held a common bond. No such luck at Stafford. It was full of Stokies from The Potteries, Black Country folk from Wolverhampton, Walsall and West Bromwich, and worst of all, belligerent Brummies from Birmingham. I'd previously heard from numerous friends that people from the Second City were warm and affable. Now, that may well be true, but the Birmingham inmates that year in Stafford must have been a bad vintage.

In the two months I was there, I only knocked about with one guy - Jim White from Rugeley, a tough ex-mining town eight miles south-east of Stafford, on the way to Lichfield. I could just about make out what Jim was saying, as he only had a slight West Midlands twang. That's more than could be said for the Brummies. I couldn't understand a bleeding word they were saying. Jim was more than happy to be my official interpreter - whenever we encountered Brummies, it all went over my head. Later I'd ask Jim what they said, most of the time he gave me the same answer, 'You don't want to know'.

It transpired very quickly that I was never going to become a Freeman of the City of Birmingham, so I kept my distance from them. I had a feeling they were all grandsons of the *Peaky Blinders*, but a few bad apples don't make a bad barrel, even though I still get a contented buzz when United beat Villa or the Bluenoses.

It took me a fortnight to work out why a lot people were talking about a big potato. I kept hearing *yam this, yam that.* Shakespeare was born only 63 miles away, what the fuck was going on? The Stafford accent was nothing like the Wolverhampton accent, which in turn was nothing like that of Stoke-on-Trent. Staffordshire was a county with just too many different accents.

There was a glint of light partially shimmering at the end of the long, dark tunnel, as my solicitor, on a prison visit, confirmed to me that an appeal date had been earmarked for the following month at The London Court of Appeal. Lord Chief Justice Bingham had been diligently working overtime, burning the midnight oil, discovering enough anomalies in the original fraud case to grant another look-see.

On a fine Sunday afternoon in the dying days of June, I filled Jim in about my close encounters with Harold Shipman. His case still hadn't gone to trial, the prosecution files must have filled a pantechnicon. 'Just a minor villain', Jim replied nonchalantly, 'We had a bloke from Rugeley worse than that'.

I sensed he was pulling my pisser, but he wasn't, and I listened intently as he recalled the life of William Palmer, the man who earned the epithet, 'Palmer the Poisoner'.

In Victorian times, Palmer, who was also a doctor, had developed an interest in horse racing, and from that day onward all his money was spent betting on the turf. Palmer's drug of choice was strychnine, which when administered, was a very nasty way to die, and unlike morphine, the victim dies in less than three hours in absolute agony. Four of his children died of convulsions before their first birthday. He couldn't afford to feed them... or he didn't want to. His wife and brother went the same way. Palmer picked up large sums of life insurance money. He even defrauded his wealthy mother of thousands of pounds. But clearly, he wasn't all bad... he let her live.

Len Bladen, a man he met at the races, lent him 600 pounds. Palmer poisoned him to save paying him back. But his luck ran out when he topped a good friend, John Cook. Palmer had two goes at Cook, the first in The Raven, a local pub, after they had returned from the races together. Palmer was potless after doing his money, but Cook had enjoyed a run of good fortune and was holding three grand. Cook immediately noticed his brandy had a funny taste, making him feel extremely queasy, he relayed this over to other drinking friends, 'Palmer has dosed me'.

He survived that attempt, as the poison wasn't strong enough. A sensible man would then have given Palmer a wide berth, but that man didn't answer to the name of John Cook.

When Cook later accepted a bowl of soup off Palmer, he asked for all he got - Palmer nailed his man and all his money. There was a huge weight of evidence against Palmer by this time, and not just circumstantial. He was arrested in 1855 and tried for murder. Charles Dickens declared that Palmer was the greatest villain that ever stood at the Old Bailey. He was convicted and sentenced to death. 30,000 people were at Stafford Prison to witness the public execution outside. Stafford Rangers never got crowds like that. Then again, mediocre football or high quality hanging - it was no contest.

The sad saga ends on two amusing accounts. As Palmer stepped onto the gallows, he looked at the trapdoor and enquired of the governor, 'Are you sure it's safe?'.

He was wasted as a poisoner, the lad should have trod the boards, his mum would have been so proud. She can have the last word though. Even after robbing her blind, killing another of her sons and putting four grandkids into early graves, she still had that special bond that only a mother and favourite son could have. As Palmer's lifeless body was being taken down from the scaffold, she solemnly declared, 'They have hung my saintly Billy!'.

It must be something in the water in Staffordshire.

I didn't sleep well that night. We were actually on the same wing as Palmer had been back in 1856. With my luck, I was probably sleeping in his bed. I didn't believe in ghosts, but I pulled the sheets well over my head. It made me think: over the last year, I'd been introduced to two mad doctors, one alive, one long gone - no man should ever get that close to evil. A move would be my only salvation. Not only did I have to get out of this prison, I had to get out of Staffordshire. They were all bonkers and I could feel the woodpecker of insanity slowly tapping at the top of my head. At that moment he only had a rubber beak, but I didn't want to be around when he went tungsten tipped pneumatic.

It had been a bad couple of months in Stafford Prison, real rotters. I'd better not say too much more about the county town, as my author was born there, as were Dave Gorman and Neil Morrissey, so that explains quite a lot. David Cameron had stood for election here two years earlier and got beat, and in my opinion he was lucky to get out of town without being beaten senseless. Anyway, enough of this jolly repartee - I was ready and primed for my miracle trip to London. Myself and two burly screws left Stafford on the Friday and I was to spend the weekend in Pentonville Prison, prior to being escorted to court on Monday morning.

The Bing - that was my new name for Lord Chief Justice Thomas Bingham. He had taken the status of super hero, being the only man in the universe who could free me from all the madness. Every yard further away from Stafford Prison was a good yard. Pentonville was calling, but little did I know it would make Stafford resemble a five-star hotel. That weekend was an eye-opener.

The prison was a sewer - a festering, filthy fleapit. Oscar Wilde had served a short sentence there, and he described the prison as 'a shit-hole'. I think that was just too kind there, Oscar being a true romantic. It was full of the very worst dregs of human society. The only things you could trust were the rats and cockroaches. Pentonville has had a terrible press, overcrowding, chronic facilities and corrupt staff. I can now give criminals this salient advice: do not get nicked in North London, because you will definitely regret it, and if that plea stops one mugging, I feel I've contributed to safer streets.

Monday morning arrived for me a second after midnight. Today was the day that freedom beckoned. I was a very early riser, so I wouldn't be enjoying a lie-in, because nobody loves a tardy type. Punctuality was a trait my father had instilled in me. If I'd actually got free rein at that precise moment, multi-coloured bunting would be adorning the prison walls, accompanied by a 21-gun salute, a full dress parade by the Dagenham Girl Pipers, culminating with a fly-past from the Red Arrows. I had to consider though the possibility of another legal stitch-up, so even second prize was better than Pentonville, namely a trip back to Stafford. You see, everything in life is relevant to where you've been before.

I was top billing in Court One. And over in Court Two, Elton John was suing a national newspaper over something frivolous; I think some reporter had called his favourite cat overweight. A disgrace, someone had to keep the intrusive press in check, rock on Reggie. Downstairs in my holding cell, I could see right up into the courtroom, and it looked bloody imposing. The bell rang. *This was it then.* My legs turned to jelly. Judgement day was here. I ascended the ancient risers in trepidation. They resembled a prop from a Hammer horror film. They were classically creaky and scuffed, being at least 300 years old. They were probably owned by our old landlord back in Denton, he wouldn't know what a tool repair kit looked like.

My heart was booming like Thumper the Rabbit on steroids. It was the height of Summer, a July scorcher, and if it got any hotter, I'd have to take off my parka. The galleries were packed, full to bursting with scantily clad female law students. More leg and heaving bosoms were on show than at the *Folies Bergère*. If I copped cardiac arrest now, it would take the paramedics a month to wipe the smile off my face.

I spotted Sharon. She was with two special friends, spymaster Andrew Balfour, my old pal from the British Embassy in Dubai, and Mike Salinger, a Manchester United fanatic who I first met the day before my father died, a company director who'd been on the boards of both Saracens and Nottingham Forest. I really appreciated them being there, but the most important man was straight in front of me, resplendent in court regalia, the highest lawman in the land, *The Bing*. The appeal stretched from ten in the morning to just after four. All the proceedings were conducted in the best Queen's English and complicated lawyer speak. I hadn't got a clue what was going on. When *The Bing* gave his final ruling and flashed me a Colgate smile, I was none the wiser. I hoped he hadn't done *a Henshall* on me. The Group 4 security guard beside me asked, 'Why the long face?'.

I sighed, 'I'm bricking it, having to go back to Stafford'.

He laughed, 'Go where you want old son, he's just upheld your appeal'. I gave him a hug. He hugged me back, a beautiful moment. I joked, 'We can get engaged, or you can remove the handcuffs!'.

He turned the key, and I was liberated. The bird had his wings back.

I drifted ghost-like out through the front doors. The currant bun rays on my face somehow felt much better as a free man. British justice had come through for me. God bless *The Bing*, a man who played it by the book. The country could do with a lot more like him. I hugged my wife, Mike and Andrew for ages on the court steps. It was our own mini Woodstock... without the backing groups. The boys eventually had to go their own way, which left just myself and Sharon to hail a taxi to take us to the Hilton Hotel in Park Lane.

We checked in. I still had my plastic HM Prison bag containing tobacco, lighter, comb, toothbrush and shampoo. I hoped the receptionist didn't think I'd just escaped. Everything turned into a culture shock - I tried to take a dump. Nothing. Not a squeak. I just couldn't do it. Nine months of squatting on a metal pedestal had temporarily constipated me. Even basic everyday things like walking on a carpet was a luxury I'd blissfully forgotten. I gorged myself rotten with fruit, feeling like Mr Creosote, especially with the bananas. For some odd reason they weren't available in prison, so a letter of complaint was duly dispatched to Fyffes for patchy distribution.

That evening old habits died hard. The £45 from prison funds went on 8 and 11 black. Inevitably the bets went down. I'd just like to personally apologise to Her Majesty and the British tax payer, but I'd had a traumatic year, and that was the first and only blow out I really needed.

The fraud trial and subsequent appeal changed the way we all banked. A statute law was brought into practice: more vigorous identity checks, credit checks, evidence of house utilities, in fact overkill information to prove you were who you said you were. No longer could one man open three bank accounts in three months with the same bank chain. Maybe a master forger could, but it put the kibosh on a lot of identity fraud. So the next time you hear someone mention that state terrorism or international money laundering is the reason for the stringent credit checks, just think back to 1998 when Madani was masquerading as three men... a real unholy trinity.

Will the real Mike Yarwood please stand up? I felt just like an imperson-ator and impressionist, but unlike Mike I wasn't fucked when Harold Wilson lost the election. It wasn't fair to Sharon sleeping with three different men, so I returned back to being plain old boring Faisal Madani. Life would become slower and simpler... well, for a few weeks, anyway.

Woe betide me if I ever came up before the beak again. Michael Henshall would never forgive or forget. It was now time to put my football contacts to work. I'd been hatching a master plan in prison.

The upcoming millennium would push the Madani brand into the front rooms of every sports fanatic in Britain.

Postscript 1

COUTTS BANK

I'd come to the conclusion most banks were economic with the truth. The more upper crust the bank, the bigger the porkies. Banks and big business rule the world, they can even bring down governments. I'm sure they all work to-gether as a cartel for their own common good, having spurious standards, codes, morals and ethics. If there is a fast buck to be made the rule book flies out the window.

Coutts still hadn't learnt their lesson from 1998, and in March 2012 they were fined nearly nine million pounds for breaches of money laundering rules. Coutts's bonus system was rewarding their own people handsomely for the opening of new accounts and a lot of the new business was administered with inadequate or scant security checks. The Financial Services Authority found that Coutts were turning a blind eye to accounts with criminal activity involved. Their conclusion was that the bank's conduct fell well below the standards that were acceptable.

The previous year Coutts had been pushing a variable rate fund that didn't come up to scratch and were fined another six million, so despite every-thing that has happened, Coutts still think they can operate on their own terms. No wonder the public have lost all faith in the arrogant 'Hooray Henrys' who control all our money.

JUDGE MICHAEL HENSHALL

My old sparring partner still crops up in the news. In 2014, still presiding at Manchester Crown Court, he granted West Ham midfielder Ravel Morrison bail, a few days after top District Judge James Prowse refused the request and put him in custody. Morrison had allegedly assaulted his ex girlfriend and her mother.

He was also sitting on the high profile rape case in which Coronation Street star Michael Le Vell (who plays the show's mechanic, Kevin Webster) was acquitted of all charges. Now, there is absolutely no truth in the rumour that he enquired afterwards how much would Le Vell charge for a service for his Bentley. Let me tell him, Phil Mitchell on Eastenders does a far better rate, but joking apart, in my opinion, he will foul up big... it's only a matter of time.

HAROLD SHIPMAN

Last but not least, it was never going to end well for Harold. He was found guilty in 2000 and sentenced to numerous life sentences. The upshot being that he would never be released and would die in jail. A day before his 58th birthday in 2004, Shipman hung himself from the window bars, using bedsheets from his cell at HM Prison Wakefield. The Sun, in their own unique measured way ran the headline, 'Ship, Ship, hooray!' - then called for all other British serial killers to do the same.

There are no redeeming factors coming out of this sad saga. More than 250 people died and they won't be coming back. I still can't erase the mental scars - *Honi soit qui mal y pense*. I want it all to go away, but it's forever in my psyche.

* * * *

CHAPTER 13

THE STUDIO OF DREAMS

Arabic saying: A mouth that praises and a hand that kills

God has made us all human, creatures of habit. We like doing the same thing, day after day, and woe betide anyone trying to change our routines. Same pub, supermarket and taxi company, because deep down we don't like change. Monotony is our forte. A good friend of mine was delivered by caesarean birth: to this day he still goes out of the house to work through the front bay window... all perfectly natural.

So when I was approached in early 2002 with the intention of joining forces and getting financially involved with a guy who talked like a crook, smelt like a crook, and looked as dodgy as fuck, I couldn't get the cash out my pocket quickly enough. The warning signs were bang there, but I still had faith in my fellow *Homo sapiens*. I hadn't had the pleasure at that stage of Michael Owen's acquaintance, so maybe my judgement was slightly impaired.

Anyhow, I could so easily have been calling it wrong. The bloke was probably a pussy cat, a prince among men, a humanitarian, a jolly good chap, even one of the boys... Nope! I had it exactly right first time, George Spitaliotis was a total cunt.

He was the man who set up the notorious TV sales channel, *Auction World* in November 2001, together with his grubby sidekick solicitor mate, Nigel Rowley. I needed those two about as much as Kojak craved an afro comb, but the upcoming *merde* hadn't yet reached the electrical cooling apparatus, so the best I could do was give Pinky and Perky the benefit of the doubt.

Spitaliotis had latched on to me through my massive portfolio of contacts and friendship with Premier League footballers. I consequently made a few discreet inquiries on the jungle grapevine. The whispers that came back indicated that an initial cash flow problem was hindering the expansion of Auction World, but it was a company with rakes of potential. That would ding dang do for me. I'd get involved with George, even though he had a surname that sounded like a contagious mouth disease.

Auction World needed a cash injection of £400,000. My reward for putting that amount in would be an honorary directorship. Whoopee-do, lucky me! An annual interest loan repayment of 23%, and total control of the supply of all football memorabilia. It was a very favourable deal. George added that there were many millions to be made. That statement was a very rare instance of him and the truth co-existing in the same room, notwithstanding that every one of those millions later rode out of town in his bulging, saddlebag pockets.

I bet you're thinking, *bloody hell Faz, 400 big ones, how do you do it?* Well, I'd breezed through the easy bit, now came the challenge. I informed Spitaliotis he could have all the money within the week, I felt just like one of the Rothschilds. I perused my bank balance at the ATM - £62.40 wasn't really going to cut it, and the roulette tables were still killing me. Back in Dubai, my uncle Abdul Rahman, was the main man in charge of the family finances, he took my call on the dog. I conferred about Auction World. He seemed impressed. And just for luck, I asked for a cheeky half million. He said it would be in my Nat West account in less than four days. Bloody hell, that was easier than going to Wonga - and they would loan to absolutely any bugger. Try them: even if you'd been a mass murderer, had 45 county court judgements, never worked since leaving school, drink gallons of Thunderbird, have an acute drug habit and your home address is a contaminated Arctic warfare tent in the middle of a Milton Keynes roundabout... expect a cheque in the post.

So that's where we were. I'd got a hundred grand spare for gambling, and Sharon could have a few bob for hair, handbags and shoes. Sharing is always caring, and at that time, it was all cool for cats.

Before going over the events that brought about the demise of Auction World - and it took three long years - I'll relate the wonderful, happy times I had with the footballers on the show... well, most of them, anyway. Auction World was diversifying into soccer, boxing, film and music memorabilia, to complement the very successful auctions of bedecked globes, watches and jewellery.

We were absolutely smashing it with the footballers. The public just couldn't get enough and the ratings were shooting through the stratosphere. Whenever big names appeared on the set advertising the footy memorabilia, the phone lines would morph into meltdown. My favourite three from Ipswich were the mutt's nuts; best mate Kevin Beattie, an unrivalled natural; John Wark, knowledgeable and articulate; and the charismatic legend, Alan Brazil, a man full of *joie de vivre*. Most probably the best sporting pundit around, he could only be described as a slightly flawed genius, having a great face for radio, but worth every last penny he was paid.

Viv Anderson surprised me. Apart from being a top man, what a wheeler dealer he was, a guy full of business acumen. There were no flies on Viv, similar to his old Forest team mates, Steve Hodge and Peter Shilton. Hodge was quiet and astute. Well, he did swap shirts with top gun Maradona after the World Cup match against Argentina in Mexico. Diego's shirt, now reputed to be worth a quarter of a million, was ample consolation for Steve's woeful mistimed clearance that culminated in the 'Hand of God' goal. But what a footballer he was... no, I don't mean Hodgy. Shilts was a one-off, a magic keeper, with great physical presence and tremendous agility, but what a complex character. One day after filming, he collared me for his overnight hotel money. After I gave it to him, he asked, 'Is it all right if I go home now?'.

I was flabbergasted. But what could you say to that? Tight sod.

Five more gold stars, former Manchester United players that were regulars on Auction World, a pair of ex-Leeds men, Gordon McQueen and Joe Jordan were both a delight. McQueen, witty and very funny, and Jordan, professional, polite and praiseworthy. Irish superstar, the precocious Norman Whiteside was great company at work and in play. Two from an earlier era, Alex Stepney and Paddy Crerand were lovely, cracking blokes, real diamonds who, in my eyes, would forever be icons. I'm not name-dropping just for the sake of it, these footballers were my heroes. Each day meeting and mixing with them was like dying and going to Heaven, Valhalla and Elysian Fields all rolled into one.

I held no grudge against Liverpool players. And why should I? They were all high up on a plateau to me. We had red legends Alan Kennedy and John Aldridge down to the studios, they never let me down. Aldridge was a terrific wit and raconteur and Kennedy, the European Cup Final scoring full back, a mellow and amiable Mackem (someone from Sunderland) - you didn't know that, I bet? Conversely, Everton toffee man Graeme Sharp would turn up for the blue side of Merseyside. He was always precise and thoughtful.

I had my own personal favourites, but tried to treat them all exactly the same. A better bunch of footballers couldn't be found. There were many, many more, but I'll finish off with four Gooners - crackerjacks, who maintained the high standard of all the footballers who appeared on Auction World, top British players, consummate internationals and each individual a top professional pundit in his own right.

Eddie Kelly, 'Champagne' Charlie Nicholas and Peter Marinello were three jaunty jocks, larger than life, who all liked a drink. Just the bills alone from the hotel mini bar would agitate the Auction World accountant into a perplexed and depressed state. These men were athletes, they would run off any alcohol in their system next day in training. Midfielder Kelly was just like his football demeanour, rock solid. Nicholas and Marinello had both been dubbed at different periods 'the new George Best'. Impossible pressure for them to live up to. I likened it to the US Republican Dan Quayle, who had been going round comparing himself to President Kennedy. Lloyd Bentsen, a senior Democrat, cut him short and swift, 'I knew Jack Kennedy, Senator. You're no Jack Kennedy.'

I also knew George Best. Enough said.

Charlie has come through turbulent times through determination and talent and is still a regular on television. Peter hasn't been as lucky. My author, Michael O'Rourke, was actually at Old Trafford for his debut with Arsenal - God knows what he was doing there, he's a lifelong Chelsea fan. Unfortunately, after Arsenal it was all downhill for the Flying Scotsman. Peter confided in me that his son had suffered from heroin addiction. On top of that he experienced some subsequent disastrous business deals and embezzlements. I hope he doesn't mind me mentioning that. He deserves a change of luck. Everything didn't turn out as expected for the once famous wonder winger, but it's better to have shone like a brilliant blazing comet for a fleeting moment, than to skulk forever in the dark deathly shadows of mediocrity.

Last but not least of the good guys was Arsenal legend Frank Mclintock, captain of the double-winning side of 1971. He oozed class, was a natural on television and what a genuine man. He was extremely well-connected in media and football circles. One of a dying breed, Frank has stood by me through good times and bad and I will never forget that. Once again, thank you skipper.

I know you're champing at the bit for the rotters, the ne'er-do-wells and the dirty dogs, but I'm only going to name two, and the worst I'm going to call them is 'disappointing'. Both of them were my former friends who, when I needed them most, were not there for me. I'm not going to slag them off, but to say I wasn't gutted would be stating the obvious.

Ian James Rush, MBE, super striker, great man. I loved Rushy, but he was very careful with his money. Others would say mean, but that made no difference to me. He cut off all personal contact while I was pursuing the elusive Michael Owen. The whole situation was probably a pain in the butt to him, but he was an important entity in my quest to be reimbursed. He semi-perjured in court, grossly understating his friendship and relationship with me, not the worst lie in the world but it did me no favours at all. I know where I stand with him now. A real bloody shame.

Michael Reginald Thomas, a one-off, an ex-red and blue, former best pal and chauffeur... Mickey, Mickey, Mickey. In the words of The Supremes, *Where did our love go*. And where did you go? Mickey Thomas is a fantastic man, but very needy and clingy. I gave him money, a car, washed and fed him. He stayed at my house many times. Sharon doted on him. We went everywhere together, the best hotels, the best casinos, there was nobody I'd rather be with when I was doing my bollocks at the roulette table. I was his go-to guy. When he needed anything, my door was always open. It's a pity then, when the shoe was on the other foot, when I was in legal and financial strife, he did a Houdini, and like a black mamba in an eclipse, slithered into the deep undergrowth. I should have realised when I once asked Mickey to break a twenty pound note for me and he passed back three sevens, that reliability wasn't his strong suit. I know he was as mad as a box of frogs and had a self destruct button, but he was one of the finest human beings I ever met. I hope that you're all right old son - I didn't deserve it, but life goes on regardless.

From a couple of very naughty boys, to a ruinous pair of heavy mountebanks - the kingpins of *Auction World*, greedy George Spitaliotis and nasty Nigel Rowley. The process worked as follows; people would tune into Sky satellite channel 651 (later 660) and bid on products, auction style. The price would rise from a supposed very low price base. Auction World claimed that all the products were high quality, and the prices were exceedingly low. The public had to take on trust that the items were indeed of the highest standard and accept the guide price, based on the supposed high street prices.

I can see you're all two paragraphs ahead. Of course this was open to abuse, especially as trading standards had all the bite of a malnourished guppy and reacted with the speed of Sloucher the Sleepy Sloth. It was a charlatan's paradise, and George and Nigel realised very quickly that they could push the envelope farther than it had ever been pushed before. They were the type of men who didn't need two chances to fuck a nation.

W.C. Fields once said, 'Never give a sucker an even break', and that was way back in 1941. People are so gullible. There is just no such thing as a free lunch, especially if the chefs are Spitaliosis and Rowley. Auction World's main staple were globes festooned with gemstones and diamonds, with validation certificates. The high street jewellery shops have a mark up of about 500%, but presenters were selling gems much higher on Auction World and assuring people that it was a worthwhile investment.

Diamonds are a minefield. Apart from the many fakes around, people think it's all down to carat size. Wrong. A one carat clear diamond, can be worth a lot more than a dirty three carat. Dealers all know the *Four Cs* - clarity, colour, cut and carat size. A good diamond has to have all the first three attributes to accentuate the fourth. I'll give a tip to anybody about to buy a big rock. Buy second hand, you will save plenty.

I'm digressing again, so back to the story. Now one would think that the public, having paid through the nose for a right pig in a poke, would get first class, speedy delivery to the front door. Well, wrong again.

Delivery times were appalling. Weddings, birthdays and Christmas all came and went before the gems turned up. That's if they ever did arrive. Auction World broke more rules than all the other television channels combined. A proud record that will probably never be equalled. The customer service was non-existent. At its peak, over 300 people worked at Auction World, so it was a bloody big operation. Just listen to this: the call centre were under orders to never, ever give the address or phone number of head office to anyone complaining over the phone.

A lighter moment occurred one day. Presenter Liz Fuller, famously dumped her omnipresent boyfriend, Paul McKenna, live on air. That was more like it, nobody likes a smart ass. The more money that was coming in, the more daring and outrageous George became. Apparently he was at it from day one. How Auction World was on the air for over three years is testimony to the adage - if you are going to tell a lie, tell a fucking great big one.

He began selling fake quality watches worth a ton for two bags of sand, 2k. Designer handbags were rarely in stock, so they were never delivered. Not content with all that profit, Rowley and Spitaliotis had my footballing mementos in their nefarious sights.

We were booming in that department, and everything was done ramrod straight, one of the few times in my life that dealings were utterly *bona fide*. Why cheat when you're coining it daily? The man leading me to the promised land was David Beckham, who had become a global icon. I was obtaining all my Beckham memorabilia from Dave Gardner, who ran Manchester-based Elite Sports. He was an agent and one of Beckham's best mates and also a partner of Sir Alex Ferguson's son, Jason.

I've had the pleasure of meeting Jason a few times, and a nicer, more honourable man you won't find. It was scandalous the way the BBC went after him, alleging misappropriation in his dealings with Manchester United. They crossed the line there, and it was the reason Fergie would never give them an interview. Alex Ferguson too, gave me utmost respect whenever I met him at Carrington, the Manchester United training ground, or at a charity dinner, or even back in Dubai.

A true knight of the realm. If Sir Alex had ventured into politics, he would have been Prime Minister. He'd have probably slapped George Bush. What a Rottweiler! His football record will stand the test of time. He doesn't need my endorsement, but in Britain, like Irish Georgie, he was simply the best.

The signed football merchandise was selling so rapidly that every dealer wanted to supply us, and it didn't take long for the UACC to contact us. Founded in 1965, the Universal Autograph Collector's Club were the self-proclaimed guardians of the authentic autograph. They just had to make themselves busy. We had a large monopoly throughout the country for the sales of autographed footballs, shirts, pictures and programmes, but, by declining to be a member of the sainted UACC, in their eyes, we were obviously at it.

Jealousy was at the heart of it. Backstabbing and bickering were common in the quest for autographs. If you had the best ones, they were called into question by other dealers. Ironically, ours were top notch, genuine, and direct from Premier League footballers. I had them contacting me day and night, to offload their signatures. It was easy money for them. We had a constant conveyor belt of mementos, but it left a bad taste for any dealer on the outside looking in.

Gary King, a jobsworth from UACC, was forever threatening court action, trading standards and the fraud squad. We told him he had *carte blanche* - *do it*. He claimed he was an expert, but he didn't know any of the players. The trouble at the time was that the autograph game was run like a cottage industry, overseen by opinionated buffoons. Hamilton Bland, the former BBC swimming commentator, was an autograph dealer. He was another who thought successful rivals were playing dirty, but what would any footballer have in common with him.

Dealers were now offering me autographed items from films, music and boxing. We were buying big from America - genuine Elvis and Muhammad Ali items were making big profits. One night, a David Beckham-signed Real Madrid shirt was sold to Kieron Dyer for five and a half thousand. And the interesting fact was the that two underbidders were his Newcastle team mates, Craig Bellamy and Jonathan Woodgate.

I was fucking furious the night George Spitaliotis got involved. It was pure greed. Top professionals from all walks of life were regular bidders, why would a man try to screw them? I can't answer that, but Nigel Rowley obviously instigated it, he couldn't lie straight in bed. He once told me that he was Princess Diana's advocate. That turned out to be a fairy tale. He was a posh sort of pub bullshitter, the one who has had trials for Spurs, been in the SAS and was a roadie for Led Zeppelin. You can't disprove it, but it's why he sits on his own at the end of the bar.

That night, boxer Joe Calzaghe bid 14k for a rare signed Beatles LP. What he didn't know was that George was bouncing the bids up to get a premium. It had nowt to do with me, but it still left a bad smell. A while back, his trainer-dad Enzo, was fronting that boxing-based Coral advert with the water and Vaseline, with the vivacious Carly Baker wiggling her world class botty as rounds girl. He really did my nut in, so I can say hand on heart, with justification, after his wooden acting, my contriteness about what happened to Joe did wane quite considerably.

Judgement day was now at hand. It was the beginning of the demise. Not only was George selling products way above their proper value, he was now running them up mercilessly. I was ready to abandon ship and I'd bullet-proofed all my contacts to take with me. I hadn't been paid my commission for at least a month, but I could live with that. All loan money had been paid back to the family funds in Dubai and my bank account wasn't exactly threadbare.

It was late 2004, Watchdog and The Daily Mirror had already torn Auction World to shreds with awful revelations. How lovely to see The Mirror involved in a story about a corrupt greedy fat twat that was just about to do a bunk with all the cash. No irony there.

The end was coming. Ofcom hurtled in with a fine of £450,000. The accounts showed Auction World had losses of £15 million. Barnes Trust Media, the owners of Teddington Studios, were owed tens of thousands in back rent. 300 staff hadn't been paid. Where had all the money gone?

Don't answer that. George was in a quandary; should he pay all the fines, company losses, back rent and staff wages, or should he fuck off with all the money to his parents house in sunny Cyprus, where there was no extradition. He must have considered that dilemma for all of a nanosecond. While he was abroad, Rowley and himself were barred from being company directors for 18 months. Big deal. I bet they were devastated. If this was fiction, you couldn't make it up.

The Law Society of Great Britain piled the pressure on Nigel Rowley. They would hold an inquiry. How was the man sleeping at night? If you are struggling to read this through tears of laughter or despair, let me tell you the worst that happened to George Spitaliosis was that Watchdog sent Nicky Campbell over to Cyprus, where he tracked George down to the family address in Nicosia. This is the only time in the whole sad, sordid affair that George Spitaliosis showed any class. He point blank refused to give Nicky Campbell an interview. Quite right too, he's another toss pot. In fact the local police turned up and told wee Nicky and his camera crew to 'do one pronto'... preferably off the island.

I'd swerved any company director ban as I was only honorary, but I should have come out of the business a very rich man. Like I said, I'd got a lot more money than I went in with, but I would still have to carry on working. George Spitaliosis had tucked me up like a kipper. Back home in Dubai that deception is known as the classic mango trick. They say you can't con a conner, but I had to get up, dust myself down, and just get on with it. Gordon Gekko had once declared, 'Greed is good'.

He'd obviously met Michael Owen.

He was up next.

*   *   *   *

INTERMISSION - Gallery

Two former football gods - David Beckham and Kevin Beattie

At Bramhall - Myself, Sharon and the great Paddy Crerand

George Best signing session

Enjoying a night out with my good friend Georgie

George Best, Mickey Thomas and pop legend, Rod Stewart -
at a Soccer Six tournament (*circa 2004*)

At the Bramhall bungalow again...
Two wonderful footballers - Paddy Crerand and Mike Summerbee

Two footballing legends - Paul Gascoigne, Bryan Robson
and my lifelong friend Sami

Superstar defender Tony Adams, my wife Sharon and me - at an awards event

Press advertising for the Libya match

One of the good guys -
United and England great,
Rio Ferdinand signing England shirts

Michael Owen

CHAPTER 14

ALL THAT GLITTERS

Arabic saying: A house divided cannot stand

There's been an awful lot written, opined, Tweeted and broadcast about Michael James Owen. Plenty of plaudits, countered by the occasional stinging barb - he's a personality constantly in the news. A very hard man to read, he was often taciturn early on in his career, but emerged from his shell towards retirement. The housewives darling was blessed with angelic babyface features and the softly spoken goal-scoring sensation celebrated a meteoric rise in the tough and physical world of Premier League football. Even the hardest nosed hacks in Fleet Street would struggle to disparage his playing achievements, especially the early pre-injury years.

I got in close and personal, and like a tackle from Ron 'Chopper' Harris, I'm still counting the bruises. 'Sharon, pass me the ointment, the Owenitis has flared up again'.

It became a painful passage of double bluff and counter claim, which is still ongoing to the present day. I know who was on the side of the angels, and as stressful as it is, let's take it from its genesis, and you, the public, can be juror, judge and executioner.

An old adage declares: *Never meet your hero, as you will end up disappointed.* Our paragons are projected onto pedestals too high. Superstar or not, they are only flesh and blood, human beings with all the foibles. Scandal, sin and excess are not uncommon, but ardent, blinkered fans and followers will always turn a blind eye to the odd indiscretion.

I'd been on a good run, mixing with my earlier matinée idols, Kevin Beattie (God), Bobby Robson (the most wonderful man), George Best (gentleman and genius), and Rio Ferdinand (friend and confidante). That fabulous foursome should have been enough for any mere mortal, but Madani could, and never would, rest on his laurels. Playing the card game of Nap(oleon), one always needs five good cards, and Michael Owen was going to be a stonewaller, my unbeatable fifth card.

What could go so wrong? He didn't come across as the Devil Incarnate, and so I became a man on a mission, speeding down the side of the Eiger with no brakes, and by the time I hit the bottom, the forthcoming detritus had spread high, wide and not very handsome.

Pre-Owen Liverpool hadn't confidently come down the East Lancs road for many a long year with a favourable chance of turning the tables on the old enemy. It had become a bone of contention, trying to usurp Manchester United in Cottonopolis, but the diminutive, precocious teenager was looking to change all that by leading a glorious Merseyside renaissance.

1997 was the year he made his debut as a confident seventeen-year-old. Already saddled with a huge reputation, he played with a carefree style that belied his lack of big match experience. In the dying embers of that season, he scored in his first league game. For the next two years he ran riot, finishing up top scorer in the Premier League. A colossal feat for a young and inexperienced player, he was even popping them in against Sir Alex's finest. Had the boy no shame?!

At international level the heaven-blessed manager Glenn Hoddle succumbed to the nationwide clamour to blood the Young Turk. And in 1998 Owen became the youngest player to represent England in the twentieth century.

Initially, Hoddle had been vacillating about giving Owen a starting place in his side, but at the World Cup in France, after previously leaving him on the bench for the first two matches, he gave Owen his head against the old enemy, Argentina. Owen was ready: *Cometh the hour, cometh the boy*. His position in the team would be cemented for years.

The planet watched transfixed, as the Northern Hemisphere pragmatists took on the Southern Hemisphere aristocrats, in a World Cup heavyweight second round showdown. It can stick in the craw, but sometimes you have to give credit where credit is due. Owen's goal against the Argentine was an all-time classic, and possibly the best goal England have ever scored at the World Cup.

Owen picked up a pass just inside the opponents' half, and with a deft shimmy he was running at retreating defenders with guile and almost indecent pace. Whatever level football is played at, the one thing that most defenders hate is a speedy forward. Owen had speed to kill for, and he was up and in their faces. He launched into a lethal diagonal run, leaving desperate opponents trailing in his wake. He found himself on the right hand edge of the Argentinian penalty area and obliquely lashed the ball into the top left hand corner of the net, leaving the goalie flat-footed and motionless.

A star was born on the international stage, though I still don't think it was as good as Archie Gemmill's mazy masterpiece against the Dutch in 1978 (15-all: Madani to serve... thankyou umpire), Owen's life would never ever be the same again. Here was a rare commodity; a man who could walk the walk, and talk the talk.

On his return to domestic football, he was top scorer for Liverpool every season between 1998 and 2004, although niggling injuries were becoming more prevalent, especially hamstring twinges. You couldn't compare him to Darren 'Sicknote' Anderton of course, as it was only drip-drip deterioration, but that, coupled with wear and tear plus the ageing process, meant the constant physical stresses and strains were beginning to take their toll.

The most important yards for a speedball are the first five. That's when you wriggle away from your marker. Cruyff, Maradona and Pele were all past masters. Watch Messi when he's on song, defenders seem to be standing still.

When that attribute starts to fade, alarm bells ring, and the crowd are the first to know. Maybe 2003 was Owen's footballing watershed, his Waterloo. Was the super nova fading? I just wish I'd have spotted it, because that was the year I first met him. We both couldn't be on the slide, surely?

It was early April on my real *annus horrbilus*. The venue was Gala Casino, Stockport. I was dining out with Liverpool legend Ian Rush, who'd brought a mate along. Dubai cropped up in general conversation. Rushy had always admired Dubai - 'It's a great country, but very, very expensive!'

That didn't surprise me, Ian had tactical long pockets and wouldn't scatter money around freely. I once saw him accidentally drop a pound coin. It hit him on the back of the neck before it hit the floor. His pal reiterated that Dubai was financially out of the reach for the ordinary man in the street. He declared that Michael Owen and his family had flown there and got no change from seventy big ones.

As a Dubaian, I knew it shouldn't have cost that amount. Thirty five thousand would have been par for the course, but if Owen had shelled out that much, he'd been seriously ripped off. This was strange really, because it was common knowledge that Owen, like Rushy, didn't have a reputation for throwing the folding stuff about (apart from a penchant for heavy gambling), and this miserly outlook seemed to be a general life strategy.

As we went our separate ways I informed Rushy that if Owen wanted to fly to Dubai again I would sort it all out for a fraction of what he had paid. It had been an ambition of mine to meet Owen and even set up a shared business. What a plonker I was!

Three nights later I took a phone call at home, 'You've got his attention, Faz, I've told him about your clout in Dubai'. Rushy continued, 'I know you've arranged holidays for Manchester United and City players, could you accommodate Ritchie Partridge and his fiancée Lesley? (Michael's sister)

Partridge was a promising young footballer on the fringes of the Liverpool FC first team, but at the time was incapacitated with a serious knee injury. He later married Lesley and it was obvious they were the catalyst for getting into Michael's good books.

I introduced myself to them at Manchester International Airport, 'Mr Partridge, I presume... knowing me, knowing you, aha!'. That quip went straight over his head, 'Hello Faz, lovely to meet you'.

We shook hands firmly. I took an instant liking to the young couple. Everything had been arranged for them, two first-class airline tickets to Dubai and two reservations at the only seven star hotel in the world, the glorious, resplendent Burg Al Arab.

It had cost me five figures, but in a fair world, my generosity would have been well rewarded. I believed in karma: what goes round, comes round. It went round all right, but when it was time to come back around, it never stopped at my platform. I didn't know it at the time, but my creaking pockets would have to stretch a lot deeper.

The Partridge-Owen combo had a fantastic holiday, and a few days after they returned I was requested to attend Melwood, Liverpool's legendary training ground to meet the golden child. It felt like being summoned to an audience with the Pope or the Dalai Lama. Ritchie had given me a blinding endorsement and, all of a sudden, Michael Owen was in a hurry to meet me.

Ian Rush was Liverpool's official goalscoring coach at the time and he relayed it back to me that I'd made a tremendous impression and things were looking distinctively hunky dory. Arriving at Melwood, the first two people I encountered were ex-Manchester City goalkeeping coach Joe Corrigan and *numero uno* at Liverpool, manager Gerald Houllier. Big Joe introduced me to the Frenchman as 'a friend from Dubai'. I found Houllier to be a thoroughly decent person, affable, but very intense, and in the short time we chatted loquaciously, he came across as a man who could definitely be a wheeler dealer.

I spotted Michael Owen over on a training pitch and waved. He came over casually with another friend of mine, Jim Cadman, a business associate who was involved in a sporting memorabilia company called *Inside Football*. I had recently sold Jim an England shirt with Owen's signature on it for sixty pounds. It was among a batch of merchandise that Jim was checking for authenticity. Michael confirmed in my presence that all was kosher, something he would backtrack on in court at an upcoming trial.

We small-talked for ten minutes. But the important thing was that we had touched base. I was hoping we could work together in the future. I mentioned to Michael that I was going to the Gala Casino, Stockport that evening, and asked if would he like to join me as my guest. Regrettably he was committed elsewhere, but suggested at some stage I join him at his favourite haunt, the Stanley Casino in Liverpool. I knew Owen liked a flutter, betting on most sports, especially the gee-gees, and sure enough, he gave me a tip for the following day. He'd built up a very strong relationship with champion jockey Kieron Fallon and this information had come straight from the Irish maestro. Before I left, I enquired about his own fitness. Disturbing little rumours were surfacing that all was not well. It was

Liverpool's last home game of the season at Anfield against Manchester City. 'I'm good... sharp at the moment. I love playing against City'. I didn't doubt it. He'd finished the season with a glut of goals, including four scored away at West Brom the previous week.

The horse - a steeplechaser - was a 6/1 chance. I rang my unofficial chauffeur Mickey Thomas (I'd just bought him a very nice second hand BMW X5), instructing him to put me a monkey on the equine flying machine. Mickey duly matched my bet.

The horse decided to throw the jockey off at the second fence, presenting a thousand quid gift to Joe Coral. How could Fallon, a flat jockey, be giving out tips for jump horses? They weren't even the same code.

We'd done our bollocks on the nag, and now there was only one thing for it. Rushy affirmed Owen's form was hot, even suggesting a hat-trick was not out of the question. Mickey had I both had a grand on Liverpool winning the match, three hundred on Owen scoring, and a pony each on the expected hat-trick. All bases were now covered. We took our places in the stand. Twenty minutes later, with City winning two-nil, Mickey turned to me and said, 'It's not looking good mate'. I had to laugh. What a pair of mugs we were.

City's keeper, Schmeichel, was brilliant. I knew how good he was after all the glory years at Old Trafford. In my opinion he's the best goalie ever seen in the Premier League. This was his penultimate match before retiring. He was beaten in the second half, but it was Baros scoring, not Owen. Liverpool limped to a 2-1 home defeat and Owen hadn't had a sniff. I rang Rushy after the match. 'Thanks for that tip Ian, don't give me any more'.

We never learn though do we? I had some business in London and Mickey had driven me down. We booked into the Hilton Park Hotel, but never slept there. We played roulette into the early hours at the Barracuda Casino, Baker Street. Mickey had a golden streak and came out three and a half thousand pounds up. It coincided with Rushy phoning, 'Michael's had the strongest information ever. When this wins, all money lost will be returned'.

I was reticent, 'I'm not sure Mickey, I've been burnt too many times'. But Mickey the eternal optimist reasoned that, 'They can't be wrong all the time can they?'

That afternoon he backed the horse to the tune of three thousand pounds. It trailed in last. And this wasn't fake money. All bets were off after that. We were quite capable of losing our own money without advice as chronic as that.

2003-04 turned out to be Michael Owen's last season in a Liverpool shirt, and even despite a persistent ankle injury he emerged top league scorer for the reds with 16 league goals, but the way he left polarised most Liverpool fans forever.

Michael Owen still had the 2004 European Championships in his sights. He flew off to the Iberian Peninsula, destination Portugal, confident he would come good for England and put himself in the shop window. Rumours were rife that he wanted away from Anfield for sunnier climes. I think Thierry Henri was the bookies front runner to finish up tournament top scorer. But Rushy wouldn't let it go, and he fancied Michael strongly to be the top dog. I wouldn't risk a bent tanner on him, and if Mickey Thomas had any funny money left, it was going to Gamblers Anonymous. We didn't have a bean on Owen. Not a sausage. Nada... zip. We were rewarded for using common sense and good gambling acumen as the mighty Michael scored all of *one goal*.

England, the beaten Quarter Finalists, had gone out to the hosts on penalties. How hard can it be to score from twelve yards? They all returned home crestfallen. I knew about half of the players and the backroom staff, so I shared in their disappointment more than most.

I'd spoken to Owen's mother Jeanette on numerous occasions since my initial meeting with Michael. Another trip to Dubai was in the offing, and Jeanette wanted to go when Michael got back from Portugal. Mickey Thomas had advised me to arrange it after the quarters, because England never progress any further. Smart ass. One of the few times he has come up trumps.

I got the Owen manifest. It was a bit of a piss-take, as there were eleven individuals on it; mother and father, Jeanette and Leslie Owen, brothers Terry and Andy Owen, Rachel Robinson (Andy's girlfriend), Ritchie Partridge and Lesley Owen, sister Karen Owen, Michael Owen and wife-to-be Louise Bonsall with their 15-month-old baby.

At no stage did any of the Owen entourage enquire if I had all the funds. I put down thirty thousand pounds myself and paid three thousand five hundred pounds on the credit card of my friend Mr. P. Hosseini. I made it perfectly clear to Ian Rush that this was not a gift and that I wanted reimbursing on their return.

Financially, I was sailing close to the wind, but I desperately wanted to be involved with Owen, and if this was going to clinch the deal, so be it. Rushy reassured me that Owen knew it wasn't a free holiday, and would weigh me in when he got back. In his words, 'It's not even half a week's wages'. Owen was an extremely rich athlete, rumoured to have 41 million in the bank. The only English player with more rhino was David Beckham.

Mickey Thomas escorted me to the airport. I wanted to see the family off. The first thing Michael Owen said to me was, 'Thanks Faz, I'll sort the money side out as soon as we get back'. This was a great relief. We shook hands, but not before Owen slipped off one of his trainers, tugging the trousers up to his kneecap. The foot, ankle and lower leg were black with bruises courtesy of a long and gruelling season, playing against defenders who were not too particular, who or what they kicked.

A couple of weeks later the family returned, but chaos intervened. Owen was being headhunted by Real Madrid, and I found it impossible to contact him. Merseyside wasn't happy, and I can't say I was over the moon either. I phoned Jeanette a couple of times. The timbre and tone in her voice suggested there would be no problems. She eventually put me in touch with a certain Steve Smith in Leeds, Owen's partner-cum-manager, and he assured me he'd speak to Owen. I began to feel people were passing the buck, and weeks were starting to turn into months.

In September Jeanette Owen rang me out of the blue. Could I meet Steve Smith and herself at the Manchester Hilton? At last I thought, they'd done the decent thing and come up in clover with my money. I'd experienced heart-stopping stress since Owen's holiday. Why would a multi-millionaire treat somebody like this? But I was prepared to let bygones be bygones as soon as they handed me my cheque. I hadn't met Smith before, and to my astonishment, all he wanted to talk about was sponsorship for Owen in Dubai. Aghast, I stole a glance into the room's ornate rococo mirror to see if I had the word 'cunt' stamped on my forehead.

Jeanette Owen pushed her luck further by asking if I could arrange another Dubaian holiday, just for her and daughter Karen. They had obviously mistaken my kindness for weakness, and wrongly assumed that I was a mindless twat. Later that day I phoned her with the new holiday agenda, insisting outstanding previous payment must first be honoured. Unsurprisingly, I never heard from her again.

Dennis Hopper, that great Hollywood actor made his debut in the film *Rebel Without A Cause*, which starred the young James Dean. During Hopper's first day on the set, one of the film crew was extolling the genius of the hot new superstar. How he was going to take the world by storm and enjoy a glitteringly stellar career. The homage was rudely interrupted by Dean bursting out of his trailer, effing and blinding, berating a young female clipboard assistant. Hopper calmly told the crewman, 'All that glitters, isn't always gold'.

That's how I now regarded Owen. A tarnished idol, someone who could crawl under a snake's belly wearing a top hat. Here was a man who hadn't the decency or morality to pay his debts. He withheld money that would be regarded as little more than a pittance to him. I'm that bitter I can't even mention him by name again. To me he's 'GLOB' - *greedy little overpaid bastard*.

I was now profoundly concerned. Rush, Glob and his mother were not returning my phone calls. I eventually got hold of Steve Smith on a private number. He broke a bombshell, informing me that Rush and Glob would not speak to me as they were now prosecution witnesses for Trading Standards in an upcoming court case involving copyright and fraudulent signatures. How very bloody convenient. Glob could now stand behind the law. What a fine upstanding citizen he was. I sought legal advice and was duly informed any personal contact could be construed as perverting the course of justice. I turned to debt collecting agencies to claw back the money, but everything hit a brick wall. Dar and Co., top Manchester solicitors got involved. Glob's side said if we could verify proof of payment, they would pay up.

Dar and Co. sent reams of overwhelming evidence, but nothing ever came back the other way. That was, until out of the blue, Glob's mob changed tactics and informed Dar and Co. that if I still persisted in chasing the money, they would inform the police about harassment for Glob's assets. Dar and Co. told me that this was a very rare circumstance: not only had Glob robbed me, he now wanted me in prison.

Rush and Glob both later perjured themselves in Chester Crown Court, but believe me, they weren't the only ones. That's coming up soon - this book is the gift that keeps on giving.

Glob didn't give a shit about my thirty three large, as he was enjoying himself in the Spanish sunshine. Not convincing at first, he belatedly got his act together and finished the 2004-05 season with thirteen goals, not great, but he warmed the bench a lot that season. Newcastle United came out of nowhere and offered Madrid nearly seventeen million the following season. As he hadn't set Spain alight and couldn't hold down a first team place, a move to the North East seemed to suit everyone involved.

He signed on for Newcastle for four years, at one hundred and ten thousand pounds a week. He wasn't known as Glob for nothing. He even inserted a 'get-out clause' in his contract at twelve million - just in case somebody more fashionable than Newcastle came in for him. He had definitely seen better days, the body was beginning to break down, his Newcastle career started with a thigh injury, and then he broke a metatarsal in his foot, followed by damaged cruciate ligaments in his right knee just for good luck. He then injured his thigh again, then suffered a double hernia, yet another thigh strain followed, before he experienced a bout of mumps and, just to round things off he incurred a calf strain. He played a paltry 71 games in 4 years scoring a pitiful 26 goals. I bet Freddie Shepherd wished he could have turned the clock back on that fiasco. Newcastle were relegated, but Glob couldn't have cared less he was off to pastures new with 24 million Geordie pounds in his pocket.

Glob's management company sent out a 32-page glossy brochure to all potentially interested buyers. He was available on a free transfer. Inside it described him as 'fit and healthy, cool, and charismatic'. What a joke! It all smacked of desperation. It backfired badly, and the media slaughtered him mercilessly. The brochure should have been twinned with the term 'turd polishing', but the publicity attracted two giants of world football: Stoke City, the only pub team in the Premier league, and newly-promoted Hull City, who had obviously sniffed out something fishy in the brochure.

Tony Blair welcomed the new brochure. A comparison with his dodgy dossier on weapons of mass destruction came out very favourably. I, like most people, had Glob down as a busted flush. The Daily Express agreed and reported no club in their right mind would go near him and suggested he retire quietly. Glob wasn't having that, and he sued the newspaper in the High Court and won damages. Maybe there was life in the old dog yet. I was still convinced only an idiot would come in for him. On the 3rd of July 2009 that idiot turned out to be Sir Alex Ferguson. Glob signed for my team Manchester United. What was Fergie doing? The bad dream was turning into a nightmare. December that year, Glob notched a hat-trick away at Wolfsburg. I didn't know whether to laugh or cry. Towards the end of the season Glob got crocked again. Fergie had signed him on a 'pay-as-you-play' contract thankfully... there were no flies on the great Scot.

The next season was like the first, he was lethargically standing up front, seldom scoring, and spending plenty of time warming the bench. Surely Old Trafford was about to see the back of him? He was hindering the progress of promising young players trying to break through. No such luck. Somebody with a warped sense of humour offered him a year extension. His stats got worse in the third and final season, not scoring a league goal - what was the point? Three seasons at the Theatre of Dreams had yielded just five league goals. For me, he had sullied the shirt. I was in no mood to forgive or forget.

Post-Liverpool, Glob had alienated a lot of people. A lot of bad karma had followed him to Real Madrid. The great people of Merseyside tried to take Glob to their hearts, but an invisible barrier of quasi-middle class pretentiousness left him just short. He would never be regarded as a Liverpool icon like Gerrard, Carragher and Fowler, working class boys who had lived the red dream. But even the regard and fondness that some Liverpool supporters still felt for him, disappeared the day he signed for the untouchables of Manchester United.

As long as I can remember, there's been a lot of rivalry between Manchester and Liverpool, some good natured, some over the top, and some downright nasty. I don't know if it goes back to 1894 when the business hierarchy of Manchester, commissioned the opening of the Manchester Ship Canal, a 40-mile navigable inland waterway which started in the Mersey estuary and cut through to Salford. The bottom line was that all the ships carrying goods and cotton now bypassed Liverpool. How would you feel if a tap that had flowed for a hundred years was suddenly turned off? Merchants and stevedores of Merseyside had to tighten their belts. Some went to the wall, while many lost their jobs at the once great port. It created a rivalry and bitterness that would pervade through the upcoming 20th century.

Alex Ferguson turned up at Old Trafford in 1986 determined to overthrow Liverpool. They were the benchmark, a magnificent trophy-winning machine that had carried all before them. He took Manchester United to the summit and Liverpool didn't like playing second fiddle. Now, with all the new money invested in the game, clubs like Chelsea, Manchester City, Spurs and Arsenal have also overtaken the Merseyside giants. Despite the new kids on the block, Liverpool versus United has the greatest and most intense rivalry, so in 2009, when Glob suddenly turned up in Manchester holding a United shirt aloft, proclaiming, 'I'd always lived in hope, that one day I would play for Manchester United'. It cut sharp, and it cut deep.

That turned more than a few stomachs in Liverpool. Whatever meagre support he had once held on Merseyside dissipated into the ether. Transfers between the two great clubs are few and far between. The simple fact is that they just don't like each other. Although Glob had circumnavigated his move round Real Madrid and Newcastle United, he had still set sail and landed hypothetically at Salford Docks. He had committed a cardinal error and the various internet footbal forums and Twitter were red-hot. You could feel the bile, bitterness and outright hate pouring out of the laptops.

Some of the more sensible ones proclaimed; 'Michael Owen cares only about Michael Owen'. Or, 'He's less durable than a cheap condom', and 'Owen's chasing the Mankee Dollar'.

Would I be right in saying then, that the opinions summed him up as a selfish man who was always on the treatment table and who would stop at nothing to earn a pound? Of course I would. People had sussed him out. You can't fool the great British public. There was hatred out there for sure, but I didn't hate Glob - I just wanted my money back. But he made me despise his actions and I didn't want my world to revolve round rancour. Life's just too short to hate.

He later twisted the knife by insisting that Liverpool had overplayed him when he should have been recuperating from his injuries, and that he'd experienced bad rehabilitation treatment there. So, according to the Gospel of St. Michael, it was Liverpool's fault. How could we all have got it so wrong?

On the plus side, he stood up to the plate at Real Madrid. Not playing a lot of games, but his goal scoring ratio to appearances were good. I'm not having people saying just because Glob owes me thirty three large that I'm conducting a witch-hunt, because his early career is spectacular, definitely world class. You have to compliment the man on his sporting prowess, it's just his personal credibility that makes me want to vomit. His move to Newcastle was for all the wrong reasons. It was led by the thirst for more easy pay days, and unlike Malcolm MacDonald, Jackie Milburn and Alan Shearer, Glob never became a Geordie legend.

Although he was quicker than Micky Quinn.

Freddie Shepherd has publicly stated that Michael Owen was the worst transfer he has ever conducted. That of course is a grievous charge, because Freddie over the years had signed some right dodge pots. I'm afraid Freddie has to take his share of the blame. Here was a footballer who was on the treatment table a little more than he should have been. It was Freddie who offered nearly seventeen million pounds. A good yardstick would have put Glob's value to maybe half that amount, but Shepherd was determined to get his man. Glob gets a contract over four years for 110 thousand big ones a week, and he banks that money, whether he plays or not.

Real Madrid were happy, Glob was over the moon, the man with all the worries was Shepherd. Michael Owen wasn't the worst transfer Freddie ever conducted, but the financial terms surely were. Glob was innocent of the charge, nobody held a gun to Freddie's head, he simply paid too much in transfer fees and wages. If Glob could have stayed injury-free for four years and blasted twenty goals a season, Freddie would have been rewarded with sainthood, but that's like stating if my auntie Agnes had balls, she'd be my uncle.

Glob's Tyneside career was akin to watching a bad episode of TV's *Casualty*. Injuries restricted him to 71 appearances in four years, scoring just 26 goals, and it was estimated that it cost nearly a million pounds per goal in wages. Shepherd said that off the pitch, Glob's added value was nil. As after a match all he wanted to do was fly home in his three million pound helicopter back to Cheshire. What did he expect, Owen going out on a bender down Bigg Market?

The Geordie fans were always going to give Glob the benefit of the doubt and back their new super signing, but as his contract was coming to an end, even these fine people had given up the ghost. Glob had made absolutely no indication that he wanted to resign... why should he? A free agent can get a lucrative signing-on fee at the next club. What loyalty did he owe Newcastle? - nothing as far as he was concerned - and the Geordie fans started to turn on him.

Soon after leaving relegated Newcastle for Manchester United, he claimed that all along Newcastle had been a poor team. Why say that, no value at all? His time there had made him a very rich man, what could he hope for by slagging them off? His answer came in April 2011, sitting on the subs bench for the umpteenth time courtesy of the Red Devils. At St James' Park the atmosphere was hostile, some say as bad as anything heard there previously. It erupted into a crescendo of hate in the 81st minute when Glob came off the bench. He'd been expecting a rough reception, but even he must have been taken aback by the ferocity. 'One greedy bastard, there's only one greedy bastard', the chant rever-berated from all four corners of the ground - fans in the famous black and white shirts were waving ten and twenty pound notes in the air.

After the match, Glob commented that he didn't realise Newcastle fans hated him that much. If he had have known, he would have shipped out earlier.

Anyhow he couldn't care less if they booed him. He wasn't looking for sympathy, he would only be worried if his own family booed him. This is my point, he just doesn't get it. Here is a man so insular and parochial that everyone apart from himself and his nearest and dearest don't count.

I've gone over the three-year debacle at Old Trafford, so all that was left was a small cameo at Stoke City. Why bother? There was only a sad caricature of a once great player turning up. In September 2012 Tony Pulis finally got his man. Glob signed on a pay-as-you-play deal with substantial bonuses for every goal scored. He must have been desperate to sign on those terms, as past performances meant he rarely played, let alone scored.

The Britannia Stadium was buzzing, oatcakes were flying off the shelves, the famous fan's song *Delilah* was booming from the windy terraces, and multi-millionaire chairman Peter Coates declared, 'Michael has something to prove, people have written him off'. Don't be a knob all of your life Peter, take a day off. The reason he was written off was because of chronic injuries, a loss of most of his pace and a preference to stand in horse shit. Why waste everyone's time in the Potteries?

Glob really excelled himself in what was to be his last footballing fun-filled fiesta, making all of nine appearances in the 2012-13 season, eight in the league, one in the cup. Long ball specialists Stoke didn't win any of the matches he played in, but Glob did score a consolation goal in the 3-1 defeat at Swansea. He knew the game was up, his money-making stream had trickled down into a dust bowl. Announcing his retirement just before the end of the season, it hardly made a mention in the papers. There were reams about Carragher, Sir Alex and Beckham calling it a day. The Golden One had become the Forgotten One. His last match was at Southampton, Tony Pulis showed his sentimental side and left Glob on the bench. Well he was used to it there. The match was petering out for a bore draw, and Pulis had a brainwave: send Glob on with 16 minutes left. A goal, and it could all be plastered over the back pages. He hadn't been on them all season. And 16 minutes later, his consistency had been rewarded. He wouldn't be on them again.

A man of Owen's stature should have had a glorious send off, but he went with hardly a whimper. He should have been a hero, a national treasure, but through his attitude and his remorseless search for the big buck, people just don't hold him in fond remembrance. Tony Pulis said that Glob had made a big impression in the dressing room - it was a pity he couldn't have done the same on the pitch. The day before Stoke's last game, Kenwyne Jones discovered a dead pig's head in his training locker. Suspecting it had been put there by Glenn Whelan, he charged outside and shattered Whelan's car windscreen. Tony Pulis could not understand the furore and unwittingly stated, 'There's always been a smashing atmosphere in the dressing room'. Jones had to later apologise to Whelan, when it was pointed out that he didn't do it. The culprit is still at large, although Glob is not under suspicion, as he would have gone for a horse's head instead. Poor old Tony Pulis got his cards a week later. He'd taken Stoke as far as he could, seven very good years a distant fading dream, the fickle crowd had turned, rebelling against the style of football. They had all developed short term memory loss.

Sometimes it just doesn't pay to get what you wish for. Take Alan Curbishley at Charlton - fans were on his back and the board sacked him. Today, Charlton are light-years away from where they were with 'Curbs' at the helm, so Stoke fans, fair warning, the only way isn't always up. Pulis hit the A500 out of town. The football hadn't been great on the eye and he'd paid way over the top for some mediocre players, but the bottom line was that defensively he was a top-notch coach. Did signing Michael Owen aid his demise? It couldn't have helped, one goal all season was not a great return for a striker. Would Owen worry or spare a thought for Pulis?

On past form - neigh lad!

Away from football, Glob has previous. That is, disputes about payment or non payment, and it's a tale of tragedy and ultimately death. In March 2004, builder Michael Flynn was found dead by his wife Susan at their Market Drayton home in Shropshire. He had taken a massive overdose and was certified dead at Telford Hospital. Flynn, a close family friend to the Owen family, had first started work in 2002 on Owen's two million pound, eight-bedroom mansion in North Wales. Michael Owen alleged that Flynn claimed hundreds of thousands of pounds for work that was never done, including tricking his mother Jeanette into handing him a six hundred thousand pound cheque for work that wasn't due.

Against this backdrop were allegations that Flynn had lent Owen's sister and her fiancé 150 thousand pounds, and was now in litigation to get it back.

On top of that, there were rumours that Flynn's relationship with Jeanette was more than platonic - probably bullshit, but in my opinion it just muddied the waters of truth. From my own personal experience, I don't believe a word the Owen family say, but who's to say they weren't up front here. The upshot was that Michael Owen successfully had Michael Flynn's business assets frozen, the value of which were just shy of nine hundred thousand pounds. Owen was suing Flynn for 1.2 million pounds, and just to kick a man in the teeth Owen was having his solicitors attempt to have Flynn jailed as well.

Now, where have we heard that one before?

Michael Flynn never had his day in court. He was in the morgue. Owen, on hearing Flynn was dead, said he was 'shocked and saddened'. Really Michael? You freeze a man's assets so he can't work or pay his bills to earn a living, then you push for imprisonment? Flynn had committed the ultimate sin: he was alleged to have relieved Michael Owen of the thing he holds most dear, filthy lucre. Michael wouldn't like that, but try telling that to Susan Flynn and her two children. Mrs. Flynn said at the end her husband was a broken man.

Madani won't be broken, Michael, I'm coming after you till my dying day. I'm not going away. You can threaten me with prison, but incarceration doesn't deter me. Do the right thing. I was in the film *Unbreakable,* I spring back more times than *Zebedee* from the *Magic Roundabout.* I've got more 'bounce-backability' (thank you Ian Hollaway) than *Bouncer* in *Neighbours.* I've made more comebacks than Frank Sinatra, I'm more durable than *The Terminator* and I've had more sequels than *Police Academy.* Talent is just a passing phase, determination is forever. But I know it's all probably falling on deaf ears, and I know you sleep well Michael Owen...

Only people with a conscience lie awake at night.

To get where Glob has got to, a man has to have a son of a bitch streak, a ruthlessness allied with a tough and insensitive demeanour. Behind his babyfaced profile is a hard-headed, ambitious, stop-at-nothing achiever. Nothing wrong with that, but you do have to run over certain people with a steamroller in the quest for riches. It's well known that if you ever get displaced from your lofty perch, you meet all the people you have crossed on the way down the greasy pole, and some of those characters have been waiting just for the day when your crown slips.

Glob's on top of the *Layer Cake*; 'You're born, you take shit. You climb a little higher you take less shit. One day you are in the stratosphere, you can't remember what shit looks like'.

Glob has 41 million in the bank, multimillion pound property portfolios, but only an acorn cup full of compassion and humanity.

Early doors, Glob demonstrated zero tolerance regarding anyone or anything blocking his path to immortality. In 2004 his agents SFX let it slip that he would not be re-signing for Liverpool and that a move abroad was on the cards. Although every word of that statement was true, Glob used it as an excuse to sever ties and promote his dad Terry to commercial manager. Gerard Houllier had informed the Liverpool board that, in his opinion, Michael Owen would stay. That shows just how much he knew as well. History tells us Glob had no intentions of hanging about at Liverpool. They weren't in the Champions League. It was all about him. SFX, who had brilliantly promoted him, were ditched unceremoniously. Anyway, he'd save a right few bob, having his dad represent him... lovely jubbly.

His gambling had already made the back pages of the red tops, and he was coerced into admitting that he had a slight addiction. Glob had a clean cut image at that stage and heavy gambling rumours were not what he wanted adorning the papers. He confessed to wagering two million pounds on the horses, losing forty thousand pounds. Behave yourself man! I've lost more than that in a year. He couldn't, and wouldn't admit what was his Achilles' heel. I can only speculate what he had put in the bookies' satchels, but I'd wager it was at least six figures - seven wouldn't surprise me. It compared with Michael Jackson declaring he'd only had one operation on his nose. I know a lot of working class people who have lost more than forty thousand.

In the long run, It was all down to damage limitation. A statement was released, 'Michael and his family know how important even £100 is to a normal household'. That sounded like a decree from Buckingham Palace, 'I know we are rich, but could you peasants out there please look after the paltry wages you earn. We didn't mean to be ostentatious'. Well, if the Owens knew how important £100 was to a family, what about the thirty three Big Ones they owed my family? The pretentious, lying rotters.

In 2007 Glob opened up Manor House, his new state of the art racing stables, situated in the glorious Cheshire countryside at Malpas. He originally employed highly regarded trainer Nicky Vaughan to nurture and improve his string of equine bloodstock. I remember previously seeing Glob on television just as the stables were beginning to take shape, talking to a camera crew about his new venture. The interviewer hinted that Glob had spent a few million setting it up, and was he worried that he wouldn't get his money back? Glob was on his usual form, replying in that monosyllabic drawl, 'Well, I've had a few sleepless nights'.

Not as many as me you tight git. I threw my carpet slipper at the TV. Luckily the cat got in the way.

If you want more gems like that, go to Twitter and follow *Mogadon* Owen, it really is gripping for news and entertainment.

2009 wasn't a good year for Nicky Vaughan. He'd only sent out five winners, and a lot of the boxes were standing empty, and Michael Owen didn't give many people the benefit of the doubt. Vaughan said, 'It came right out the blue', trying to sound surprised. He was told to empty his wardrobe, grab his P45, and on the way out, don't look back on what could have been. Glob had terminated Vaughan's contract and replaced him with up-and-coming Tom Dascombe (Great trainer). I would advise Tom, if you ever hit a real bad patch watch your back, you never know in life when a pike staff will hit you right between the shoulder blades.

*   *   *   *

The biggest and most costly criminal investigation in British sporting history commenced in 2007, costing ten million pounds. The City Of London police - their fabled (nay, legendary) fraud squad - had arrested three jockeys and charged them with conspiracy. At the centre of the trial was six times champion jockey and Glob's pal, Kieren Fallon, along with fellow riders Fergal Lynch and Darren Williams. The charge: they were all stopping horses, deliberately making them lose, so profits could be made on Betfair.

A case such as this has been very difficult to prove in the past, and of course with The City of London police involved it could all go *Pete Tong* for the CPS. Fallon mentioned in court that a certain Michael Owen texted him everyday for tips. I now realised ironically, that me and Mickey Thomas should have been laying all Fallon's information. Every tip we received via Glob had lost. If only we had been backing them to lose, we could have retired rich men.

Of course, true to form, the trial collapsed. The mistakes and incompetence of the City of London police came roaring to the fore. The judge, Mr. Justice Forbes, directed the jury to return *not guilty* verdicts on the three jockeys. Two months and ten million wasted. If I had somehow been called to give evidence it would have saved a lot of time and money. Fallon rarely sent out any winners. He wasn't stopping horses, his selections were just crap.

My personal fight against Glob goes on, but I hope I've been transparent, fair and not too partisan. It's a battle between the little man and the big corporation, between right and wrong, between good and immoral (I don't think he's evil).

I only want my money back - it's not too much to ask is it? Let me finish on this fact: if some of you are undecided, Michael Owen doesn't ever deny taking my thirty three and a half grand holiday. His defence is that it was a gift from me, because he had signed a batch of autographs.

With that, I rest my case.

*   *   *   *

CHAPTER 15

TRIALS, TRIBULATIONS, TROUBLE

Arabic saying: At the narrow passage, there is no brother or friend

The legendary rocker Frank Zappa once declared that, 'Hydrogen wasn't the most common element in the universe - stupidity was'. I'm reluctant to disagree with the late, great maestro, a freethinking man who christened his eldest daughter 'Moon Unit', but as an alternative, I'd like to suggest *avarice*. The world is full of greedy bleeders and Premier League footballers are right up there in the vanguard.

The obvious way for me to progress at this stage was to accentuate my efforts via the football contacts. Every man and his dog wanted Premier League collectibles, so I was in prime position to earn a lucrative living for myself and Sharon. I still had adequate funds, a Filofax full of football superstar phone numbers, plus the will and drive to become the undisputed ace autograph agent of the North West of England. What a position to be in. I was King Kong, I was Jimmy Cagney ('Top of the world, ma!'), I was the angel standing in the sun, I was invincible.

Do you know what I really was though?

I was a bloody gormless twat. I sleepwalked into a partnership with a new business acquaintance. Why, you say, you didn't even need one? Listen, nobody's perfect. This chapter wouldn't be half so good if I'd gone solo, made a shitload of money and retired back to Dubai. As it stood, I'd be fronting the newspapers and appearing on the television again, and I was doing it all without a publicity agent.

Jordan eat your heart out.

The man who I teamed up with was Graeme Walker, a guy from Connahs Quay in sunny Flintshire, who had business premises - namely a shop called 'Sporting Icons' of Chester. There are two important words in business law - *due diligence*. This is the necessity that one must be robust in finding out everything possible about a future business partner. He didn't come across slimy like George Spitaliosis. After all, I couldn't keep meeting wrong-uns could I? Surely there was one honest man operating in the North West. Even though his name wasn't Louie, I gave him my heartfelt Humphrey Bogart lisp including, 'I think this is the beginning of a beautiful friendship'.

The Madani investigation into Graeme Walker's past hadn't amounted to a hill of beans, but I'm sure my three word reason, 'Can't be arsed', won't go down in business law terminology, but it certainly had a lazy, lethargic ring of suicidal self destruction. The portents weren't good though. Unbeknown to me in 1999 Graeme Walker had been convicted of manufacturing and selling fake Calvin Klein perfume. The Trading Standards had shut down his factory and were still watching him like omnipresent hawks, especially a stubborn ex-copper who had a permanent, raging hard-on for him.

Perversely, it had all started so promisingly. Graeme Walker was a good man, the worst I can say about him, was at times of stress, he would become delusional - a bit like Greg Dyke who says England can win the World Cup in 2022. Just for the record, I'd like to make love with Shakira: let's see which one happens first. Graeme came down to the bungalow in Bramhall three or four times, spending up to two thousand on signed shirts, photos and pictures, it was all temporarily going swimmingly.

It was around this time I experienced my first and second heart attacks, one in 2005 and the next in 2006. It was a good job neither were fatal, as this book would be a hundred pages shorter. This is down mainly to the magnificent National Health Service, a British, God-given institution, run by inspirational doctors and angels in uniform. I cannot thank them all enough. They are the true heroes and heroines of this great nation.

2006 turned into another *annus horribilis*. First the heart attack, then the knock on the door by Trading Standards accompanied by the Old Bill. I didn't know if the delay of two years for my expected day in court was a blessing or a pain. There is the theory that it was a long way off, so hey man, just relax. But the other rule of thumb, as anyone with a future court date will tell you, there isn't a bleeding day that goes by without you thinking about it.

Right, that's the only downbeat paragraph in the book done - I don't want to be known as 'Morbid Madani'.

The trial was set for February 2008, and I had gleaned through my *Walsingham spy network* that Trading Standards had what was as good as a personal vendetta against Graeme Walker. There were at least twenty other traders in the local area with records worse than his, but he was the one in their telescopic sights, and by association, the authorities decided that I might as well go along for the ride. One small blessing was it wasn't far to go, as Chester Crown Court was selected as the arena of choice. I'd have rather gone racing at the Roodee, but like the condemned man on the gallows, I wouldn't be hanging around for bets.

Months earlier, a golden shaft of light had burst through the turbulent storm clouds. My solicitor Steve Fox had negotiated a plea bargain at the magistrates' tea party. A *guilty* entry from the both of us would result in suspended sentences... oh happy days!

Graeme Walker was approached with the proposition, but he killed it stone dead, after bumping his gums with the declaration, 'I am an innocent man'. Just remember again that word: *delusional*.

The case at Chester had caught the media imagination, and it was going to be a doozy for the great and the good. On the first day all the TV channels were there, every red top and broadsheet were reporting with paparazzi cameras flashing, like a Hollywood premiere. I felt just like Russell Crowe, but without cursing and throwing punches at the cameramen. Was my left side more photogenic? The public would only want the best for this spectacular, fun-filled extravaganza.

The entrance to the court brought me right back to my senses. It was known as 'The Castle', a type of building which filled me with dread. Many bad things had happened behind the ramparts of similar fortifications throughout the ages in British history. Events such as King Edward II having a red hot poker thrust up his jacksy in Berkeley Castle. Now, that would make your eyes water. Holy moley, this was serious business. A prison sentence was a distinct possibility. The Chester judiciary, not often associated with clemency and sympathetic understanding, had the reputation of a hanging court. OK, that's a slight exaggeration, but you follow my drift. Thanks to the bloody sainted Graeme Walker entering a not guilty plea, I was committed to do the same. If I pleaded guilty, I was advised that I could cop for the lot. I wasn't a greedy man, if the *merde* was going to hit the legal cyclone, I was prepared to share it out evenly. My charitable traits could even come up trumps, but I had a sinking feeling that things would turn sour and bite us both on the *derrière*. I still couldn't utter the word arse, I was still reminiscing about Teddy Two... gives a whole new meaning to the term 'piledriver'.

The events that unfolded next at Chester Crown Court are probably unprecedented in the historic annals of British law. It made Rumpole of the Bailey resemble the Nuremberg Trials after WWII. I once knew someone who had a trial at Nuremberg, but he ended up in FC Kaiserslautern's second team.

Life's strange like that.

The trial got off to a bad start. Most of the first day was lost when a woman juror declared after dinner that she knew Graeme Walker. The judge David Hale was exasperated. Believe me, it wouldn't be the last time His Honour would be put under pressure and lose his rag. Anyway, Walker had lost a golden opportunity in my opinion. The Mafia would pay big bucks to have a situation like that. And the fun and games kept on coming. Before the replacement juror was sworn in, we were approached by the prosecution, 'Do you have any objections about the new juror? She is an ex-policewoman'.

My barrister Peter Davies (now a judge by the way, all my legal briefs seem to go to the top), suggested to me that if we objected, it might appear to the other jurors that we had something to hide. I couldn't speak for him of course, but Hadrian's Wall wouldn't hide my indiscretions. At this stage I was past the point of caring. Your mother always told you to trust a policeman. And it's not like they ever lie and perjure in court is it? The ex-bill was sworn in. I'd made my bed, so I'd have to lie on it. The trouble was, I had no comfort blankets.

February could be such a cruel month, I felt a cold snap run right down my Trossachs. The policewoman, unbelievably, started giving me the evil eye, and it snapped me right out of my malaise. I had to rediscover my Great Balls of Fire. I'd give it the notable Madani countercharge - it was time to fight the good fight. What's that judge, finished for the day? Fuck a duck - just as I was coming good again!

These contrasting feelings of euphoria, and then desperate depression, were going to fester on throughout the whole trial. It was a tough one to call, as my emotions were going up and down faster than a thermometer in Cleethorpes. Coming out of court, the cameras were popping like Chinese firecrackers. Why are you cretins taking photos of me? I looked exactly like this when I arrived in the morning - apart from my six o'clock shadow of course. The uproarious cabaret show went on for everyday of the trial, hitting warp factor six when the footballers eventually turned up to testify. Fame is such a fickle beast - today's news, tomorrow's chip papers. Bollocks to you too, Harry Ramsden. Fame could do one for me, I never did like that Irene Cara anyway. Vivien Leigh was my gal, 'Tomorrow is another day'. I would return. They don't write them like that anymore.

Coming back to court for the second day felt like 'Groundhog Day'. And the third. And the fourth, etc. Well, we were in February after all. There were multitudes of pressmen and photographers, and more and more of the general public each day. It was gripping the nation. I decided to call myself 'Punxsutawney Faz'. It had a certain ring.

The prosecution weren't playing the game though, and they started referring to me in court as 'Mr. Dubai'. What the fuck was all that about?

Ah, wait... I saw their little ruse. They wanted the jury to think here was a man of position and power: someone who could grease palms, coerce and influence people, a demigod, a mover and shaker, the new Messiah. And all I was doing meanwhile, was calling myself after a giant American rodent with massive front teeth. I suspect the truth was somewhere in the middle, but the jury would have to come to their own conclusions. This was heavy psychological shit, and I prayed we could all come out of it unscathed.

This trial would set the tax payer back one and a half million big ones. They say the criminally insane are all in Rampton and Broadmoor. I wasn't sure our fraudulent acquisition of four and a half grand warranted it, but I've never studied law have I. These people knew best: ours was just to serve and obey... after we'd doffed our caps, of course.

Making themselves a right little earner were four handwriting experts: one for moi, one for Graeme and two for the Crown Prosecution and Trading Standards. No stone would be left unturned. The ironic conclusion was that not one of them agreed with any of the others; they only agreed to disagree. That's one week of my life I'll never get back I can tell you. What a complete waste of time, money and effort.

Sharon was at court everyday. On getting home after the pantomime she asked me, 'What the hell was that all about?'.

I shrugged my shoulders and replied, 'Don't ask'. Even the barristers and judge couldn't make head nor tail of what was going on.

The momentum of the trial was vacillating one way and then the other. Nobody knew where it would end up. Ladbrokes were going 4/5 guilty, 4/5 innocent, 200/1 compensation to Madani. Even they got it wrong, the runaway train was out of control and about to career off the tracks. If this debacle was ever published in weekly episodes, you'd have paid good money to find what happened next.

But then, right out of left field, came a swerve ball from Trotsky Meadows, my old nemesis... City of London police turned up and reaped a bloody carnage.

They burst into the court conference room, interrupting a private discussion I was having with my barrister. Deadly duo, detectives David Evans and Steve Derry announced I was under arrest for false representation, and they started reading me my rights, including the one to remain silent. There was every chance of that, I was dumbstruck. Peter Davies tried to intervene and was brushed aside. I was being taken back to London and that was that. They escorted me out to an unmarked police car. No cuffs were involved due to my ongoing health issues.

Within half an hour, our merry band was cruising down the M6 towards The Smoke. I'd have loved to been a fly on the wall of the judge's chambers when he was informed that Madani was on tour, as apparently he went apoplectic. To be fair, it was a tad irregular. Back in Chester the dust had just about settled, as prosecuting QC Andrew Thomas informed the bewildered jury, 'Faisal Madani has been arrested in relation to alleged use of fraudulently obtained credit cards, including one from Wonderbra model, Eva Herzigova. No charges have been brought as the investigation is still ongoing'.

With that, the trial collapsed. What a great day for British justice. The rest of the world holds our law system in envious regard - no wonder O.J. and Michael Jackson walked. The news lines went bonkers. Local media, national papers and all the television channels reported that one of the *Mr. Fakers* had been arrested. In a fair world it would have been construed as a mistrial and I would have walked. No such luck here, and the sequel trial was arranged for March. The damage was done, and I wouldn't get an unbiased verdict. Still, at least all the legal teams were on double money - little Prudence and Bunty could now go to Roedean... what jolly hockey sticks.

I was grilled mercilessly by City of London police for six hours solid. I broke my Commonwealth and European record for replying *no comment*. I was on superb form. It was like a breath of fresh air being far away from the stuffy Chester courtroom. The world record held by Dan Dann the Daggerman from Dagenham was still safe, I wasn't in his class thank God, but then I didn't work in a dimly lit abattoir, as a short-sighted slaughterman.

The police were trying to nail me for using moody credit cards to send various footballers on holiday to Dubai. England captain John Terry was one of the recipients, and he needed this adverse publicity like Battersea Dogs home needed rabies.

I'd been commandeered in Chester at just after nine-thirty in the morning, but I was back home at the bungalow in Bramhall for the ten o'clock news that night. The police are always complaining about lack of funds, but if they moonlighted as a taxi service they would make a fortune - they are shit-hot. Alighting from the back of police car, I waded into a posse of newsmen. Didn't these guys ever sleep?

'Can we have a quick word Mr. Madani?'.

It had been a long day and I wasn't in the mood, 'Hypersonic... now the lot of you, fuck off!'.

I slammed the front door shut on Murdoch's minions. A cup of tea and Eccles cake would put the world to rights.

The next morning I staggered out of bed about half past eleven. I was knackered, yesterday had taken its toll. Sharon burst into the lounge clutching half a dozen red tops and a couple of broadsheets, 'You've made headlines again!', she exclaimed.

'We've got to get rid of those corduroy pillow cases.', I countered. The body was weak, but the mind was razor sharp. All the gay banter in the world couldn't get the trial cancelled though. Methinks they wanted a showdown. The dreaded day in March came all too quickly. The three ring circus was in town again. It was cruel really. I'd decided between the two trials not to take the witness stand, firstly not to make a fuck-up, and secondly to protect some of the footballers that were my friends. I couldn't just go after the few greedy rotten bastards. Graeme Walker's barrister, Paul Lawton, came after me when he heard I wouldn't be testifying. That was all I needed. It went without saying that Trading Standards prosecuting brief Andrew Thomas was also attempting to do a Madani hatchet job.

Lawton told the jury that I was an outrageous fraud. No shit, Sherlock. He said that since 1996 I'd been passing myself off as the brother of the ex-Manchester United director Armer Al Midani. Not entirely true, but if someone ever suggested the connection, I didn't go out of my way to deny it. And if you look at the surname spellings, they are different. Lawton actually started to do me a favour, as he was coming across as a blusterer. When cross-examining witnesses, he was letting them all off the hook. I had him sussed from the start; an upper class, useless tosser.

Andrew Thomas was a different matter, it was hard work fending him off, and it was quite a relief when he went for the throat of Graeme Walker, as there was a lot more incriminating evidence against him. I sat back and relaxed while Thomas ripped to shreds Walker's claim that he was an innocent man. Cheshire Trading Standards had taken the decision to raid Sporting Icons - Walker's house of ill repute. The ex-copper with the hard-on led the charge inside, he had multiple ejaculations after falling on copious amounts of dodgy gear.

The raid revealed large quantities of unsigned stock sat on a desk which was kitted out for signing goods, with a selection of pens and specimen signatures from which copies could be made. Thomas looked full square into the jurors faces and said, 'This is clear evidence that Mr. Walker was forging signatures on his own premises. We also know he had boasted to people about his ability to forge signatures'. Well, bugger me! Game, set and Indian rubber. I looked over to Lawton. He was looking decidedly hangdog. He had told the jury that I had supplied all the bent signatures, and his defendant was a paragon of virtue. So that was all his credibility shot to pieces. Even Judge Hales was looking him up and down like a piece of rancid, maggot-ridden offal.

Thomas had no intention off letting Walker off the hook, so he upped the ante. He said that apparently the shop had sold 40 Liverpool shirts from the 1977 European Cup Final, signed by Ian Rush and others, and adding that this was like the miracle of the loaves and fishes.

This caused a titter in court, but the only two not smiling were Lawton and Walker. Even the judge had a pleasing countenance. In cockney parlance, Graeme Walker's quest for salvation was *brown bread*. The punishment kept on coming; 58 full England caps, all fakes. It transpired that his shop in 2005 had a turnover of nearly 200 grand, with autographs from Laurel and Hardy, Mae West,

Rock Hudson, Sylvester Stallone, The Beatles, Buddy Holly, Nat King Cole and Queen. This was a piss-take. He was taking home four grand a week, a lot more than fell onto my lap. Where did he get the balls to suggest I had supplied him with all the fakes? Andrew Thomas finished his demolition job by declaring, 'Graeme Walker knew full well he was trading fraudulently. The evidence is there before you'. I actually felt sorry for him at that moment. He'd tried to pass the buck to me, but that was never going to happen, and I don't think there was one person in that courtroom who considered him innocent. The irony of the present situation was that at the earlier magistrates hearing we both could have accepted a bender. That ship had long sailed, and it was now time for self-preservation. I could tolerate bruised shins... rather that than a drop-kick to the bollocks.

That afternoon, post trial, the good wife was accosted by Mrs.Walker outside the court, 'I hope you are happy Sharon, you took all that money off us!'. Sharon had the class to ignore her and not retaliate, but a few of the national papers picked up on the spat. Talk about delusional, Mrs. Walker was obviously taking lessons from the master forger.

It was now time for the footballers to take the stand. Mercury was rising, and the media loved it. Michael Owen put in an appearance. He wasn't going to do me any favours. Dressed in a whistle and flute, he started off by praising me, and I actually started warming to him. But that didn't last long. He said he met me through Liverpool legend Phil Thompson: not true. I've never met Tommo. But why would he say that? It was Rushy who got me the meet. Maybe he was protecting him.

He declared every specimen signature put before him was a fake. Well, they would be - most of them were allegedly signed by his dad and brother. Don't forget, Michael's a family man. He wouldn't be dropping them in it.

Steve Gerrard - one could tell he didn't want to be there, turning up like an angelic schoolboy in his demure jumper and tie. The Liverpool dynamo declared he didn't know me and studied a couple of signed photos on which, he said, were bogus signatures. He was gone in fifteen minutes, the relief was palpable.

Next up was one of the greats, and my former pal, Ian Rush. My barrister (and Liverpool fanatic) Peter Davies went in softly, softly, 'You broke my heart when you went to Italy'.

Rushy came back with, 'No, I didn't go there, I went to Juventus'.

Ripples of laughter permeated the courtroom. Davies tried to suppress a chuckle. I knew Rushy wasn't the sharpest tool in the box, but what he said next astonished me. Peter Davies was armed with the names of all my personal connections that Rushy and I had met socially, and on business, hundreds of times. He asked about the friendship. Rushy said that he had met me on a couple of occasions. Davies couldn't, and wouldn't, let that go.

'But you've been to his house, met him in hotels, worked for him on shopping TV World. You've even been to Dubai twice on holiday, courtesy of Mr Madani'.

Rushy was adamant. 'That's right.. a couple of times'. I laughed myself, as did the jury, Rushy was on damage limitation. He wanted out of there.

All the footballers who turned up crapped on me from a great height. The majority of the specimen signatures though were from my own club, Manchester United. What I'm going to say next was never disclosed in court. I decided not to give evidence. I would take the medicine - to protect the players and, equally important to me, not be a snitch in court. Maybe if I had the time again, I might have played it differently, but I doubt it.

Sir Alex Ferguson advised any of his players who had made statements not to go to court. He didn't want the season disrupted, and there were requests for both Wayne Rooney and Gary Neville.

Rio Ferdinand had made a statement, but it was favourable to me, and so that one wouldn't be read out in court, along with statements by John Terry, Ashley Cole and Jamie Carragher. I'd helped Jamie's family enjoy a great holiday in Dubai. These were real people, and his dad and uncle were right behind me - great Liverpudlians. What a man Carragher is. Someone who has never forgotten his roots. Conduct a poll with Liverpool fans: who do you think was better for Liverpool - Carragher or Michael Owen? It would be a landslide, one was a giver and the other wasn't. It's food for thought for the departed Raheem Stirling.

Ex-Liverpool, double-winning manager and superstar footballer, Kenny Dalglish, also told Trading Standards to go forth and multiply. I cannot thank him enough for his support and loyalty, a great man with a wonderful sense of humour.

The only person who turned up for the Red Devils was Andrea Murphy, daughter-in-law of former Manchester United assistant manager, Jimmy Murphy. She told the court that Graeme Walker was using the United club crest without their permission. Not that heavy, but another demerit mark against someone who was starting to resemble a broken man.

It's been well documented that Gary Neville has been at the forefront of a crusade in the fight against bogus signatures, but before anyone asks for future beatification for Saint Gary, I'd like to input my two penn'orth here. Let me first say, Gary Neville was a tremendous right back for England and Manchester United, a loyal one-club man who, since his retirement from Premier League football, had switched to punditry on Sky Sports with an ease that was nothing short of miraculous. As good as Gary Lineker is, it has taken him years to get to that standard. Neville made the transition in months and is probably the best in the business. Love him or loathe him, he is always worth listening to... are you reading this Michael Owen?

I've had the pleasure of meeting Gary - who went on to coach Valencia - on at least six different occasions, and I even shook hands with him. I'd be astounded if he said he didn't know me, or was oblivious of what I did for a living.

Let's get down to the nitty-gritty.

Premier League franchises: *greedy.*
Premier League clubs: *greedy.*
Premier League players: *greedy.*
Premier League agents: *greedy.*
Premier League fans?

Financially strapped...

Anyone disagree?! No? Right, let's carry on.

In 2004 - this was before the 'philanthropic' Glazer family took over - Manchester United banned their players from signing shirts and footballs. Another kick in the teeth for the genuine fan. Post-Glazer they cancelled the half a million pounds pool for players who appeared on Manchester United TV giving interviews. Were the players happy? Nah... Remember what they are of course: greedy.

Gary Neville was a player, so he wouldn't have been over the moon. They all love their big paydays. I heard that Gary would go up to the Arctic Circle if he knew an Eskimo had a fiver, just to get it off him. With the MUTV money a distant memory, the players set up another independent hush-hush pool. I, myself, put in thousands of pounds in brown envelopes, and that's without my holiday flights for players and stays at the best hotels in Dubai. Gary Neville would definitely have known about this arrangement. I could have brought all this up in court, but what was the point? It would look like I was blindsiding. The money I put into the players' pockets was a considerable amount, and I wasn't the only trader paying top dollar.

The one and only thing I expect if I am paying for signatures at Old Trafford or the training ground at Carrington is genuine stock. Rumours were coming out that the groundsman or clerical staff were doing the signatures. I've got no proof where my brown envelope money went, but it would be naïve to think the players were in the dark, or went without. When Gary Neville started making himself busy, aghast after discovering a bogus signature of himself, it was definitely the tip of the iceberg. In all the years I was selling autographs, I had only sold one of his, and his brother Phil never troubled the scorers either. I should have got a knighthood for that. Absolutely nobody ever showed any interest in the Nevilles. In fact, Gary should have been flattered that someone had actually gone to the trouble of forging his signature.

The Neville brothers had a reputation for tight pockets. A little-known snippet about them was that when they were school kids, they invented the commodity known as *copper wire*. They simultaneously found a two pence coin in the playground and neither would let go, pulling in opposite directions. The rest is history, as they say. They remind me of the Jewish Chuckle Brothers, *'To me... to me again'.*

Some players took part in my signing sessions for cash or holidays. So I knew all those signatures were authentic. Others from Manchester United, I had to take on trust, relying on the discretion and the honesty of all those involved. That's sad really. When it came to the crunch at Chester Crown Court, where was Trading Standards' golden boy Gary - a man so vociferous and passionate about people making money out of his name. That's a joke in itself. It was a date with destiny he should never had avoided. Was he worried my barrister would have had a plethora of awkward questions for him, or was he too busy signing autographs? Either way his absence speaks volumes. I would be prepared to take a controlled lie detector test. I wonder if Gary Neville would be as confident... *'to me, to you'.*

Back to the trial. All of the footballers had presented their evidence, and a few more witnesses for Trading Standards were ready to rock. Johnny Wilkinson's agent was giving evidence about his client's supposed signature. He told the jury it was definitely not one of Johnny's. Hey, what did I care - it was another one of Graham's. I looked across at him. His posture was stooped. He'd aged ten years. I know he had tried to saddle me with the blame, but I felt so sorry for him.

Up next was George Best's agent. I had been really good friends with George, right up to his death, and the signature in question was genuine. I can even remember the pub in which it was signed. His agent said he thought it was a fake, it took a lot of restraint not to shout out. But what can you do. I was being penalised for a proper signature... a right *karma chameleon.*

So, all the prosecution witnesses had come and gone, Graeme and I had been put through the grinder, but at least I'd come out the other end with some fragile dignity still intact. I prayed Graeme would do the same as me and refrain from taking the stand. No such luck. It was like watching Chinese water torture. *Drip... you are a liar. Splash... you are a forger. Deluge... you are a cheat. Cloudburst... you are delusional. Monsoon... you are going to jail.*

It was now time for the legendary Madani comeback. I had a Triple Alliance of all talents. It was the last refuge of all undoubted scoundrels: the appearance of the character witnesses. These people can definitely influence the jury, and apart from the judge and the barristers, they are the final orators. First up: England and Ipswich superstar Kevin Beattie. I had made a cardinal error here. One the size of Richelieu's ego. I really should have sent a car down to Suffolk to pick him up, instead I purchased him train tickets. He got absolutely rat-arsed on Network Rail and turned up in court paralytic drunk. Slumped on the stand, he slurred out his name, that was as good as it got. After two minutes of blather, claptrap and yammer, they slung him out of the building.

A total, unmitigated omnishambles.

Good friend Gary Ashburn was up next. He was extremely nervous. Before proceedings restarted, I quietly reassured him outside, that it was only my head on the block, and that he would be going home afterwards. *Just think straight and relax.* He broke down in the box under lukewarm pressure from the prosecution, suffered a panic attack and became the second witness helped off the stand. *What you gonna do?* These circumstances were way beyond my control... but at least I had one last shy.

On the third and final leg, up confidently strode a man who had a longer criminal record than I did. Prior to his appearance, I had conscientiously vetted his overall condition, and he was neither nervous or pissed. Top banana - we could pull this off yet, especially with a fair wind in our sails. The jury might just forget about the last two nimrods. Ray Balding was a fellow businessman who hosted from executive boxes at Old Trafford.

It didn't take long for the exchanges to disintegrate into chaos. He had a stand-up screaming match with the prosecution, but not before helpfully inform-ing the jury, 'Faisal might be a crook, but he is definitely not a conman'.

Why would he say that? Those three muttonheads would probably add at least three months to my sentence. Yes, I could certainly find them; a piss artist, a quivering wreck, and a bolshy pragmatist. To my astonishment, Judge Hales personally thanked Ray Balding for his contribution, 'It's quite refreshing for a witness to come forward with such candour'.

Ray gave me the big thumbs up on his way out. I didn't know whether to laugh or cry. I was fluctuating in a land of confusion, but thankfully, barrister Peter Davies still had tomorrow with his closing arguments. He was sure to earn his corn. I scampered home that evening, accompanied with a brittle confidence. I craved for leniency, but I wasn't over optimistic of ever getting it.

The trial was reaching its high water mark. Walker's legal beagle, legend in his own lunchtime Paul Lawton, was up and I'd like to relate that the courtroom was crackling with electricity, but I'd be perjuring if I did. The jury was rapt; one woman was filing her nails, another was studying the ceiling, the foreman was checking his watch every five minutes, while a guy on the front row had the facial tics and expressions which were akin to the experience of stepping on a giant dog turd. Lawton had a pop at me again. *Give over mate, you're like a broken record.* He was swimming upstream against a tsunami - even he realised it. Thankfully he kept it reasonably short, even the judge looked relieved.

My ace advocate was up next, Peter Davies, and he was on top form. 'Much has been said about Mr. Madani's decision not to give evidence to the court. He has his own personal reasons for this'. Then, turning to the jury, he continued, 'Ignore the nudge-nudge, wink-wink innuendo deployed by the prosecution and Mr Lawton, the bogus signatures have not been supplied by Mr. Madani. He is not a Walter Mitty character. Throughout any week he is constantly on the phone to Premier League footballers, they are all friends of his'.
Don't stop the man now, he's smoking.
'Why would Mr Madani deal in bogus stock when he has a vast network of contacts who supply him with ample signatures?'
The jury were then reminded that two hostile witnesses, Ian Rush and Michael Owen, had both gone on expensive holidays paid for by me. That put the cat amongst the pigeons. Peter Davies stepped down. He got a ten from Len, and Janice Nicholls from *Thank Your Lucky Stars* announced, 'I'll give it five'. Lovestruck Madani had him down as number one and wanted all his babies.
It was only fair that the prosecution had a go too. Andrew Thomas was very competent: on Madani, 'Here is your classic middleman. He knew he was dealing in fake goods, or, at the very least was turning a blind eye to what was going on'.
Adding, 'Business was being conducted with payments of cash in brown envelopes, using back door methods.'
Not all entirely factual, but Trading Standards had taken my pants down, and all I could do was wait. I doubt if I was a candidate for penal solitude on Devil's Island.
He didn't really need to wallop Walker, as he had him by the curlies on day one. A lot of evidence had Walker bang to rights. He dismissed the absurd allegation by barrister Lawton that I was supplying all the bogus signatures and that Graeme was an innocent victim. Thomas finished succinctly, but with a deadly clarity, 'Graeme Walker, an electrician by trade, and a counterfeiter by choice'.

Ouch! Cancel what you had planned for the weekend, my old son.

It was time for judge David Hale to start his summing up. We hadn't heard a lot from the learned man, but he came across as a competent and balanced chap... not a bad old stick. He droned on all morning, and for an hour after dinner. He was sending me to sleep - *Go back to your constituencies and prepare for government.* I was having a nightmare, only semi-conscious at the Liberal Party Conference. I came round to shuffling noises reverberating round the courtroom. The jury were retiring. They looked a sharp crew, and it was odds-on - a verdict would be just around the corner.

Ten long days later I was still twiddling my thumbs. How wrong can you be? On practically every day that had passed, I'd fantasised about getting a full acquittal. I knew full well I was getting a custodial sentence, but there's nothing wrong with having a positive mental attitude. Damage limitation was the name of the game.

We got the call. The jury had their verdicts, and I wasn't looking forward to it. An air of inevitability pervaded the court. As expected the foreman gave out a deadly double. Guilty for me on 18 of the 20 charges of breaching the Trades Description Act. Bummer. Graeme Walker guilty on 51 of the 53 charges against him. Judge David Hale would consider the moot points and reports, and announce the sentencing tomorrow. I requested to go straight into custody that night. It was pointless going home, and I needed to get into the new regime as quick as possible.

Graeme Walker's brief requested that he return home for the night, on medical grounds. Apparently he had contracted a heart condition and he wasn't in the best of health. I knew he had gone downhill during the trial, but this revelation was very upsetting. After all, I was the one before the trial with a medical record the length of a hypochondriac's copy of 'War and Peace'.

The meat wagon couldn't have travelled far in half an hour, and I arrived at Altcourse Prison, Liverpool. I was a bit apprehensive. One would have preferred Strangeways, but it was off Trivago's usual itinerary. I couldn't believe the startling reception at Altcourse, all the cons had been watching the trial highlights day by day on television, and when I walked in I got a standing ovation. I had shaved my moustache off that morning, and everyone was chanting, 'There's only one Avram Grant'.

I suppose there was a slight resemblance, and I took it as a backhanded compliment. They all wanted fake signatures on Liverpool and Everton shirts and shorts. It was fantastic, and it was the first and last time in my life that I felt like a real celebrity.

I slept remarkably well that night. Tomorrow was *Judgement Day*. The offences weren't the worst in the world, but the trial had cost seven figures and the judge would be under pressure to make an example of us. Trading Standards had put a monumental amount of effort into it, so they would be awfully pissed off if we only got a slap on the wrist. For that reason alone, I was speculating a stretch between one and three years. Any more than that, and I would suspect a conspiracy.

In three shakes of a lamb's tail, we were both standing back in the dock. David Hale wasn't wearing a black cap (the man was all heart). Graeme Walker was sentenced first; three years. There was a gasp from his relatives in the gallery. Jesus, that was a stiff one. It wouldn't have done his ticker any good. *Give it me judge, do your worst...* 'Faisal Madani *(pause like the X Factor)* - nine months'.

Jackpot! What a result! It was all I could do to look moodily reflective. But inside of me there was a party going on. I walked solemnly past the gallery, 'Lying sneak' wafted down. I hadn't heard that standard of slight since I was 13. The Walker clan certainly knew how to cut a man to the quick. If it had been followed up with *dirty rotter,* it might just have finished me off.

There was no time for ceremony, as it was back for two more days and nights in Altcourse Prison. Graeme Walker was coming along for the ride too. We were both pawns in this great game of charades. I suspected our relationship would be fraught with anxiety, mistrust, or even anger. But I couldn't have been more wrong as Graeme Walker was a total gentleman. We talked, put the past behind us, and wished each other all the best. It meant a lot to me to depart on amiable terms after all the friction. Graeme Walker was really a top man.

I was on the move again - Buckley Hall, a category C prison in Rochdale, was my destination. I think Graeme was heading for Kirkham Prison. Our paths probably wouldn't cross again, so never say goodbye my old friend, just wave farewell.

What I'm going to say next isn't in anyway meant to sound flippant, cocky or condescending. The Buckley Hall Prison experience rivalled a Butlin's Holiday Camp. Don't forget, I'd been behind bars at Stafford and Pentonville, which represented Purgatory and Hell respectively. It's a tough one to call, but prison for white collar crime is a walk in the park. The old Victorian prisons are a cesspit of murderers, rapists and perpetrators of violence, but the new modern forward thinking institutions are full of IT, credit card and stock market fraudsters... different strokes for different folks.

Here's my time at Buckley Hall then. Even with the prison's largesse, it still didn't all go to plan. You know me, I could fuck it up in a Carlsberg advert.

This was probably the best correctional facility in the world. If Buckley hall was a health spa I'd probably subscribe. It boasted an on-site pool table, table tennis, a football pitch and top quality gym apparatus. There was also a more-than-adequate library, plenty of educational courses and workshops, good hairdresser and excellent health centre. Definitely a brave new world, and a million miles away from slopping out, inedible food and primitive 'comforts'.

On the first night I arrived, tucking into sausage, egg, bacon and fried bread was very nice indeed, but not the best fare for my dicky heart and shot pancreas. I didn't want to leave Buckley Hall in a mahogany overcoat, so I had to seriously consider my personal dining arrangements. In all, I converted to three different religions during my short spell at the prison, entirely in the name of finding a healthier alternative.

Initially I turned to Mecca. A couple of months digesting halal food and drink were fine, but I fancied a change and travelled pole to pole for a kosher kebab. Again the Jewish food was appetising and filling, but they seemed to serve up chicken soup everyday, so after two weeks, the golden city of Amritsar was calling. I went Sikh, but drew the line about wearing a turban. That lasted all of a day. The food was foul. Guru Nanak must have had iron guts. I went full circle and returned to Mecca for the remainder of the sentence. The prison chefs must have thought I was a secret Iranian Egon Ronay.

The prison population was three-quarters Muslim, mostly Pakistani, with English being a minority language. But there was absolutely no aggro, everyone got on, it was a lovely experience. The prison mosque was a point in fact, Sunnis and Shia all mixing together. The imam should have got the Nobel Peace Prize, as the two factions had been knocking lumps off each other for 14 centuries - mostly over fundamental differences about a new Islamic prophet. It didn't apply at all to Buckley Hall.

Mobile phones seemed to proliferate daily in the prison, and everyone seemed to have one. When I first arrived, I couldn't help noticing inside the perimeter fence, a dead pigeon or two... 'Is there a killer goshawk in the area?', I asked Eric the Embezzler.

'No, mate, not at all. See that huge fat one lying on it's back? That's big Lionel's new Blackberry... special delivery', he chuckled.

Of course the screws were in on it. People on the outside were lobbing the latest technology over the fence, giving a whole new meaning to the term carrier pigeon. Some of the more brazen prison officers would just bypass the pigeon route and simply smuggle mobiles in for their captive customers.

If anyone is shocked by this, sit down now. Most people need or want more money. What have politicians, lawyers, policemen and most professions with influence got in common? Correct - they like a backhander. Not all, but more than you think. The practice has been going on for hundreds of years. It's

146

never going to stop. In other countries it's endemic. In truth, at Buckley Hall, I was expecting to come down to the canteen one morning and find a Carphone Warehouse kiosk in there... stranger things have happened.

I was coming up to the last few weeks of my sentence, when I had the one and only bust up in my pleasant sojourn at Rochdale. I wasn't feeling top notch the previous evening and when I awoke the next morning, my head was banging like a jack hammer. After refusing to go out on a work course, the administration felt I was swinging the lead and wouldn't accept my predicament, or even accept my malaise. They then made a cardinal error. As punishment, they decided to take my in-cell television away. Big mistake! The 2008 Euro Football tournament was just commencing.

So they were playing dirty, were they? Right... I'd come back at them with the prisoner's ultimate deterrent: a hunger strike. I was going to need a man on the inside to help me, so I befriended a guy whose company had appeared in two different seasons of Rogue Traders, as well as a special hour-long edition. That was just the sort of consistency I was looking for: a man who was keeping Matt Allwright in work. Nigel Hudson and his young wife had been extradited from America. Trading Standards and the plod had been hot on his trail and pursued him half way round the world. We bonded immediately. He was a keen football man, a Wolverhampton Wanderers fanatic, having been brought up 21 miles away from Molineux, in Stafford. That bleeding town will go on my gravestone.

Talking about Matt Allwright, what about his big swarthy leather-clad Iberian motor cycle mate, Dan Penteado. One tends to lose the moral high ground exposing alleged dodgy dealers when your cohort is committing benefit fraud. What's laughable is that Dirty Dan claimed housing benefit for four years total-ling 25 large, while all the time appearing on prime time television. No wonder Ian Duncan Smith wanted change. Anyway, Daniel did a little time. Just don't expect a glorious comeback with his old mucker Matt on Watchdog any time soon.

All the governor at Buckley Hall wanted was a quiet life. It was the cushiest number in the prison service regime. His most stressful part of the day was completing The Times crossword. A Madani hunger strike was his biggest crisis since somebody had purloined some Pontefract Cakes from the canteen. Though this was on another level, especially with my medical files filling an entire front room. He visited my cell, imploring me to reconsider my position. I told him *not bloody likely*, as taking away my football was a declaration of war. It was now a matter of honour and principle, even a noble death, if that's what was called for. He fell for it hook, line and sinker, insisting on having round the clock health workers in my cell. I say *round the clock*, but they all knocked off at six o' clock. Still, it's the thought that counts. He was covering his own back, and the last thing he wanted on his watch was a roster minus one.

On the first day of the hunger strike, I slept mostly, and the health workers took it in turns to sit with me, making sure I was taking regular sips of water. I think the governor had come up with a cunning ploy, because all they talked about was food. I was made of sterner stuff than that though. What sort of jessie would quit after a few hours? I was playing the long game. The oppressive and brutal prison system couldn't have their cake and eat it. But fuck me, what I wouldn't have given for a hot buttered crumpet at that moment.

Day two, the governor sent in the heavy artillery in the form of the prison chaplain. Nice bloke, but after two hours he was starting to bore me shitless. My water diet was keeping me hydrated, but the sky pilot was doing my nut in.

'See you tomorrow Faisal', he gushed. It was late afternoon and I grimaced back, 'You don't have to, surely you must be busy?'.

He wouldn't have any of it, and he'd be in first thing. How much more of that could I take? It was time to make my ground-breaking move. The Euro quarter finals were commencing in two days.

Three days in, and I started to feign sickness, falling in and out of consciousness, blathering clap trap in a strange voice, *'Lord Palmerstone has demanded a veal and ham pie for his cat'*.

The chaplain was convinced I was sinking fast, everything was reported back to the governor. He was popping his head round the door every few hours. I carried on regardless... *'Aunt Evie, is that you? I'm coming...'* .

The chaplain took that as spiritual, and he began to hyperventilate. I came in with the money shot. It was a glorious sunny day, *'Is it a solar eclipse? ...it's all going dark'*.

The chaplain summoned the governor. He burst in 'Faisal, Faisal... what's it going to take to end this?'

'Football match...'. I mumbled back.

The TV was back in my cell in less than half an hour. I was now sitting bolt upright in bed being spoon fed tomato soup, and the health workers wanted to check my weight. I'd been weighed three days earlier when I started the hunger strike.

But in the meantime, I'd put on two pounds.

The health workers looked at me in astonishment. They decided the mechanism must be faulty, so they tried another appliance. Same result. I was the first prisoner in British penal history to come off a hunger strike weighing more than when I started. I shrugged my shoulders, insisting my metabolism was a rule to itself. They knew I was at it somehow, but couldn't put their finger on it. Conspiracies abounded, but only the truth counted: calories in, calories out.

The explanation was simple. After six o'clock, skeleton staff, plenty of mobiles, quick call to *eat.com*, delivery to Buckley Hall, over the fence, with Nigel making sure the meal arrived in my cell. On the first night I tucked into lamb bhuna and on the second, good old favourite, chicken tikka, both accompanied with large naan breads and lashings of Coca-Cola.

I'm amazed on that third day when I was hallucinating, that nobody noticed the cell absolutely stunk of chicken tikka. They must have thought I had crapped myself and were too polite to comment. The prison chaplain was convinced there was more to it, 'God works in mysterious ways, Faisal'.

I reminded him: *so did my bowels*. He declared that he hadn't seen or heard anything like it since the time of Padre Pio. A thorough examination of my hands revealed no stigmata, but there were still remnants of chicken tikka. In his mind miraculous phenomena had occurred, people would bypass Lourdes and make the pilgrimage to Rochdale. I couldn't see it myself, but he was over the moon, and I didn't have the heart to tell him it was all down to the Star of Bengal.

While I was at Buckley Hall, England and Manchester City legend Mike Summerbee visited me. I'd been friends with Mike for years, but it was wonderful to see him. Most people in prison are forlorn and forgotten, so it wasn't just a great treat for me, because the whole prison morale went up.

Buckley Hall always had a high air of contentment, but morale went into the troposphere after Mike arrived. Screws and cons were queuing for autographs, everyone wanted to speak to him. My standing in the prison went up as well, happy days. On a personal note Mike told me, he was ashamed by all the footballers who had taken from me, but were not ready to stand up and be counted. That was nice of him. A true gentleman and great human being.

Nigel Hudson and myself would talk for hours on end. He had been on an incredible journey like myself, and he suggested his pal write my life story. I enquired, 'Who is he, Dostoyevsky?'

'Dusty who?', replied Nigel.

'No... his name is Micky O'Rourke. I'll get him to contact you when you're back home'.

He sounded like a hitman for the IRA. But he was English. I'd wait for him to ring.

I didn't have long to serve at that stage, I'd developed a soft spot for Buckley Hall. Even now I get quite nostalgic thinking about the place. The people working there all seemed to care, and it was a credit to the penal system. If Her Majesty is reading this, ma'am, all is well in your little lock up in the foothills of the Pennines. The town hall's not too bad either.

So it was home to my beautiful bungalow in Grange Road, Bramhall. And back to my wonderful and caring wife. A serene and uneventful life in the suburbs was a possibility for most men. Alas, I was moulded from a different strata of clay, and the twists and turns would keep coming. My public demanded action. Soppy Joe here wouldn't disappoint.

Micky rang up, promising to send his newly-published book in the post, to see if I liked his writing.

Black Eyes and Blue Blood is a 'can't put down' read. The life and times of Liverpool hardman Norman Johnson. As Alan Partridge would say, 'Lovely stuff'. Seriously though, myself and Sharon would face financial hardships in the next three years, culminating in the loss of our bungalow, and Norman and Mick became good friends, both helping through difficult times.

City of London police were still on my case, and their ongoing inquiries weren't going away. Any force that would gatecrash a crown court trial had to have a streak of ruthlessness, but we will put them on the back burner. In the decade they call 'the noughties' I lost two great football friends; one to cancer, one to the bottle. Both left an indelible mark on our great game, but in the credit margin I gained the friendship of two international footballers who play in royal blue, both men completely different from the public perception of them. My pal and confidante Red Rock Rio was still in my corner, amongst other dear and close friends that just happen to have been top footballers.

Talking of the 'Big C', it took Norman Johnson as well in 2013. That man stood shoulder to shoulder with me, and he was a hugely popular man in London, Liverpool and Stafford. I'll never forget him. Fair, fearless and generous to the end.

George Best, Bobby Robson, Rio Ferdinand, John Terry and Ashley Cole, all unique individuals, but blessed with that winning mentality. Their lives are all well-documented, so I'll try to keep it novel, brief, informative and interesting.

P.S. What a five a side team they would have made in their prime! Robson managing, with 'The Cat' Madani in goal... blimey, I'd be redundant.

Football's coming home.

*   *   *   *

CHAPTER 16

SIMPLY LEGENDS

Arabic saying: A horse of good breeding is not dishonoured by his saddle

Anyone born with a God-given talent will reach the top of his chosen profession. This universal truism should be applicable to all sportsmen or women. If only it were that simple.

I believe it takes a lot more than that. Giving 100% should be a 'given' for every sportsman, but they don't all put it in, all of the time. Luck plays a part of course, and it's been quoted a million times, *The more I practise, the luckier I get.* That was a Gary Player sound bite from donkey's years back, but it still prevails today. Determination and persistence are also the friends of the aspirational, as is arrogance in small doses. If you think you are superior, with skill, luck, determination and bottle, you are on your way.

Bev, the young lady behind the counter at our local convenience store, is an avid Liverpool fan. She was complaining to me the other day that in her opinion, Manchester City and Chelsea were both arrogant. I told her they had plenty to be arrogant about. I don't suppose the Liverpool side of the eighties were shy, retiring, modest bods. Cantona and Henri had a Gallic swagger, appearing to own the pitch on which they played, although that was obviously a French trait as well. Managers Clough and Mourinho had and have a self-assured hubris. Football fans of opposing sides love to hate these big heads, but all would kill to have them rock up at their club.

Hubris in other sports is well-documented, but the crucial factor being all the sportsmen mentioned here have oodles of talent; Ali and Mayweather in boxing, McEnroe and Sampras in tennis. Ronnie O'Sullivan would play left-handed when the urge took him, still out-potting his opponents. Fred Trueman played for a great Yorkshire cricket team at a time when one had to be born in the county to represent them. A team of huge egos, Boycott, Close and Illingworth being just three. Fred not only thought he was the best player in Yorkshire, but truly believed the universe had never produced a player as good as he, and never would.

Playing against a southern county, Fred was at his hostile best. Yorkshire had ripped through the top and middle order, leaving a few hapless tail-enders to bat. Fred came roaring in towards the batsman, standing petrified like a rabbit in headlights, the ball pitched just wide of the off stump, but veered back violently knocking his leg stump out the ground. The wretched number ten trudged back to the pavilion, but not before passing his tormentor and saying, 'Great ball Fred'. Trueman was not known for his magnanimity, and he told it in a matter-of-fact manner, 'Aye lad, but it was wasted on thee'.

This is what we want in sport; characters who do the biz. While we are on cricket, a quick postscript on Don Bradman. *The Don* was regarded as the greatest batsman ever. He knew he was good, but unlike Fred he didn't go out of his way to tell people. He retired from test cricket with an average of 99.94, his batting career sadly culminating in a duck in his last innings when he only needed to score four to have an average over a hundred. That figure will never be beaten and it's miles ahead of the next best. Years later on, at a speaking engagement, a young reporter from a small town paper had the temerity to ask Bradman what he thought his batting average would be against modern day cricketers. The great man was pensive for a moment, then replied thoughtfully, 'Around the mid-forties'.

'Strewth', retorted the cub reporter, 'I didn't think cricket had improved that much'.

Don reassured the young man, 'You must remember son, I am now 74'.

That brought the house down. All great sportsmen know they are good - but some tell you, and some don't.

What I can't abide are drug cheats. I was devastated when Lance Armstrong was busted, and I hope to God Chris Froome is clean. I won't watch athletics, it's a dirty charade. Ben Johnson, Flo-Jo and Marion Jones were three phoneys, and there are many others. How did average Irish swimmer Michelle Smith start overtaking speedboats? She was at it, even the Irish nation can't accept the results, and it's not like gold medals are the norm for them. When our old pal filthy lucre raises its ugly head, standards deteriorate. The only way to save athletics is to have a free-for-all. Let them *all* take drugs. The Olympic Flag can have five anabolic steroids on it instead of the rings. They will definitely go, faster, higher, stronger, but at least we will know who really is the best. I'm bloody miffed and angry about the whole situation... I'm signing off now - to relax with a spliff.

Right, now I've got that off my chest, back to the fab football men. I'll go in chronological order, starting with the past master of Portman Road; Bobby Robson was a rare freak of nature, a genuinely nice guy who made it all the way to the top without changing his quiet, caring, likeable personality.

Kevin Beattie introduced me to Bobby in my mid teens. What a beautiful human being, charismatic with not a trace of edge. A real substitute father figure to me as I was enjoying the rise and rise of Ipswich Town. Bobby was a tactical genius, who got the very best out of his players. He won trophies in England, Holland, Portugal and Spain as a club manager.

He is still the only England manager to have got the national side to a World Cup semi-final on foreign soil. That balmy night in Italy, so nearly a glorious one, only to go out once again in a penalty shoot out to the pesky Germans

Bobby, a proud son of the North East, was born, raised and died in County Durham. A very useful inside forward in his playing days, he was deemed good enough to be awarded twenty England caps, but amazingly, his trophy cabinet was bare. He never won a thing at domestic or national level.

It was apt and fitting when Bobby was installed as manager of Newcastle United in 1999. The boy had returned home to his roots, an arena where he had watched his boyhood heroes Len Shackleton and Jackie Milburn grace the hallowed St James Park turf. I'd not bumped into Bobby that often after his earlier stint at Ipswich and before his eventual return to Newcastle. Ipswich Town always had two annual players and staff reunions, one for the FA Cup winners and one for the EUFA Cup winners. Bobby would always try to make it, as would I, but it wasn't always logistically possible.

I had Bobby's mobile number, so we kept in touch that way, he was never too busy not to speak and I hoped he would always call me first if he needed anything. I'm going to relate two tales from personal contact with Bobby that have never been published. I know he had his own unique way of communicating with people, often forgetting their names. He once went to the room of England captain Bryan Robson and called out, 'Come on Bobby, the coach is leaving'. Walking to the lift, Captain Marvel retorted, 'Ready boss... but I'm Bryan, you're Bobby'.

After a midweek match down South, the Newcastle team were returning home on the cripplingly long haul back to the North East. Robson fell fast asleep shortly after they set off. Later on the driver swapped steering duties with the relief driver at Scotch Corner service station. Robson woke up a few miles out of Newcastle, to find the original driver sitting next to him, sipping coffee. He jumped straight to his feet and shouted out, 'Who the hell is driving?!'.

So that was the world according to Bobby. I hope you enjoyed my two new anecdotes. It was September 2004, and Robson had recently been sacked by Freddy Shepherd at Newcastle, unfairly in my, and a lot of other people's opinion. Let me firstly just tell you, Bobby's personal assistant, Pat, was older than he was, not relevant on this occasion, but just to show you how the man operated, he did his own thing. Secondly, he absolutely hated flying - if he could avoid doing it, he would. The less time up in the air, the better. He was a feet on the ground, *terra firma* man.

My mobile rang. Bobby's name lit up the screen. I got in first, offering my heartfelt condolences, but he was pragmatic. He wouldn't be the last manager to be hooked unfairly. He needed a break. 'Faz, can you book me a flight any time in the next fortnight from Newcastle to Dubai? I know you're the boy... how long is the flight?'.

I told him it was seven hours. There was an awkward silence. He was contemplating. 'Listen, I can get to Manchester next week, how far is it from there?', he asked.

I told him seven hours again. I could hear him cussing under his breath, he was getting desperate. 'Right, I'll get Pat to arrange for me to travel down to London. How long will it take from the capital?'.

I was like a broken record. *Seven hours...*

He went ballistic, shouting down the phone, 'Is that the only bloody thing you can say?! Don't you know any other bleeding words than *seven hours* ?'.

I was laughing that hard I nearly burst a blood vessel in my temple. Bobby started guffawing at the other end - if anyone was eavesdropping, we would have been certified. Bobby had the last word, 'Newcastle it is then mate. All the best'.

Killer.

In the year 2000 somebody with a warped sense of humour entered Middlesbrough FC into an end-of-season, round robin tournament in Libya. Bobby Robson is only on the periphery of this, but still plays his part in a bloody good romp to North Africa.

I was contacted on the phone by a lifelong friend, Sami, a man I regarded as more a brother than pal. He was extremely excited. It was the first time in more than a decade that an English Premier League club would be playing a match in his native Libya. He wasn't going to miss it, and I told him to count me in. There was a charter flight from Newcastle International Airport... the boys would be migrating to the Sahara.

The trip had the full backing of the Foreign Office. Britain and America had sensed Libya was making an attempt to come in from the cold, as relations had been delicate to say the least, especially on these shores.

The recent memories of the murder of WPC Yvonne Fletcher outside the Libyan Embassy in London in 1984, and the alleged state terrorism involved in the downing of Pan-Am Flight 103 over Lockerbie in 1988, were events that could hardly be forgiven or forgotten. But Gaddafi had appeared to be willing to change direction and could even be prepared to make future concessions. If this football tournament could help improve the relationship and prevent further bloodshed, then everyone was a winner.

What could possibly go wrong ?

Well for a start, goalkeeper Mark Schwarzer refused to travel 'on principle'. In other words, his wife wanted him to take the kids to Disney World instead. That left Ben Roberts as the only gloveman in the squad. No problems surely. It would all be a walk in the park. Bryan Robson and his assistant Viv Anderson had assembled a talented bunch of players that had finished comfortably in mid table, ably supported by reserve coach, big Gordon McQueen.

The fateful day was upon us. Everyone arrived nice and early, bright-eyed and bushy-tailed. Star man Paul Gascoigne was the ultimate professional - he'd only gone and forgotten his passport. It needed a man built for speed, and Jimmy Five Bellies was sent out to retrieve the missing document. He must have been gone over two hours, and Gazza was sweating bricks, but a jubilant Jimmy finally waddled back into the lounge, holding the passport triumphantly aloft, reminiscent of Neville Chamberlain returning from Munich after meeting Hitler.

By wicked coincidence, Newcastle United arrived at the airport on their end of season tour to Barbados. Their mickey-taking was merciless towards the Middlesbrough players about the trip to Libya. Bobby Robson was not shy in dishing it out, but like a lot of names, people or places, Bobby got it completely wrong. He'd only got it into his bonce that we were off to the Lebanon, which at the time was being bombed daily in a full scale war between Hezbollah and the Israeli army. He was still laughing his socks off as we finally entered the departure lounge. The last thing we heard was, 'Keep your heads down lads'. Sami and myself had to have a chuckle. It was golden Robson, which set us right up for Libya.

This was going to be a one-off experience.

Channel 5 must have had some dire ratings that season, because they decided to do a fly on the wall, 'warts and all' documentary, fronted by fanatical Boro supporter, Stephen Tomkinson. He'd starred in the over the top, up to date news comedy *Drop the Dead Donkey*. He didn't know at the time, but this trip would easily top that.

On arrival, the coach at Tripoli Airport bore the legend *Meddlesbrough FC*. Something would go right sooner or later. I'm sure not all the players' hearts were in it, but a good night's rest would put the world to rights. On the eve of the first match against a Tripoli XI, goalie Ben Roberts contracted a dicky tummy. In other words, he converted to the Shi-ites. He was literally having to take a dump every twenty minutes, and there wasn't a lot of 'substance' involved.

At this stage Stephen Tomkinson was still perversely upbeat. He started interviewing the players on the coach heading for the stadium. He asked Middlesbrough born and bred, carrot top, chunky midfielder Phil Stamp, what were his impressions of the new environment. 'Libya is shit. We all wanna go home. The food is shit too!' replied Stampy. A man obviously primed for the diplomatic corps after his football career finishes.

At the ground, the Italian team Bari, the other outfit in this 'round robin' competition, generously offered to loan Bryan Robson their third choice goalie, but surprisingly, Robbo politely declined their sporting offer, because he had an ace up his sleeve. Phil Stamp would play in goal. Was there no end to the man's talents?

Everywhere around Tripoli there were large posters of Gaddafi versus Gazza. It was an ad man's dream. Well, it would have been ten years earlier, as Gazza was now a sad and pale shadow of the vibrant football genius that once rampaged through Western Europe. He was in the very late Autumn of his career and there weren't many leaves left on his footballing tree. At least he could be temporarily reunited with his former Lazio team mate, Saadi, favourite son of Gaddafi.

Gazza was left in no doubt by the Middlesbrough management not to mention alcohol in any interviews he might give the press. Libya was a dry state, drinking was off-limits and totally unacceptable. Not too much to ask of a senior player, but this was Gazza...

Libyan TV got him and Saadi, together in front of the cameras to discuss their time playing for Lazio. The very first thing Gazza comes out with was, 'Do you remember the time we both got rat-arsed in Italy?'. A little was lost in translation, but Gazza was forcefully bundled away before he got everyone locked up.

The arena had a grandiose title, *The Great Man Made River Stadium*, in honour of the contractors who had built the world's largest irrigation project. They had laid four thousand kilometres of pipes, bringing new life to The Sahara and the barren Mediterranean coast.

Middlesbrough were useless. They lost to both Bari and Tripoli, 2-0 and 1-0 respectively. Phil Stamp could hold his head high though. He was blameless. After the football finished the lads privately went on the lash. The price of black market whisky doubled, and the British Embassy put in an official complaint, as there was a severe shortage of the hard stuff. It made you proud just to be there.

What good came out of the tour, we will never know, but before the upcoming season of 2001 was over, Robson, Anderson, McQueen and Gascoigne were all gone - sacked or transferred. A sad ending really. But was the desert escapade the beginning of the end?

Back to Bobby Robson. He was knighted in 2002, inducted into the English Football Hall of Fame in 2003 and had two life-sized statues erected to him outside Portman Road and St James Park. That was the least he deserved. He beat cancer on five separate occasions, until terminal lung cancer took him in 2009. No man should have had to go through all that. In all the years I knew him, I never heard him complain about anything.

Rest in peace Sir Bobby. A dazzling light went out that year, but his money-raising cancer foundation will live on forever.

How many people can say they were friends with a football all-time great, a man who started soccer iconography? George Best - the Belfast Boy - a fleet-footed genius in size five boots was my pal. Over my lifetime, I'd met him as a small boy in Dubai, as a young gambler in many of the great casinos, and as a more mature man, privately at his home and publicly in the restaurants and public houses of the Metropolis.

I saw him most frequently in the last half decade of his life, and if anything he was more famous and popular at the back end of his dazzling career, than when he was in his pomp as the darling of the Old Trafford faithful. With modern footballing TV coverage at saturation point, and the internet showing every game ever broadcast on the medium of YouTube, George was well known to not just the wrinklies, but to all the spotty adolescents who weren't even a twinkle the last time he went on a dribble.

His football career has come under the microscope many times, so I'm going to concentrate mainly on his post-playing days, how events and circumstances went beyond his control. As a lad he followed Wolverhampton Wanderers, but contrary to that, had the brains and intelligence to graduate to a grammar school, not ideal for a football fanatic, as their school sport code was rugby. He soon got a switch back to a secondary modern, and was spotted a few years later by an alert Manchester United scout, who sent back a recommendation just shy of the second coming. After an initial bout of home sickness he eventually became a regular at United, and from thereon a top class international superstar.

At the age twenty seven, he was unceremoniously booted out the door. Tommy Doc decreed George was history after he had missed training yet again. How many players are more successful after leaving Manchester United? Not many... Peter Beardsley springs to mind, but he was hardly an early developer. Apart from some minor accolades playing for various clubs in North America and one and a half stellar seasons for Fulham, George was freewheeling down towards retirement. He had lived the dream, but he was his own man. Something else would turn up.

George liked a drink. Is the Pope catholic? Do bears crap in the woods? Does Dolly Parton sleep on her back? I know this isn't a groundbreaking journalistic scoop, but it does hide a serious message about the dangers of alcohol. Many are too blasé about our relationship with the bottle or the carafe. If alcohol was newly discovered this week, the authorities would probably ban it as a dangerous drug. Tobacco probably kills more, but how many lives are ruined by the demon drink? I'm not a killjoy, do what you like, take recreational drugs, smoke 40 fags a day, drink ten pints a night, just don't expect to make your three score and ten. Moderation is the name of the game. Starting the day with a Full English, fish and chips at dinner time and round the night off after coming out of the pub with a curry takeaway, will kill you quicker than a tracer bullet. If that's the lifestyle you enjoy though, don't expect the phone to ring offering you a role in the latest James Bond film, unless they need a fat, flatulent, wheezing, sweating villain called Dangerous Porky Pie.

The drinks industry in Britain is a very powerful entity. It is a billion-pound industry, and alcohol is available everywhere; the corner shop, supermarkets, even petrol stations. It's advertised every night on the box. Don't be fooled by all the pubs closing, people are buying cheaper and stronger booze, and imbibing it at home. Half a bottle of Vladivostok Vodka for the wife, six cans of Special Brew for hubby, and watching Geordie Shore the sequel. It doesn't get any better than that... no wonder we lost the empire.

The surprising revelation about George was, he never drank or had booze in the house. His problem was, once in the pub at dinner time, he would drink continuously until closing time. He wasn't the classic alcoholic either, as he could go days or even weeks without touching a drop, but once he started on a session, it was a case of *last man standing*. Against all expectations, George was an incredibly shy and gentle man. As his football career was taking off, he initially started drinking to relax in the company of strangers.

Pundits might say George had an excessive drink problem, but I classed it as an incurable disease. Nothing, absolutely nothing could derail his Chablis Choo Choo. His mother, father, two wives and only child, tried and failed. I never judged him, it was pointless, I just went with the flow. It wasn't going to end well, but he knew that more than any expert.

1978 was a watershed year for George. In January he married Angela MacDonald Janes. He had met her in America whilst playing for the Los Angeles Aztecs, and she became universally known as Angie Best.

By the way - whatever happened to that chocolate bar called Aztec, the one in the purple wrapper? I used to like them, it just disappeared one day. I'm still traumatised.

Anne Best, his beloved mother, a women who had also hit the bottle after George's troubles became too stressful for her, spiralled deep down into alcoholism. It culminated in a fatal cardiac arrest later that year. George now had a legitimate reason to drink, and heartbroken, he went on a guilt trip. His drinking got so bad, that he even had a drug called Antabuse stitched into his stomach. This is a process where chronic alcoholics experience unpleasant side effects if they partake in the consumption of liquor.

All bets were off in 1981, as Angie gave birth to bonny, bouncy, Calum Best. This was the catalyst for George to clean his act up, and he went on the wagon. He now had another dimension to his life. At that moment, George should never have so much as smelt the barmaid's apron again. As a non-drinker, I cannot imagine how strong was his urge to hit the bottle. Calum should have been his first and only priority, but within a year, he was down the pecking order. Angie had seen enough, the relationship deteriorated and they went their separate ways. That was the moment: he was in the power of a greater force, slave to the bottle. He would always submit to the lure of alcohol. He didn't mean to hurt his loved ones, but this was one match he couldn't win.

There are many types of drunks - we've all met them; the friendly one, ('You're my best mate'), the aggressive one, ('I'll rip your throat out'), the sleepy one, the stupid one, the loud one, the quiet one, the boring one, the talkative one and worst of all, the one whose pissed his pants. George was none of these. He was a classy drunk. He never said a bad word to anyone, including me or his wife. Maybe he had built up a huge tolerance to drink, the same way that poison seems to have less effect on rats over time. He had certainly put the hours in. His favourite tipple was white wine, but he had his own little slogan, 'As long as it starts with an 'A' and ends with an 'L', that will do for me'.
Why he loved the month April so much is still a mystery.
So the next time some barrack room lawyer tells you, beer and wine are harmless, give the twat a wide berth. He probably works for Greene King brewery.

A million drink-related crimes are committed in Britain every year, but we still regard drinking alcohol as a 'bit of a laugh'. The Scottish like a tipple, but it can lead to tragedy. Last year a distillery worker in the Highlands tripped over and fell into a vat of single malt whisky and drowned. The coroner's report stated that he was in the vat for over an hour and a half, but had came out twice for a piss before he finally went under.
After his marriage collapsed, George returned to Britain, and the drinking became a proper stinking. In late 1984, he was jailed for three months for drink driving and punching a policeman. Clever clogs George Orwell never saw that coming. He turned out for the Ford Open Prison football team, a morale booster for the cons and screws. What a tale to tell the grand kids.
He was earning plenty as an after dinner speaker and also as a football analyst on TV. Sure, he was pissed most of the time, but the love and clamour of the public meant he was always in demand. In 1995 out of the blue, he married former air hostess and model Alex Pursey. She was 26 years his junior. A brave decision by both, as the generation gap and drink problems are never easy to overcome.

Sharon and I were both fond of Alex. The couple had two wonderful red setters called Red and Rua, which they regarded as their babies. All you doggy people will know the feeling, you can't beat a four legged friend. Mike Summerbee and I visited Chateau Best a couple of times. Mike had been a business partner with George back in the halcyon days of young glory. They owned fashion boutiques together, a good move, blue and red combined covered all the customers who supported either United or City. George would sign my football memorabilia, and years after he retired, his autograph was still fetching premier money. We both did very well from the arrangement.

George was partial to Lebanese food, it was his all-time favourite. We would meet in a Lebanese restaurant in Mayfair, and they were very happy occasions. He was in his element and I would give anything to share those memories again. The management and waiters loved him dearly, and I discerned very early on that all nationalities were in awe of the man. Benfica supporters had dubbed him *El Beatle* and with that epithet he was probably worshipped in a 'Norwegian Wood'.

Around the new millennium, after over three decades of heavy drinking, George's liver decided to wave the white flag. It had been working overtime and handed in its P45. George was coughing up blood, his shaking hands were upsetting to see. And the only solution was a new, younger, fitter model had to be found in the form of a liver transplant.

The situation seemed to shake George regarding his own failing mortality. He initially didn't consider himself worthy, but his supporting family and friends insisted he push for the transplant. Two and a half years later George, who had cut right down on the drinking, was found a suitable replacement liver. He entered the private Cromwell Hospital near Chelsea, wherein after a successful nine hour operation, George came round. There were more tubes emanating from his body than a map of the London Underground. The room resembled Kew Gardens, bedecked with an abundance of flowers. A large vase of blooms by his bedside caught his attention. Norman Whiteside had sent them, accompanied with a tag card, 'Best wishes, can I have your old one?!'.

Norman liked a bit of black humour, and his own liver must have resembled a pork scratching. It's the big boys' way of showing the world we're tough. Nothing worries the lads, but the reality is that the majority, when entering the unknown, are scared shitless. You ladies have got far more steel than any of us. George had previously been promised by a wealthy Middle Easterner with connections to football, that the cost of the operation would be taken care of. That scenario didn't materialise, so I deposited ten thousand into his private account. I was happy to do it. The man had been through the mangle, it wasn't going to rain on his parade.

This was a day when Hyperion shone like a red giant from the heavens, sending down a multitude of golden rays, and cumulus nimbus and cirrus clouds had blown a hasty retreat. The Archangels were blowing silver trumpets, Seraphim and Cherubim sang from the choir invisible. Even The Devil gave a begrudging nod. God was bouncing about wearing the emerald green Northern Ireland shirt. He hadn't worn a white one since 1966 as he had to be seen to remain neutral.

I hear he didn't even own a Scottish jersey.

A man... a great man had been given a second chance, a renaissance was at hand. This would be a good time to conclude the George Best saga, but we can't because the reality doesn't allow it. Within months he was drinking heavily again. Alex beseeched all the local landlords to desist from serving him drinks, on the premise that it was slowly killing him. George resented that intrusion. Remember, our man cannot beat this foul addiction, all he hears are the dulcet tones permeating from the vineyard... *drink me, drink me.* Just like the ancient Sirens who lured unsuspecting sailors to their death by shipwrecking their vessel on the rocks, George was subconsciously being lured to *The Red Lion* and there wasn't a life jacket in sight. Everyman and his dog wanted to buy him a drink. But they were killing him with kindness.

Alex had turned into a nervous wreck. The whole escapade had worn her right down. The nine-year marriage was over, and they divorced in 2004. My heart went out to both of them. No victims, just circumstances. It had been miraculous for the bond to have lasted that long. My four wives can attest to that.

I didn't see the end coming, but George had actually adjusted to his lot. He had cheated death once, and it now held no fears for him. Reminding me of the film excerpt from *Bill and Ted's Bogus Journey* where they meet The Grim Reaper. Ted introduces himself, 'Yo Death, how's it hanging?' .

That was George's attitude. But he was also thinking about others. If just one person could be saved by not following his footsteps, it wouldn't all be futile. On October 3rd 2005, George was admitted back into the Cromwell Hospital. A lung infection had now taken hold, but this was possibly not as bad as thought as he had previously shaken off similar infections without too much trouble.

The first three days in hospital showed no symptoms of alcohol withdrawal, but the lung infection slowly spread to his kidneys. He was also experiencing internal bleeding, because his misfiring liver was causing the blood not to clot. People don't realise that the liver is an extremely complex organ that performs hundreds of functions. The doctors later on appeared to have pulled off a minor miracle when George actually improved over a ten day period, but they still couldn't eliminate the original persistent lung infection.

Other complications came and went, and then returned again. I visited him about a month after he'd been admitted. He'd had hundreds of visitors, many great footballers had popped in to wish him well, but what I saw shocked me down to my boots. In the bed was a frail, emaciated, shadow of the man I loved. It was heartbreaking. I couldn't take it all in. I knew he was on the point of no return. Outside in the car park I burst into tears. I was sobbing uncontrollably. It had been a massive effort not to break down in George's room.

On returning home, Sharon sensed something was wrong. I filled her in, and she started the waterworks and that set me off again. It was like losing a family member and there was not a thing we could do about it. George then developed pneumonia, followed by a bout of septicemia and still that infernal lung infection wouldn't budge. Late on, George invited in the News of the World to take his picture, which appeared on their front page, coupled by the caption, *'Don't die like me'*. That was almost heroic on his part. Most mortals would have wanted to sign off with a photograph showing them flying down the wing in their prime. George wanted to warn people; don't mess up your life, like I did. To this day I still can't look at that image.

George died five days after the picture was taken. He had been in hospital for over seven weeks. What a fighter he was. Amazingly, alcoholism wasn't mentioned on the death certificate, he'd suffered multi-organ failure. He had gone peacefully, firstly sedated, then after consultation with family members, the life support was switched off. He never felt a thing. The world mourned. There was a shining new star in the heavens, a hundred thousand people turned out for his funeral procession. His son Calum was magnificent throughout, another class act. He has all the good looks and charisma of his father.

I struggled to sleep that night, until I recalled a night out in the mid eighties. Dining in a restaurant, I overheard a guy on the next table say to his group, 'Name a better front three than Dixon, Nevin and Speedie?'. I suppose he was talking about contemporary players, but before anyone could say anything, I leaned over and said, 'Charlton, Law and Best'.

He grinned and said, 'That'll do.', and carried on eating. I nodded off, smiling. George Best will live on forever, especially in this digital age. When we are all dust, he will remain a real diamond and an immortal.

We can all drink to that... mine's a cup a tea.

* * * *

What have Stepney, Peckham and Barking got in common - apart from being arguably some of the rather less salubrious parts of London? They are the birthplaces of multi-millionaire, contemporary football men, Ashley Cole, Rio Ferdinand and John Terry. Three men, who in the noughties and beyond, were the backbone of the England defence. Each captained the side, Cole was the best left back in the world, while Terry and Ferdinand were supreme central defenders. At domestic level they won more medals than Audie Murphy.

It was actually my old friend Rio, who introduced me to both the Chelsea boys - John Terry at Old Trafford in 2007 (the night that Steve McClaren insipidly inspired England's defeat to Spain), and Ashley Cole at the Lowry Hotel, Salford, Manchester.

John Terry has been slaughtered in the press over recent years, but I can safely say, he is one of the most generous men I have ever met. I know he is no angel, he'd be the first to tell you that he's fouled up time and again. Footballers are not role models, they never have been. They're young men with time and money on their hands. The last God-fearing player was Peter Knowles, so if you want a waffle on The Watchtower, head for Wolverhampton on Wednesday.

The media like digging the dirt, good news stories don't sell copy, apart from The Sun's *Freddie Starr Ate My Hamster*. Even then, there was no up side for the rodent. If John Terry ever built an orphanage, discovered a cure for cancer or brokered everlasting peace for the world, the papers wouldn't touch it with a thirty foot hop pole.

Near the Chelsea training ground at Cobham is a hair salon run by Toni Terry, John's wife. JT arranges for everyone at the club, from the juniors upwards to get their hair cut there. Nobody pays, that wouldn't get reported, it might give the wrong idea. It's not all been a bed of roses - John bought a large red brick mansion in Oxshott, a short drive again from the training ground. He decided to build a bigger one on his own land adjacent to it, a project that would fulfil his ambition to construct a dream home for Toni and the twins Georgie and Summer.

He won't mind me saying this, it's been well documented in the press, but the costs of the new build spiralled and he had to keep re-mortgaging upwards. The papers were having a field day, hoping he'd do his bollocks and eventually go bankrupt, but a surge in the housing market meant he has since sold both for massive profits. Well done old son, I've got no time for the lovers of schadenfreude... or even Clement Freud.

Four months after my first meeting with John, I was delighted to receive an invitation for myself and Sharon to attend his and Toni's wedding. He doesn't like doing things by half, so he'd only gone and booked Blenheim Palace in Oxfordshire, ancestral home to the Dukes of Marlborough. The late, great Winnie liked men with grit, guts and determination, but he'd have never made a centre half himself as he was only five foot six tall. Sharon was ecstatic. I knew it would cost me, as she needed a new outfit and she didn't shop at Matalan. I decided to go my own way. Suits for the wedding were costing five grand, so I went native as a billionaire sheikh. I already had all the Arab robes, all that was missing was the headdress. In different parts of the Middle East it's called a *keffiyeh* or *ghutrah*, but on the Edgware Road it's called a large tea towel. Cost - seven pounds and fifty pence. Wallop, back of the net!

On the 16th June, the Madanis headed off with Sharon driving, and the Desert Fox navigating. It was a typical Summer's day: it was persisting down. We arrived at the picture postcard market town of Woodstock, surely Jimi Hendrix wasn't making a comeback...? No, it was 37 years too late for the greatest guitarist who ever lived, we would have to make do with Lionel Richie. And there wasn't even a Commodore in sight, unlike the paparazzi who were on every street corner. God, it was going to be a big event. OK Magazine had paid serious money for exclusivity inside the palace. The Daily Star, Mail and Express would have to slum it outside the gates in the pouring rain, huddled up to the hoi polloi.

I've never seen security like it. The Queen and Bill Clinton had both visited Blenheim under less surveillance. I was expecting to see gun turrets on the towers. The men on the gate were really sceptical when we rolled up, but we had our official invites, and they radioed up three times before we were allowed to proceed up the drive. Quite right too - I could have been masquerading as The Sun's *Fake Sheikh*.

Inside, a multitude of the great and good were there, people of all races. I say that just to clarify that John Terry is not a racist. And never has been. It was bang out of order that he was accused in court of being so. He may be a lot of things to a lot of people, but that's not one of them. I'm not exactly *pasty* myself, so I wouldn't associate with him if he was prejudiced. Everyone at Chelsea knows he isn't, and so do all the people who know him well.

The guest list was a *who's who* of football: Wayne Rooney, Ashley Cole, Jamie Redknapp and Frank Lampard amongst many others. Oh yes, and little Michael Owen. The colour drained right out of his cheeks when he clocked me, I was in the mood for confrontation, but Sharon steered me away saying, 'Wrong time, wrong place'.

Female intuition - a lot to be said for it.

We settled down on our designated table - accompanied by wives and girlfriends were, Jody Morris, Michael Duberry and Chelsea fanatic - star of Soccer AM - Tim Lovejoy. All good people, and we couldn't have picked a better sitting. John Terry had been pushing for Billy McCulloch, the Chelsea masseur and club joker to make guest appearances on TV's *Soccer AM*. Here was his big chance, he was due up on stage in an impromptu comedy act.

A free bar had been operating all day, courtesy of JT. He was picking up the tab. Most people are responsible, but there are always more than a few who smash it out the park. It's only human nature, flying in the face of the adage - *There's no such thing as a free lunch.*

Beer, wine and spirits were being imbibed in copious amounts, so a perfect atmosphere, one would assume, for Billy McCulloch to bring the house down with his comedic genius.

Introduced as Billy Blood, he cavorted onto the stage like a neurotic Lee Evans. But the audience was never with him, and he went down like a lead zeppelin. It was embarrassing really, he probably is a funny man, but we can all have an off night. He finished his act to a smattering of applause, I looked over to John Terry, his biggest fan, I read his lips, 'Thank fuck that's over'.

Tim Lovejoy was open-mouthed. A glazed paralysis covered his face. Helen Chamberlain wouldn't be having the pleasure of an introduction to *the world according to Billy.*

We tucked into fish and chips brought to the table in posh newspaper. It was brilliant. This was the era of the *nouveau riche*. We could eat what we wanted, when we wanted. Heston Blumenthal could stick his snail porridge right up his jacksie.

Still the ale flowed. The British aren't lightweights in raising a glass, then again it was a occasion for rejoicing. It's not every day you get married - unless you're name is Mickey Rooney or Madani. The lights suddenly lowered, the star turn was imminent. Lionel Richie was rumoured to be picking up a cool quarter million. You could get fifty Lionel Blair's for that. But then again, if he was playing in my back yard, I would draw the curtains. Talented Lionel had played Las Vegas, the O2 Arena, The Olympic Stadium Rio and Glastonbury, probably every major venue in the world. He'd originally signed for Motown Records and sold over a hundred million records, but as he made his grand entrance, all that permeated my mind was, 'You poor, defenceless bastard'.

Most Lionel Richie crowds have paid good money to see their lifelong hero, but he was up against it at Blenheim. This crowd were four sheets to the wind and had musical tastes ranging from Hawkwind to 50 Cent, I knew he was in trouble when he sang *Hello* and the crowd chanted it back. Three or four times he appealed for quiet, but he was swimming up river. Toni Terry looked round the room anxiously. A shame really, but alcohol loosens peoples inhibitions. Lionel came off stage saying, 'Now I know what it's like to play a British social club'. 250 big ones would make the flight back home feel a touch more cosy though.

Frank Lampard came over to the table. He knew Lovejoy, Duberry and Morris well, but spent half an hour putting me and Sharon at ease. Previously in the early noughties I'd made Frank's acquaintance a couple of times at the Chelsea training ground. Claudio Ranieri - *The Tinkerman* - was manager at the time. Mickey Thomas and I were amazed that when Concorde came over, all the training stopped for everyone to admire the big bird. What a lovely man Frank is, polite and soft spoken. He went out of his way to make us feel comfortable.

Sharon fancied a potter round the palace. When we bumped into strang-ers, I introduced myself as *The Sultan of Drof Las*. That's 'Salford' spelt back-wards to the lay man. OK Magazine were intrigued by the mysterious man from the East, so they had to have a photograph of Sharon and myself for the latest wedding edition and for posterity.

Later that evening, the greatest fireworks display I've ever witnessed rounded off a fantastic day. Thank you John and Toni Terry. My wedding present of a luxury holiday to Dubai didn't exactly hit the spot, there was going to be repercussions, with most of the detritus cascading down on me.

Rio Ferdinand, River Phoenix, Old Father Thames and Nile Ranger - all men named after waterways, and amazingly all allergic to fish. No, not the battered type, but the ex-lead singer of Marillion. Not one is a prog rock fan. That's the Rio I know. He never, ever played Kayleigh on his car stereo system. He was determined to reach the top without any outside distractions.

The young Rio stood out like a shining beacon, accelerating through the youth ranks to rapidly become a first team regular at West Ham, a club that has produced internationals galore from it's academy. Moving on to Leeds United, a world record transfer at the time for a defender, he quickly cemented down a place in every England squad. Leeds's financial woes meant a move to Manches-ter United was on the cards, and in 2002 after two short seasons at Elland Road, he crossed the Pennines. Again, the fee another world record for a defender.

Sir Alex had his man. He'd paid top wonga, but he had the best ball-play-ing centre back in the business. Silverware wasn't long in coming, in fact the Premiership trophy arrived in the very first season. The Mancunian scotch mist dissipated, a rainbow straddled the stands of Old Trafford, and at the ticket office, George, Zippy and Bungle queued for season tickets... *ay caramba.*

Ironically, years before I met Rio, I had the pleasure of meeting Rio's dad Julian. He was working the doors in London's West End. An imposing man, and one could see why, and how, Rio and Anton were superbly conditioned athletes. I first encountered Rio in a Manchester restaurant, shortly after he had signed for the Reds. We're still good friends today. He's the football man I'm closest to, and I trust him implicitly. We phone each other frequently. He's very opinionated about football and he's rarely off the mark. Sharon used to enjoy visiting his family in Alderley Edge, and vice versa. If we were dining out in Manchester, we'd gravitate towards his beautiful restaurant 'Rosso'.

In recent years we've both had some disappointments. In 2015 Rio lost his beautiful wife Rebecca to cancer. Sharon and I were devastated. For the kids to lose their mother at such a young age is heart-breaking, but we know Lorenz,

166

Tate and Tia will pull through. Rebecca was Rio's soulmate. They married in 2009, and in a break from recent family tradition, they were the first Ferdinands to tie the knot for many a long year.

I'm not going to dwell long on the Anton Ferdinand - John Terry spat. There's been more than enough written about it, with the lawyers filling their pockets yet again. Top England defenders on opposing sides, verbally kicking lumps out of each other. For me personally, it was really sad. Relationships have improved recently, and I do hope that John Terry, Ashley Cole and Rio can put it all behind them. But, like everything in life, things don't come easy. Rio has recently retired from the great game. Whatever he does, punditry, business affairs or managing a football team, he will be a great success. The man is astute, but more importantly he is a loyal friend.

Lastly, a man who, when in his prime, was the world's finest left back - Ashley Cole. A recipient of 107 England caps, he claimed three Premier Leagues, both the big European trophies and seven FA Cup winners' medals. The vast majority of all the football clubs haven't won that many. That record will last a thousand years. He would never need a sat nav to get to Wembley. At Arsenal, he was a tremendous attack-minded full back, before moving to Chelsea, where he became a better defensive player. There are different schools of thought where he played his best football, but the bottom line was he performed well, week in, week out.

He was labelled greedy after angrily knocking back a 55K a week offer from Arsenal during contract talks. I don't blame him actually, as I think he was worth double that. He got stuck with the epithet 'Cashley', which seemed to follow him around for the rest of his career. The acrimonious divorce from Cheryl Tweedy, in which certain papers had a field day, didn't do his cause any favours either. In certain households he was about as popular as colic at the stud.

I loved him. He was maligned, but misunderstood. I was there at his wedding - *fuck me*, I can hear you all shouting, *freeloading at another posh bash, you scrounging Iranian twat!*

Not quite... my wedding gift to the happy couple was another luxury holiday to Dubai. Invite Madani and you won't be disappointed with a bread maker or canteen of Taiwanese cutlery. You know it makes sense.

Ashley actually got married a year before John Terry, at Wrotham Park, Hertfordshire. The mansion is in fact the setting for the Hollywood Oscar-winning period drama *Gosford Park*. A lot of people might think Ashley is a brash, loud-mouthed poser, but nothing could be farther from the truth. He's quite a shy man, who has stayed close to his roots. The wedding wasn't on the scale of John Terry's, but still must have cost over a million. There was a beautiful horse-drawn stage coach on hand, from which Cheryl emerged. She looked like a fairytale princess.

The wedding dress was designed by Roberto Cavalli, but to be fair she could have been wearing an outfit made from black bin liners and still looked a million dollars. She'd come a long way from the council estate in Newcastle. She really is tiny, a little petite poppet. How she managed to batter that toilet attendant, God only knows. Ashley was wearing a silver lustre suit. Not many could have got away with it, but there was no chance of upstaging the bride.

We were sitting on the same table as Gary Lewin the Arsenal and England physio, a cracking fella, who'd previously introduced me to Arsene Wenger. The food was magnificent, the floral decorations were stunning. All in all it was class affair. What else could it have been, the man getting hitched was an all-time class act.

Four more footballers I'd like to mention: Cesc Fabregas, Shaun Wright Phillips, Michael Ballack and Didier Drogba. I'd met them all briefly, fine men, intelligent and a credit to their profession. The game needs footballers of that calibre. It has made me quite nostalgic looking back - happy, happy days, but the near future held darker omens.

City of London Police were lurking, just like time share reps, traffic wardens, cold callers and Michael Mcintyre, they weren't going away on a quiet request...

*   *   *   *

CHAPTER 17

TALE OF THE TAG

Arabic saying: The crazy man talks and the smart man understands

Back in Bramhall, I tried to relax, but knew I wasn't out the woods. City of London Plod had sharpened their claws and were determined to send me back to the big house. On top of all the shenanigans, my luxury bungalow was also in their sights. David Blunkett's insidious Proceeds of Crime Act had his goons attempting to clean my bank account out and put myself and Sharon on the streets. Bramhall is quite an affluent suburb, but how many residents there could prove where every penny had come from? Bottom line, none. The area is known as the least lonely place in England. I can vouch for that, there were policemen knocking on the bleeding front door every ten minutes.

A lot of things in life are never what they seem. Take the names of pop groups like 10cc, the Scissor Sisters and Steely Dan. The first is named after the average amount of semen in the male ejaculation, the second is a sexual position between two consenting ladies, while the third is a powerful steam driven dildo from Yokohama.

I'm not going to drop Joe Cocker in it, so don't ask.

That's when I decided to get away from Greater Manchester for a few leisure days down South. I couldn't foresee see any circumstance which could suck me down under the quicksand, as I was already up to my Adam's apple and lacking in any water wings. In London, I'd accepted a lift from an associate, David Grant - not the well known singing coach - but a dozy pillock who happened to drop me right in it.

We were cruising past Regents Park, approaching Lord's cricket ground in St John's Wood, when they came out of nowhere. No, not Albanian windscreen cleaners, but the Metropolitan Police Force. 'We cool Dave?', I asked.

I could feel droplets of sweat forming on my brow. He looked a trifle sheepish, a bit like a knackered ram with attached electrodes at the abattoir.

'Nothing incriminating in the motor is there?'. He didn't have time to answer. The Met emerged from the boot with ten thousand in dodgy money. I gave a nervous laugh and looked to the skies. Why do we do that? I could have cried my eyes out.

As we were escorted in handcuffs down to London Bridge police station, it went through my mind that they might be putting me on the next Virgin express back up to Manchester with a slight admonishment, 'Off you go then, you old rascal.'.

No such luck.

After a sleepless night in the cells, I was grilled in the morning and bailed in the afternoon to return in three months. I had pleaded innocence and ignorance in the interview room to a pair of incredulous detectives. It didn't look good. Who would believe a word I said with my record of forged passports and driving licences? And it didn't help matters that ex-best friend Mickey Thomas was a convicted money forger. It was only circumstantial, but it meant I couldn't call him up as a character witness... *As if.*

Sharon was not best pleased when I arrived back, forlorn and dishevelled. If she had packed her bags there and then, I wouldn't have blamed her one iota. Trouble was, it was only going to get worse in the weeks that followed. I needed her in my corner. There was never a doubt of course, rock solid that lass. Within a month, the authorities sent down a shit storm of biblical proportions. The first to make themselves busy were the City of London storm troopers. They raided the bungalow and turned the premises upside down on the hunt for more incriminating evidence. Sharon spent more than a week getting it back something like it was, only for the Met to turn up uninvited and trash it once more.

Squatters would have taken one look, cocked a snook and given it the cold shoulder. It was heartbreaking to watch our home being squeezed through the wringer. Then came the thunderbolt: they were taking the bungalow off us. We had to get out. I immediately appealed against the decision, if only for Sharon's sake. I had to fight my corner, but the establishment is a big hulking machine. Not many little men come out on top.

The appeal could drag on for years, but the reality was that we were homeless. The only thing I wouldn't miss was the next door neighbour. He was a high court judge. We were on our arses, but I scraped up enough money to land a rented property in Fir Road, Bramhall, a bungalow about a third of the size of our old one. Not as good a postcode, but beggars couldn't be choosers. The crappy sequence continued; our beloved Persian cat, Lily, was run over and killed in the street. She had been used to playing in a private part of Grange Road which was traffic-free. I was very fond of Lily, but Sharon was devastated. She absolutely adored that cat. It was akin to losing a family member.

Have you ever noticed in life that when you are at your weakest, they all come for you. It must be an universal truism. People who have experienced traumatic times will know exactly what I'm talking about.

Sharon was close to breaking point and behind my poker-faced facade, I wasn't far behind her. The mental and physical duress was sapping us both. Then one night, wham-bang! - it came right out of the shadows. I had a heart attack, a bad one. That just about put the cherry on the iced bun. A lesser man might well have given up there and then and taken the easy way out. Had all my chickens come home to roost? If they had, then make my eggs scrambled, poached and boiled - and throw in an omelette for good measure. I'm a gutsy little son of a gun, a fully fledged paid-up member of the British and Persian empires and that's the next best thing to being immortal. The ticker was letting me down, but to be fair, I'd been going through a bloody gargantuan bout of stress. The silent killer was doing his worst. But I wouldn't swallow it though... he was a thoroughly bad egg.

I was rushed into intensive care at Stepping Hill Hospital, Stockport. It was touch and go at one stage, but I came through. How many times has the National Health come up trumps for me? Once again I owe my life to those brilliant and wonderful doctors and nurses. Nye Bevan, I bloody love you.

Loads of footballers came in to wish me well: my friends Mick and Norman even came up from Stafford. It gave me a real fillip. And the weeks in bed helped me see reason. Sharon was visiting every day, and we decided that when I was well enough, a move away was on the cards. The last year in Greater Manchester had turned into a right rotter. It was no fault of the city, fate had turned its fickle back on the Madanis. All the events recently had been bad experiences, and we simply couldn't take any more negative vibes, so we decided to move to my first homestead in England - sunny Colchester.

It needed to be ecstasy in Essex.

I was on the road to recovery, not exactly in fine fettle, but the old line came to mind about the optimistic leper when asked how he was feeling - *mustn't crumble*. I decided to ring my old teenage pal from Colchester, local taxi driver, Payman. Another Iranian, he must have the best name ever for a cabbie, even though he might take the scenic route every now or then. The Tetris parts were falling into place, as it turned out his uncle had a two bedroom flat available for rent. I told him to put my name on it. The cheeky sod said, 'Which one?'.

We were on the road again - but Willie Nelson declined to come, full of shit he was. M6, A14, and A12 all faded into the past. We were back. The large sign loomed into view declaring - Colchester - Britain's oldest recorded town. We were home, and it felt right. Memories came flooding back. I'd experienced many happy times here, and if we could recapture just a fraction of days gone by, the move would be a bloody belter. We signed the lease and settled in. For the first time in months, everything was prime time.

171

On Sharon's birthday, I went the extra yard, buying her two Persian cats - Troy and Millie. One of the best things I've ever done. She was thrilled, and it exorcised a few ghosts, besides bringing two electric bouncing balls of fluff into the flat. It was winner, winner, chicken dinner. The whole family were partial to a wing.

Three months had elapsed since the discovery of the funny money in David Grant's car. I had been bailed to report to Paddington Green Police Station. This was most worrying because Paddington was a very high security establishment, specialising in the detainment and questioning of dangerous terrorists. If the Met thought they could up the ante and intimidate me, they were bang on the mark. I was wearing my lucky brown underpants. It was damage limitation time.

They gave me an ultimatum, now I don't know about you, but I never ever respond to an ultimatum. Ambrose Bierce once said, 'The definition of an ultimatum is the last warning before resorting to concessions'.

Sure enough, after further intense interrogation, I was given extended bail from the most secure cop shop in the country. Houdini couldn't have escaped from there. I would advise any would-be terrorist: take up botany, stamp collecting or morris dancing. It must have affected David Grant, as he did a bunk to the Dominican Republic. If this was a feature film, the audience would be yelling: *pull the other one, this is bullshit.* The stark truth was, I would be taking the flak unilaterally.

What a bummer to start the Summer.

Could things deteriorate?

You betcha. A few months later, they came for me. It was early September 2009, and I was just enjoying the last remnants of a breakfast for champions; half of last nights cold kebab, two roll-ups and mug of tea with five sugar lumps. City of London Police arrived at the flat with an arrest warrant. It was nice to feel wanted. I now had both the capital's finest fighting over me. They wanted my nuts on a plate. If they formed an orderly queue, I'm sure all the minor misunderstandings could be resolved amicably. It was nice to be the voice of reason. The charge was twenty three counts of alleged false representation of credit cards, including one from Wonderbra model Eva Herzigova.

I was taken to City of Westminster Magistrates' Court. I knew it well. Not personally, but it was originally called Horseferry Road Magistates' Court, which was the place a good percentage of football hooligans had their cases heard. A few naughty boys of my acquaintance have had their wrists slapped there. I would settle for that myself, but there was more chance of Snoop Dogg winning a rosette at Crufts.

There's not a lot one can do at a hearing. The charges were read out, the magistrates had that stern, steely look of disdain. I'd seen more compassion in a glass eye. The police were on form, and they opposed bail. I don't think it mattered, a change of scenery was definitely on the cards. The upshot, three months' custody in the Wandsworth Hotel. Could have been worse, it did have a bad reputation once, but recently the authorities were making a concentrated effort to improve conditions.

All I wanted to do was get my head down for ninety days. Is that too much to ask? Confrontation is a young man's game. By some warped coincidence, I discovered a man called Victor John Terry had been one of the last men to be hanged here in 1961. The next day his modern day namesake was requested to attend his local police station to answer questions in the ongoing inquiries of the case.

At this juncture, I'd like to apologise profusely to John Terry. He was the innocent recipient of a Dubaian holiday, paid for originally by me with a dodgy credit card. At no stage was he wittingly involved in any attempted fraud. He was swiftly exonerated of any involvement, but the national papers published the connection between us. The old *nudge-nudge, wink-wink* brigade were rampant. The phrase, *No smoke without fire* was mentioned, but John Terry was blameless. He didn't need this bullshit, he had enough problems of his own without me driving a Chieftain tank onto his lawn.

Derek 'Let him have it' Bentley, and William 'Lord Haw Haw' Joyce were two amongst many that were hanged here. Blimey, the last bloke only spoke on the radio... It was a tough world in those days, they even dished out the Cat o' nine tails and the birch in the fifties. Ronnie Biggs did a bunk in 1965. What was he thinking? Nearly forty years living by the Copacabana Beach with an exotic leggy nightclub dancer. What a waste.

All in all, it wasn't a bad regime there. I got in with the landing screw. He was a good old boy who'd seen many changes in his career as a turnkey. I was having a gripe after dinner one afternoon, and he says, 'Faisal, if you can't do the time, don't do the crime.'

I'd heard it hundreds of times before, but I made out it was a blinding new witticism. I broke into feigned and uncontrollable laughter, 'Stop it boss, stop it, you're killing me.'

'Have you not heard that one before lad?', he asked. I was shaking my head like neurotic head banger. I told him he was wasted here, and that he should be doing stand up. Off he strode down the landing, a spring in his step. A star was born.

The rest of my time there was a doddle. He looked after me like a surrogate son. All I had to do was laugh profusely at a couple of lame jokes every day. To be fair, by the time I was due to go back to court, he was actually making me laugh for real. He had really improved and it was lovely to see him come out of his shell. He was definitely funnier than Jack Dee.

At the second preliminary hearing at Colchester Magistrates, it was another fine day for British justice. It was known in the trade as a *total fuck-up,* and it would live long in the memories of this fine establishment. I didn't feel great on the way to the court, and the security thought I was swinging the lead, but by the time we reached the entrance hall I was feeling, as the Aussies say, *bloody crook, Bruce.* I'm not sure how much stress I could have taken that day, but it was taken out of my hands.

The CPS were there, the lady barrister had turned up, I was present and correct. In fact all the gang were in town. Pity we didn't have a court room to proceed any further. The two independent London police forces had amalgamated the different charges into one case. There was one hell of a crossed wire as both forces thought the other had booked the court room. You really couldn't make it up.

I wanted to laugh, but felt like a bag of rusty nails. I was sinking into oblivion, and they realised I wasn't faking it after I collapsed in the corridor. An ambulance was sent for, and the next thing I remember is being administered oxygen and being loaded onto a stretcher. As I was being wheeled through the hall, I spotted the clerk of the court, head bowed, chin on his chest, talking to himself, 'We've housed three Roman legions, survived two World Wars, numerous blizzards and floods, now he turns up and it all turns to crap'.

As we went past, I was going to give him the thumbs up, but wasn't up to it. The scene resembled the last minute of a Fawlty Towers episode. My only regret was that I was feeling too ill to enjoy it at the time. The ambulance headed straight for Colchester Hospital, where I spent two nights before being transferred to the medical wing at Chelmsford Prison. There are a few football connections here: the 1979 film *Porridge* was shot here. The script revolved around an organised celebrity football match in the prison. I can't believe it was that long ago, Rene Artois was the coach driver... I mean Gorden Kaye. Fletch and Godber come up trumps once again. This was one of the few television situation comedies that morphed successfully onto the big screen. Richard Beckinsale died shortly after the film was released. One of the good guys, he went too soon.

Tony Adams and Ian Wright have spent short holidays in Chelmsford, and I know Tony liked a drink, but Wrighty served a fortnight for having no car tax and insurance. That's a strange one though - I can't believe that's worth a custodial sentence.

He later fronted the excellent *Football Behind Bars*, a TV series set in Portland Young Offenders Institution, based on the premise of setting up a prison football team and academy. Wrighty's enthusiasm, coupled with genuine concern and interest for the teenage inmates, shone through in every episode. The man's a winner and a very talented pundit.

The medical wing at Chelmsford was top notch. It was better than BUPA. The facilities were great, but I was itching to get home. Behind the scenes the police had been the subject of a good rollicking after the debacle at Colchester, and my brief was pushing for bail. Apparently the Met and City of London were nowhere near finalising their enquiries. They simply wanted me to rot in jail. Remember, at this stage, I hadn't actually been found guilty of anything. A combination of police ineptitude and my vulnerable medical condition meant a proposed middle ground solution. So, in December 2009 I was released on electronic tag. *Ding dong merrily on high, Madani's home for Christmas...* sing that, it scans lovely.

I was as happy as a thirsty cat under a leaky cow. Of course there were pros and cons, but I was home with loved ones and everyday I wore that tag, it was a day off any prison sentence that would be dished out to me in the future. On the reverse side, I had to be in the flat between 7 pm and 7 am, so no more night matches. Thank God for Sky TV.

Do you know how long I had to wear that electronic tag? Try two and a half years. I'm sure that they weren't designed to *Big Brotherise* you for that length of time. I was sick of the sight of it after 900 days. Don't forget the police hadn't got their act together in bringing the case to court. If you add the four months I'd already served in Wandsworth and Chelmsford, it had taken just shy of three years to put a relatively uncomplicated case before the beak. The police couldn't be totally sure I was guilty, but they were prepared to nick three years off my life if they could. Now I'm not griping for myself, you know me, my pain is self-inflicted. I can do the time for white collar crime. I know the pitfalls. I'm rooting for the poor innocent sod after me that has to rot away in custody, while the police vacillate with the truth.

It's happened before and it will happen again. Someone spending two years in custody, only to reach the courthouse and then be informed there is no case to answer. Heavy politics all this, but somebody high up in authority must legislate soon about the scandalous amount of time some people are imprisoned for pre-trial periods.

For me, it was a blessed relief when the Eva Herzigova case - as it became known - finally came to court. It had knocked the crap out of me mentally. I was even calling out *Eva, Eva* in my sleep. Sharon wanted to know who this other woman was. She was a laugh-a-minute, but she had been through a lot, and the curfew meant we hadn't gone out socially at all at night or been back up to Manchester to see her mum. A holiday was absolutely out the question. All these activities are the norm for most households. Lots of things we all take for granted taken away, not fair at all for her.

D-Day was set for late June 2012 at Southwark Crown Court. The daddy of all fraud courts. If you get a gig there, some serious shit is going down. They don't entertain run-of-the-mill goldbrickers. I arrived to find a healthy posse of press, but the majority had lost interest, retired or died waiting for closure.

It was the end of a long, tortuous, dusty dirt track to justice. I had hoped I would get a fair trial, and with the tag accumulation, in the eyes of the law, I had already served the equivalent of 34 months behind bars. The Judge Alistair McCreath seemed a just man. He had presided on the acquittal of Tulisa Conto-stavlos, and the conviction of Gary Glitter. Nothing wrong there. My worry was, he was obliged to give me more bird. There was no way I was walking out, time served. I prayed he wouldn't hand out a six or a seven, but I had started to become a bloody nuisance to the authorities. I was 48, not old, but mature enough to know I was beginning to get on their tits. There was even a rumour floating about that a deportation was on the cards. There was nothing to do but throw myself on the mercy of the court.

I put my hands up to trying to spend 110K on other peoples' credit cards, for top footballers to travel to Dubai, seventeen counts of fraud and three counts of possessing fake ID papers, including Greek and Tunisian passports. I was bang to rights. I wasn't the mystifier, but a very naughty boy. Just for good measure the prosecution weighed in with David Grant's counterfeit currency.

Nice.

Helen Malcolm QC stated that I claimed to know some footballers. That was the equivalent of saying Red Rum has jumped a few fences round Aintree. It was all low-key, and she informed the court of nothing we didn't already know. The case was a cinch. I wasn't denying anything. My lawyer Chris van Hagen came up with a cracker in mitigation, 'The hallmark of most con men is financial gain, here is a man who suffers from vanity'.

I don't even own a comb or mirror, and he'd only known me half an hour. I think he'd been on the wacky baccy. An ounce of Dutch Haze had turned him into Hercule Poirot.

All I was interested in was the sentence, and I didn't have long to wait. It was all over in 20 minutes. Judge McCleath waded in with four and a half years. Extremely fair, all sides satisfied, the funny money tariff was four months to run concurrently, another problem sorted. I worked out in my head that I had ten months still to serve. Not bad really. The nightmare was receding, but I had seen the light.

It had become crystal during the discourse, that all my money was going to the footballers. I had turned into a modern day retarded Robin Hood, robbing the rich to give to the even richer. Van Hagen had come up with vanity, but it was sheer stupidity that was driving me. Most of the footballers were using me. I knew in my heart the ones that mattered. I was on the road to Damascus, not physically, that was too dangerous, but in my mind I had been converted... no more gifts, no more charity.

My designated jail was Highpoint, a Category C in Newmarket, Suffolk. It didn't look that high to me, that area must be the flattest part of Britain. The records say the highest football ground in England is The Hawthorns, home of West Brom, but what about Summit Park, home of Scafell Pike Rovers? Definitely a serious contender.

I quickly settled in. A very progressive prison with educational courses and numerous workshop projects - a thinking man's establishment. The screws were superb, and there was no tension or malevolence. It would be a toss-up between Buckley Hall or Highpoint on which was better, both had excellent facilities. This is the way to treat many offenders, respect was a satisfying two way street at Highpoint. The authorities investing time and effort in cons who had been forgotten and written off, but then this being reciprocated by the same people trying to better themselves.

I'm starting to sound like a Liberal Lefty, which I'm not. Murderers, paedophiles, rapists and terrorists should still do hard labour, eat frugally and sleep on the floor for three years. OK, maybe a bit harsh, but I'm a secret admirer of Anne Widdecombe. I like hard women and she's five-foot-one of mean machine.

Colchester was only an hour away, Sharon could take a leisurely drive up, swerve past the odd racehorse and take in all the scenery round Newmarket. It really was a stunning part of the world. I was content. There was a TV in my cell, I was getting plenty of sleep, the food was great and my health was holding up. If it carried on like this, I was considering putting in a request to stay longer.

Tony Martin the ex-farmer had done a stint at Highpoint. And there was a rumour going round that the governor, for some reason, would never turn his back on him. George Michael had done four weeks, for driving while under the influence of drugs. A sad saga, but it was never reported that his chauffeur was lying on the back seat, pissed. Where was Andrew Ridgeley when you needed him.

One of the workshops was involved in the destroying and recycling of counterfeit goods that had been intercepted by customs officers in the busy freight port of Felixstowe. This was a plum job at Highpoint as you can imagine. The possibility of smuggling some designer gear out of the workshop into the general confines of the prison was very tempting and beneficial to the inside workers.

177

For all the good intentions of the authorities, when one analysed this situation and peeled back the many layers of skin to the bone, the gist of the matter was obvious. Here was a large establishment full of men, the majority of who were thieves or fraudsters, so if security was lax, some or all of those involved would take advantage. It was human nature. I've never studied psychology, but one didn't need to be Freud or Jung to know that even the elite like something for nothing. The MPs expenses scandal bore that out. The very worst being champagne socialists, as once they get their snouts in the trough they never come up for air, so they could hardly excuse men on the bottom rung for moving a few togs.

I'd like to say the odd shirt found its way out, but it was like Milan fashion week: on a good day, you could get anything - Burberry coats, Armani jeans, Hugo Boss suits, Gucci shoes with accessories like Louis Vuitton belts and Ray-Ban sunglasses. A few of the black guys looked like pimps from Chicago. The bloke three cells down from me was from Eltham, but he was the double of Huggy Bear from Starsky and Hutch. I acquired a brown leather jacket for half an ounce of tobacco - very nice indeed. We didn't have our freedom, but by God we had some dignity.

The ten month tail-end of my sentence, came and went in the blink of an eye. I'd vowed no more monkey business. I was approaching my half century, and enough was enough. Sharon picked me up. It was time to enjoy the simpler things in life. I had no idea though, what was around the corner.

They say God laughs at those who make plans.

After what came next, he certainly had a unique sense of humour.

*　*　*　*

CHAPTER 18

THIS OLD HEART OF MINE

Arabic saying: A known mistake is better than an unknown truth

The nightmare was finally over. No more tags, no more police raids, no more appearances in court. I now had the rest of my life to live and ponder. What was wrong with just getting by? Not a lot. I was feeling healthy and relaxed, which was much more preferable than being the richest bad dude in the morgue.

Sharon had suffered from bad colds and flu all that long last Winter, which were still persisting right into the clement Spring. I had noticed some sinister black mould in the bedrooms and bathroom, which weren't apparent before my unpaid sabbatical, so we enlisted a damp specialist to have a right good gander. It turned out, not only did we have bad condensation, which in reality looks a lot worse than it is, but also penetrating damp which is extremely unhealthy, especially long term.

I made the decision there and then, slugs were not our pals, so we were definitely moving. Whilst in jail, the family in Dubai had rallied round for moi and remitted over to England a tidy lump sum. Not a fortune, but enough to make a difference. An ongoing legitimate business enterprise had also yielded a dividend, so wonga worries were on the back burner. Another big consideration for the move, were the cats, they had never been outside before. We'd find a place with a big garden so they could then have a run and a romp.

I was extremely grateful to Payman and his family, but I had to put my family first. We gave him a month's notice and Sharon went house hunting. We loved Colchester. If it was good enough for the Romans to make it the capital, that would do for us. In the end we only moved a quarter of a mile from Hanbury Gardens to Northfield Gardens. She found a cracking four bed house. We hadn't had 'an upstairs' for years, so we were figuratively going up in the world again.

Of course, we were renting, and a mortgage was out the question. Even if I'd got enough funds to buy one outright, I'd have knocked it back. There was still a bitter taste concerning our bungalow in Bramhall. An English man's home is his castle. Many people have lost their residences for a variety of reasons, and it is a traumatic experience you never forget. There is an old English word called *rapine* - it means to lose your property by pillage. Well, I had been rapined all right, and embrocation wasn't going to do justice to my sore fiscal regions.

We settled in right away. I had another surprise for Sharon, as I came back home one day with another two Persian cats - Rio and Oscar. You can't have too many moggies. There were now six mouths to feed, but Madani was up to it. No more money was heading for the millionaire footballers, they'd just have to slum it, with their huge pay cheques and promotional rights,

With my hell-raising days behind me, I settled down to enjoy a less hectic, more mundane, slower-paced life with Sharon. Together, with a fair trade wind and a following current, we could both retire from public life gracefully. I would have happily taken that plunge, but kismet was about to give me one last buffeting - that's a euphemism for a fucking good thrashing. I would be writhing on the floor, four skinheads kicking seven bells out of me, and every time I attempted to rise, a size twelve scuffed Dr. Marten boot would dispatch me back down again to mother earth.

June 4th 2013 was a day like so many other Summer days. I'd kept my nose clean for two months, Highpoint was a distant memory, and Sharon and myself were enjoying the sunshine allied with the hustle and bustle of shopping on the Edgware Road. Health-wise I'd been in the pink for over two and a half years, but this was to be my Mt. St Helens moment. My chest felt like it was being gripped in a giant vice, sweat was cascading off me, I was as groggy as a man who hadn't slept for three nights and then walked into an uppercut off Tyson Fury.

With absurd optimism, we returned home after I felt considerably better on the way back to Essex. I never like to make a drama out of a crisis, but once back, the pains started shooting through my body again. Sharon phoned 999 and I was rushed into Colchester Hospital. It was so serious, that I was knocked out there and transferred, under sedation, straight over to the Basildon Cardiology Unit. One of the best departments in the country - it's full of talented heart specialists who have, over the years, performed many groundbreaking operations, some in dire circumstances. I was, at least, in good hands.

Apparently, I died twice on the route between the two Essex hospitals and was painstakingly resuscitated by the phenomenal ambulance crew. I owe my life to them. Thanks lads, you're amazing. Can anyone believe scumbags throw stones and bricks at these medical paragons?

Stretchered into the high dependency intensive care ward, I was in a world of pain. Two nurses were on standby twenty four hours a day. There were more wires coming out of me than a dysfunctional Dalek. A gruesome 24-inch needle was pumping oxygen through an artery to the heart from an opening in the top of my thigh. Heavily dosed on a morphine drip, I'd been in much better situations.

I was bedridden there for three weeks, most of the time unconscious. Sharon was coming in everyday providing a welcome and pleasant relief, but I was out the game for hours on end. The powers that be wanted to perform open heart surgery, but I was too weak. It was a very risky proposition, my pancreas was only operating at ten per cent. I was very poorly, and the future prospects weren't that great either.

I came home as weak as a blue baby. Ten pills a day were the only things keeping me alive. I was immediately referred to Papworth Hospital in Cambridge, home of some of the World's greatest heart and lung specialists. On five different occasions we consulted five of Papworth's best heart surgeons. At least they were unanimous - a heart transplant was the only way to go. None of them were prepared to operate, but the consensus was I had - give or take - six months to live.

At this stage I was a dead man walking (or shuffling in my case). I was scared stiff. I'd not been this worried since Sharon phoned me late one night and said she'd broken down on a deserted forest lay-by waiting for the RAC to come out, when Stan Colleymore tapped on the side window.

I could still laugh, even in troubled times, and they didn't come much worse than this. One had to be strong, cry a river, then build a bridge.

But a complete fluke gave me hope. A friend from Ipswich named Vic, recommended his brother-in-law, an Indian heart surgeon called Rakesh. He'd performed surgery on ex-Aston Villa manager John Gregory, and also on actor-comedian Rowan Atkinson... although he had drawn the line when asked to remove the late Lemmy's facial warts. If Mr. Bean was prepared to go under the knife, then so could I, but at that present time the particular risky operation that was required had only been attempted four times worldwide and had never even been considered before in Britain. I was game though. A plucky trailblazer. Nobody remembers who finishes second. I could even find my name in The Lancet. The trouble was though, I could also find it in The Times obit column. Nothing was out of bounds, all I needed to throw was a double six.

In truth, I was shitting myself. As I grew older I'd acquired a degree of humility, so I decided any future epitaph would read: *He aimed low in life... and missed.*

People would appreciate that much more. God loves a modest man. It reminded me of the new priest in his parish presiding over a funeral for the first time. He gave a short eulogy for the deceased, who hadn't been the best of men, followed by an appeal to all the people there for a last kindly word. There was an awkward silence for over a minute, until a voice from the back piped up... 'His brother was far worse'.

We met Rakesh at Wellington Hospital in St John's Wood. It was only 200 yards away from where I was arrested with the funny money. This time I needed almighty providence in Middlesex, as the opposite wasn't worth considering. The maestro took me to one side, and he was candid enough to tell me the odds weren't on my side, but if I was willing to go through extensive tests and there was even the slightest possibility of a favourable outcome, he would operate. I clasped his hand, I would happily take my chance. The stents from previous operations couldn't and wouldn't uphold minimum health requirements, blocked and diseased arteries would have to be replaced in a sextuple open heart bypass.

After three months of tests, the team were ready to rock. I was really scared, but that's how I rolled. Triple bypasses are not uncommon, six of the best however was cutting edge. In 1492 Columbus and his crew imagined they would sail off the edge of the World because they were heading into a situation unknown for mankind. I had since run out of options leaving me no choice but to follow their example and plunge head first into the black abyss of uncertainty.

On the 18th November 2014, I went under the knife. Two hours in, I died yet again and came back. I was making more comebacks than Take That. The operation used grafts from my left leg, culminating in 86 staples being used to hold all my body parts in place. The ultra complex operation lasted eleven and a half hours, with a further five days on top, as I lay helplessly in an induced coma. While I was under the effects of the anaesthetic, I bounced a cheque for five thousand pounds.

Sure, old habits were dying hard even in my sleep.

The Wellington Hospital was charging five hundred pounds a day. It was a dear do this living, but I didn't fancy the alternative. I came round on the Friday night, and I swear to God this is true, the television screens were beaming out Jackpot 247 the interactive roulette game on ITV. I focused just as the ball fell into red 30 - one of my favourite numbers! At that moment I thought I had died and gone to heaven.

For ten minutes I felt like a Roman God, but it was JUST a passing phase, and for the next 18 days I felt like a decomposing turd. Certainly not the best nine grand I've ever spent, for sure. It was going to be months, not weeks, in recuperation, but the main thing was, I was alive. Dr. Rakesh had come through. 95 per cent of the heart had been under-performing, but I now had a second chance. However, my life's ambition of replacing Michael Flatley in Riverdance was shot to pieces. But what can you do.

I'm forever in the debt of Rakesh, a great man, who will go right to the top. It took until February 2015 for all the incisions to heal, but the side effects were harder to shift. More chest pain, bouts of depression, sleep disturbance, mood changes, dizziness and diarrhea. My nasal sinuses were constantly bunged up, and I was beginning to feel like Toxteth O'Grady, but as he was world champ, I soldiered on. The daily pill dose had gone up to sixteen. I was only averaging one erection a month too. Scrub that...

I wasn't getting that many when I was well.

I was picking up bucketfuls of medicine at the chemist dispensers at the local Tesco. I shouldn't laugh, but one day they mixed up the prescriptions. A local guy who needed blood pressure pills got my sleeping tablets and I got his pills. It could all have been fatal. He kept falling asleep at work, but of course it made no difference to me. I was a walking, talking medicine cabinet. My solicitor Mark Lomas is currently on the job, so is the other side. Tesco have lost so much money recently, that another payout won't hurt them too much.

So that was the *operation to end all operations*. Every single day now is a bonus. And whether I live six months, six years or sixty years, I walk around with a smile on my face. Football is huge again, and I've been to see games at Manchester United, Arsenal, Ipswich and Colchester.

There's a lot of life left in the old dog and many more matches to see before that big game in the sky.

* * * *

CHAPTER 19

HIS FINEST HOUR

Arabic saying: He who plants thorns must never expect to gather roses

This is the first day of the rest of my life.

I'd heard that statement many times before; the violent man who had turned to pacifism, the wicked man who had found God Almighty, the drinker who had beaten the booze, the drug addict who had cleansed his body and the reformed man who had changed to win back his wife and kids. Now at 50 years of age, dying three times on and off the operating table meant it really was a new concept I was undertaking. Dr. Rakesh had giving me the gift of life, the most precious gift in the universe. I was still having a crafty puff on the odd roll up, madness I know, but it was a great relaxative. Sharon had suggested acupuncture to wean me off smoking, but I've never understood how sticking needles in your cigarette could stop you smoking.

Everything post-operation is a different ball game. You evaluate things differently, see things that weren't evident before. One's priorities change dramatically, but most of all, every morning after you wake up, golden sun majestically rising in the sky, curtains gently wafting in the cool breeze, birds merrily chirping in the back garden, you thank the Lord Almighty for all these underrated experiences - for all the things you once just took for granted before your scare. You lumber lazily down the stairs towards the beckoning sunbeams permeating through the coloured leaded glass of the front door, and there's only one message you can relay to your beloved wife, a woman diligently preparing your early morning muesli, 'Sharon, that bloody paper boy's late again... lazy little sod'.

To be fair, I wasn't feeling too shabby after what I had been through, but nobody lives forever and all us mere mortals have deteriorating standards of health as the body physically implodes, but never-ending ambition and a noble challenge can still help one get through the day. There was still life in the old dog. Maybe I wouldn't write a pop classic like The Killers' *Mr Brightside*, score a try like Gareth Edwards for the Barbarians against the All Blacks or get a pound in front of Warren Buffett, but I still had a bunch of piles to make Powerful Pierre the Beaujolais grape farmer gasp, 'Que c'est delicieux!'.

I took an unexpected phone call one evening - it was my old prison buddy Shane Martin, a man I had befriended at Highpoint. We had gelled like yin and yang and discussed going into business together straight after we both got out. You know the scenario: most of the time it's just old lag talk to get you through the monotonous months, namely a whimsical pipe dream, never to materialise.

He'd set up a Gibraltar-registered firm, Welgelee Holdings. Did Mr. Fix-it want to get involved? Could I have a week to think about it? No, that wouldn't do... Would it all be kosher and politically correct? Forget about it... I was gagging. In a nanosecond I was on the board. Any future profits would be going into our pockets, not the filthy rich footballers. They would have to now pay the piper, because the Madani gravy train was on the Dr. Beeching line.

Shane Martin had come to prominence with his involvement in an attempted audacious sting which had became universally known in the media as *The Fake Sheikh's Fraud*. It had nearly come off, only to unravel at the last knockings. Man, that was brilliant out-of-the-box thinking, which one could only admire from a distance and think: *I'd have liked a piece of that action*. Although it was criminality, I love ingenuity and balls, and that case had tanker loads.

So the boys were back in business. Without getting technical, Shane knew all about company law, loans, mortgages, tax and VAT. Yours truly: men back in Dubai, who would assist the right companies for share rights and profit on their outlay. I'm yawning here myself, but for all you young ambitious empire builders out there, this is just what you want to hear, ways of getting your semi-fledgling company to the top, very quickly.

We traded successfully for about eighteen months, both of us noting that a lot of the people we were helping were a lot dodgier than our good selves. *Swimming with sharks* is a well-known euphemism which is particularly appropriate for our predicament at that time. We had set off a million alarm bells on that glorious day we opened shop. The unholy alliance of Martin and Madani was never going to go unnoticed by the boys in blue. And, sure enough, City of London police were monitoring us from the very first phone call. More importantly, we perceived that, as inept as they were, the authorities were in for the long haul. What we didn't anticipate was enough foul play to make the 1962 World Cup match between Chile and Italy - known as The Battle of Santiago - resemble a tea dance at the old folks home. They came at us hard. The rule book was rewritten *Panzer style*. They wanted us on our knees. They sent in the dogs of war to crush us. And we didn't even have a pair of shin pads between us.

There is an unhealthy relationship between City of London police and Her Majesty's Revenue and Customs - they are both guilty of going after high profile collars. If the truth gets squeezed now and then, so be it. A conviction for a well-known star is worth all the crap they take when they don't play fair.

When I was about to be sentenced for my last indiscretion and on tag, City of London frequently implored me to give evidence about Premier League players and managers. They hate with a passion the glamour and glitz, not to mention the vast amounts of money swilling in and around the game.

They wanted me to dish the dirt on players and managers I had associated with; John Terry, Ashley Cole, Rio and Anton Ferdinand, even Michael Owen (by God I was tempted there). There was no way I would ever do that, not for remission of a sentence. In fact nothing could make me do it. They wanted to know what I knew about Sir Alex Ferguson's dealings. He would have eaten them for breakfast. What did I know about Harry Redknapp's tax affairs? I knew he would thump them in court. That's what I knew. That case was so unfair, bringing a large slice of undue stress on Harry and his wonderful family. Just remember at this juncture, who brought that pantomime to court? You're ahead of me... City of London and HMRC. Suffering Succotash, there's a pattern emerging. Keep reading, the stench will become unbearable.

Clothes pegs a pound a bag...

City of London wanted me bad, and in Detective David Sutton they had a man who was willing to cross the line. In fact he would have crossed the Maginot Line, the Brighton Line and illegally parked on every bloody double yellow line, in his holy quest to bring Madani to book. It became an unhealthy obsession with him. It reminded me of Craig Lovato, an American Drug Enforcement Administration agent who hounded cannabis king Howard Marks all over the world. His life just revolved around busting Marks. It's nice to feel wanted, but it got to the stage where I expected to see Sutton looking up at me from the confines of the dustbin when I emptied the trash.

One of the remits of Welgelee Holdings was to help companies who were under the cosh from HMRC (remember them?). They weren't very keen on that arrangement, and their favourite bloodhound, the hapless City of London police were handed the bone to sniff out any underhandedness.

No one was safe, even the companies we helped were under suspicion. In their eyes everyone we were involved with were up to no good. A tug was inevitable, and mine came in unusual circumstances.

It was Christmas Eve 2015 when an unhealthy *rat-a-tat-tat* on the front door awoke me from my partial slumber on the sofa. The television was exuding relaxing alpine music, James Garner and Donald Pleasence flying over the snow-peaked mountains in a stolen German plane. I knew what was coming. I screamed inside, *don't fucking say it*. Too late. Garner said to his blind passenger mate, 'Another twenty minutes and we got it made'.

'You stupid twat, look at the fuel gauge!'. Engines all stalled, the landing wasn't going to be pretty.

I had a sinking feeling myself. Standing in the front room was Detective David Sutton. Sharon had let him in. 'Just popped round to tell you, official charges are now ready, three counts of conspiracy to defraud and two counts of fraud, this one is big enough for the Old Bailey'.

He had a smug, self-satisfied grin on his face. My reply soon wiped that off, 'Thank you detective, it's been a life's ambition to appear there. I've done the whole circuit now, magistrates', crown courts... and now the big one: the Old Bailey. That's the best Christmas present I've ever had! Would you like to stay for a drink?'.

Sutton was nonplussed. He had expected me to lose my rag. He declined the offer of a stiffener and skulked out. I had the upper hand. He couldn't fathom out if I was an evil genius, or a total nutter who was out of his depth.

Over the following months it was becoming crystal that individuals who had dealt with Welgelee were being offered a *get out of jail card* in the form of immunity from prosecution if they became witnesses for the CPS against the two Anti-Christs - namely Shane Martin and Faisal Madani. At this stage it was turning decidedly dirty. Truth was leaving town, an unwelcome interloper according to the prosecution. At the Westminster Magistrates' hearing the depositions were so shocking that for the first time in my life I was utterly speechless.

I had to pinch myself. An African businessman called Francis Arhin, who we had helped pay his HMRC bill, stated in a deposition that myself and a gang arranged a meeting at the Hilton Hotel, where we allegedly threatened to kill him unless he handed over £200,000. Anyone who knows me well could testify that was a crock of shit. I haven't a violent bone in my body. I've never even swatted a fly. That was a good start, an attempted murder charge. Francis apparently didn't know anything about it and suggested the offending wording was added after he had signed his statement. Surprise, surprise, there was no sign of any murder mayhem to put before the beak when the case was transferred to the Old Bailey. Had City of London shown mercy and turned a blind eye to extreme violence, or did the encounter never happen?

The silence was deafening.

Mischief was still abounding. The Preston Constabulary in the shape of the Serious Organised Crime Agency (SOCA) got their two bobs-worth in also. This one was a cracker. Apparently, I'd only gone and paid a convicted drug dealer's 'proceeds of crime' bill to Her Majesty's Courts and Tribunal Service. It was processed using a Bradford primary school's credit card to the tune of 26K. I was supposed to have paid it in person in Leeds. Two things were wrong with this top quality police investigation... one, I didn't know the recipient (nor had I ever heard of him), and two, I've never been to Leeds in my life. If SOCA were going to pull this one off, they would need divine intervention. They had no chance, barring miracles. I was slightly disappointed when that charge passed muster, but I thought if that was the standard of accusation, their bar must be set pretty low. I willingly accepted the three counts of conspiracy and two of fraud, confident that they could all be put to bed, but we would only really know on Sept 26th 2016 - location, The Old Bailey.

It would go down in history as one of the greatest trials ever heard there, the jury and judge are still talking about it.

After the Westminster hearing events were unfolding behind the scenes. The London papers had reported the transfer to The Old Bailey and my mobile was red hot with incoming calls. Amongst them were three or four from an ex-London Bridge Flying Squad Detective Constable, Lester Oakley. He offered his services in the upcoming case. Procuring a top quality solicitor and barrister were just two things he could do for me. Friends were telling me to be cautious, because in their eyes, he was a *wrong-un*.

He'd been involved with the force up to 2008, that was until he was unanimously convicted of six counts of theft involving the disappearance of 5K from police evidence storerooms. He copped three beautiful years for that, and when he came out records say he resigned from the force. Is that a nice way of saying *pushed?* Anyway, he never paid back the money. I don't blame him for that, but when The Met cut his pension in half he appealed, ironically, in 2011 at the Old Bailey. The poor lad was having a wretched run of bad luck. Case dismissed in double quick time, the judiciary can't abide bent coppers. To be fair, there's hundreds of the buggers out there, they just don't get caught, or their plight is covered up. (Sorry, I'm a terribly bitter and twisted old cynic).

So that was the man standing in front of me - a thief, a liar and a dodge-pot. What would you have done? Probably run a mile or told him to *do one*. Well, there were two ways of looking at this situation. I took the opinion that he would have a grudge against the Old Bill, more probably, a rancid, fermenting hatred. Here was a broken man who wanted deadly revenge against a formidable official body who had deprived him of his liberty, cast him out into a darker world and, for good measure, kicked him forcefully in the nuts with a huge pension reduction. The man was obviously looking for a saintly crusade, to heroically battle - cage fighter style - while bonding as tight as Gorilla Glue with the Madani campaign against the Blue Satan.

Obviously...

How fucking wrong I was! (I know I never back a winner, don't rub it in, I'm just very trusting).

The legal team Lester had assembled for me were Criminal Defence Barrister Quentin Hunt of Bedford Row Chambers (just North of the Thames near Regent's Park), and Solicitor Ian Kelcey, a rotund cove from Bristol. They both seemed affable and competent, so all was well at this stage.

I next received a letter from City of London, requesting my participation on an identity parade, courtesy of David Sutton. I didn't like the sound of that and phoned my new pal, Lester Oakley. He suggested that I go, so as not to antagonise them. But I wasn't having it.

'Listen Lester, my face is all over the internet. I'm on the telly more than Ant and Dec and I've been in the newspapers more than Brexit'. He was adamant it would help us, but I couldn't see an upside, so I gave Lester a compromise

'Ring Sutton up and tell him to drop his kegs and show his arse, because that's what my face looks like'. He responded that I couldn't say that to a serving officer. That's when I twigged on. Oakley was a plant. A fifth columnist.

And sure enough, when the trial commenced, he was a witness for the prosecution. They really were scraping the bottom of the barrel. The odd bad apple never falls far from the tree. Lester was batting for the home team again, and believe me, he was no Kevin Pietersen.

With the revelation that the *blues brothers* were an item once more and the trial imminent, I would have to keep a beady eye on my legal beagles, Hunt and Kelcey. I didn't have a lot of confidence in them after all the prior shenanigans, but we were where we were. (Try saying that, Jonathan Woss)

So, as a tribute to the aforementioned omnipresent Ant and Dec, *lets get ready to rumble* would have been appropriate.

Our friends from the paparazzi were clicking away merrily upon our arrival. They'd followed my career since the halcyon days of the magistrates' court visits. It brought a lump to the throat knowing that these fine, hard-working men of the street with their unsociable hours were still following their prodigal son - undoubtedly a flawed favourite, but always good value for a quote and an Everton Mint.

It was a star-studded extravaganza. The top man in court was judge Richard Hone QC. In the prosecuting corner was London Barrister Nicholas Hearn. Shane Martin had Barrister Gelaga King, a man with connections to Sierra Leone, and Yours Truly was represented by Quentin Hunt. Ironically, there would have been less carnage if Quentin Tarantino had actually scripted it all.

The prosecution main witness was restaurateur Ammar Wafaie, a man I had known for twenty years, and followed by other alleged wronged company executives, including Paul Beck, a man who had visited Shane Martin at Highpoint and even offered him a job when he finished his sentence. They had even drafted in my regular taxi driver, Eric, so they could validate my movements and track me by my mobile phone call records. If they could turn back time, they would have left him well alone, reading his paper back at the rank.

A week into the trial, it was turgid and tedious, with neither side emerging from the mire with any credit. When, *wallop* - the Madani curse struck again. The proceedings were suffocating me, and my poor old pancreas was underperforming and about to throw in the towel, while the heart palpitations were racing away like an over-tuned Subaru. The medics were sent for and they recommended five days rest away from the stress of court. Judge Hone was brilliant, telling me to take as long as I wanted. I informed the great man, that five days would suffice nicely. Easy as you like, the court adjourned for a one hundred and twenty reinvigorating hours.

During my recuperation, Sharon and I discussed what route we must now take, as a tactical switch was now needed, and therefore we decided heads must roll. I must admit the break did me a power of good and I emerged fully refreshed and eager for confrontation. I felt like a cross between Superman, Albert Pierrepoint and an albino - one for the purpose of strength, two for stringing my defence up and three to show the jury my lighter side. On returning bright-eyed and bushy-tailed, and bang on schedule, it was time to be proactive.

Somebody hold me back. I was on fire.

Outside the court room, Hunt and Kelcey approached me in the lobby, using my recent malaise as a reason to sound the retreat, Kelcey initiated, 'We can make an advantageous deal if you plead guilty and don't go in the box'.

I had seen this coming, but I needed my defence to fight to the death, as these two looked like they would jump a mile if a miniature poodle had cocked his leg near them. I countered somewhat curtly, 'This isn't over until the fat lady sings... not when the fat man waffles'.

I said this to see what reaction I would get back. Kelcey just looked down at his brogues. He was history. It was Quentin Hunt in my headlights next, 'Are you a fighter or a deal maker?', I demanded to know. He advised me to go for damage limitation. I now knew where I stood. It was time to go our separate ways - 'With a defence like you two, who needs an enemy? I can find milksops on every street. I'll defend myself and I'll do a better job!'.

Our jolly band met Richard Hone in judges' chambers, and about half an hour later Hunt and Kelcey tendered their resignations. Not the usual protocol at the Old Bailey, but at least destiny was now allied with my favourite person. If I was going to the slammer, it would be down to me, and me alone.

The common and well-advised line of the judiciary is as follows: Conduct your own defence in court, expect days of pain, followed by days inside. Most people who try and then fail are either arrogant, deluded or mentally unstable. Myself? - I was cocky. Always have been, but I was under no illusions about pulling this one off, and lastly, not all the lunatics were in the asylum and I did have the word *mad* in my surname. Nobody saw what was coming over the next two weeks.

Nostradamus couldn't have come close.

Mentioned earlier, star witness Ammar Wafaie was City of London's supposed white knight who had been fleeced. The defence would have to find a few chinks in his armour. Between Barrister Gelaga King and myself, his version of events made him look like the Black Knight in Monty Python's Holy Grail - utterly limbless and with nowhere to go.

I won't get into the minutiae of the totals involved, as everyone's tax affairs are of a personal and private nature, but you can rest assured, most of the amounts were a lot bigger than the postal order your auntie Kath sent you for your birthday when you were a nipper. A ballpark figure will suffice when we get down to the nitty-gritty. The following court minutes are not religiously in order, but just to get the maximum impact of the trial, so that's the way I'm rolling.

I had previously introduced Wafaie to Shane Martin when he was struggling to pay a large VAT bill. Through Welgelee Holdings we attempted to alleviate some of the pressure, and he later needed financial assistance as he was experiencing cash flow problems during a two million pound refurbishment of his second Lebanese restaurant, *The Mamounia Lounge* in Knightsbridge. I had been a patron of his other restaurant, *The Al Sultan* of Mayfair for two decades. In that time, I had brought many Premier League footballers there, in parties of up to ten.

To be fair to Ammar, he stated in court that, 'Mr. Madani would always ask if we needed anything or if could he help in any way. He would bring in signed football shirts, tickets, everything. He was very popular with all the staff'. That was very nice of him, but a lot of his evidence didn't make sense and there were irregularities that contradicted his version of events.

Shane Martin's pitbull Gelaga King was having none of it though. Wading in, he suggested Wafaie was not being honest with the jurors over his offhand remark that Madani was, in his opinion, a regular customer. He asserted, 'Madani in fact, was a very, very good friend, who was putting large amounts of money into the Al Sultan coffers by bringing famous footballers including England captain John Terry to his restaurant'.

Amazingly Wafaie couldn't ever recall seeing JT. (Tell little lies, and they all add up and come back to bite your backside).

King continued, 'You definitely knew Mr. Madani had been arrested and convicted for credit card fraud, which had John Terry answering a few police questions on his behalf. (Terry totally absolved) It was in all the papers and on the BBC'.

191

Then adding, 'What I am suggesting is that you and Madani used my client as a buffer. So, if anything went wrong, for example, the past problems Madani had when dealing with the footballers, would not come back to your front door'. (Jesus, even I hadn't seen that one coming. That put a different slant on it. Gelaga must be a chess grand master. The jury was looking totally bemused, even the judge raised an eyebrow.)

Wafaie was made of sterner stuff. He'd seen Lebanon fall, stone by stone, and the star witness would come back with an Oscar Wilde electric riposte. He stuck out his chest and meekly offered, 'I don't think so'.

A bit of an anticlimax, but that was the Prosecution main man. There wasn't a lot of depth following the Lebanese Lip.

When I was up in the box, even though Wafaie was a mate, I had to stick the knife in and twist it until he cheered up. Barrister Nicholas Hearn was the prosecution's Alpha Male. I had to better him not by law, but by unorthodoxy. I was asked what was my profession, 'I'm a conman'.

The jury gasped, and the judge commented that although out of the ordinary, it was pleasing to hear such candour. (Remember earlier, don't tell little lies)

I continued, 'I didn't go to prison for jay walking. I went for fraud'.

A few titters from the jury, and the judge was smiling. I carried on regardless, 'I look like a crook, even Stevie Wonder can spot me'.

There were hoots of laughter now, even the ushers and some of the prosecution bench were chuckling. Hearn trying to keep a straight face, continued, 'Mr Wafaie denies any knowledge of your criminal record'.

I knew that was a porkie. 'He was well aware. 98% of people who go to the casino or his restaurant have a criminal record. If you don't have one, you don't get in'.

The court was now in uproar. Hearn had seen enough... no more questions.

This case came to be known as the one in which the prosecution witnesses were far dodgier than the defendants. My last word on Ammar Wafaie - he was a humble waiter when I met him twenty years ago. Six years later he owned the *Al Sultan* in Mayfair, and today the *Mamounia Lounge* of Knightsbridge is his, including two million pound refurb. Not exactly backwater postcodes. You have to sell an awful lot of hummus and shish kebab to cover those overheads. I was in the dock for fraud, and he helped put me there. I had my little rented two up two down in Colchester, so you decide which of us were at it.

No contest.

Next up for the prosecution was company director Paul Beck. If this went tits up like the last, City of London only had a few minor financial indiscretions to rely on, but not enough clout to get a conviction. I was gutted for them. Paul Beck was impressed by Shane Martin and as the aforementioned had visited him in prison and a job offer was on the cards when Shane returned to Cheshire. On release Shane told Paul about my connections in Dubai and a meeting was arranged.

Again, through Welgelee Holdings, a deal was proposed. Beck to pay an up front fee to cover his tax commitments, with a three million pound loan to follow. His firm went into liquidation that year for well over three quarters of a million pounds, after pressure from HMRC.

Ouch.

Beck's time in the witness box was not very convincing. He could not answer the question - why would he associate with two convicted fraudsters, notwithstanding the handing over of a very large amount of money to them, on the premise he would receive back that amount tenfold. The judge had him sussed and took an immediate dislike to him. Here was a man trying to save his own skin and would say anything that helped that cause.

I decided I would give the *coup de grace* to the wounded hyena when I entered the witness box.

We were off and running again, and Nicholas Hearn stated, 'Mr. Madani, you took advantage of Paul Beck. He is a very generous man'.

I countered, 'You must be joking... Name one Yorkshireman in history who has thrown his money around'.

That stopped them dead in their tracks. I knew whose side the judge was on, when he commented, 'You may have a point there'.

Without stereotyping, I added that there was more chance of borrowing a penny for a pay toilet in Golders Green or Glasgow than in Batley. The sound of laughter was again on the rise. I was on a good run, so I kept it going.

'With a chief executive like Paul Beck, who needs a recession?'.

The jury liked that, and the judge was smiling. I went for the showstopper, 'In fact, Paul Beck is the Donald Trump of Cheshire'. (His company was there).

Hearn asked why, 'Because of his financial acumen?'.

'No, his bullshit', I replied. That brought the house down. The judge was laughing uncontrollably into his handkerchief, and I finished the hatchet job with an old saying from back in Dubai, where Beck would be compared to a Chinaman flying a chicken.

It was going very nicely at this stage, and outside in the lobby I didn't need a pollster to tell me we were winning on points. A knock-out might just save the prosecution from further embarrassment. A reporter from The Sun, shook my hand, 'You've got the judge and jury in the palm of your hand'.

I modestly told him that *it wasn't quite over yet.*

A barrister from another case which had finished earlier had ambled into the courtroom after hearing howls of laughter, 'Wonderful stuff, you should have sold tickets', he snorted, patting me on the back. The best was yet to come though. I spotted David Sutton getting a bollocking from a senior detective. I just caught, 'He's fucking running rings round you... an unmitigated fucking disaster!', before the 'tec stormed out the courthouse. That was the sweetest compliment of the three, and the ironic outcome of all this, City of London Police never turned up again for any of the last six days. They bottled it. Never a good sign for an institution.

There were still plenty of highlights to come, mainly from the defence. The minor prosecution witnesses were useless, the barristers were just going through the motions, but taxi driver Eric brightened up proceedings. The prosecution were establishing my movements over certain days with mobile phonecall records, and, of course, my taxi destinations. This was a pointless exercise that went nowhere, so when I had the opportunity to cross-examine, what harm could it do? Eric was extremely nervous when he was gently quizzed by Hearn, and if anything, had badly deteriorated by the time I confronted him. He didn't want to be there, so I made it easy for him, 'Eric, you usually pick me up from my home address or from Colchester railway station'.
'That's right sir'.
'Would you say that was a few times a week Eric?'. He nodded.
'I'll take that as a *yes*', I said.
The normal itinerary was, my house to the station when time was not pressing, but straight to London if I got behind the clock. I asked Eric about the fares; London was 44 miles away, the station was 3 miles. He said the journey to London was £8 and the trip to the station was £95. Titters of laughter. I asked him to reconsider. He really had cracked. He repeated, London £8, station £95. Hearn had his head in his hands. He'd put up with some duffers, it looked like he was the next to lose the plot. This was a chance for comedic gold.
'On that basis Eric, if you took me to Scotland, would you owe me money?'.
The blank look on his face was priceless, akin to pressing him for the secrets of alchemy, I put him out of his misery, 'No more questions'.
The laughter just kept coming.

Hearn wasn't happy about being a bad second with yours truly, and back in the box he started punching below the belt, 'I've heard you do all the dirty work for the footballers. When they want prostitutes or loose women, you're the man they call'.

That was a gross misrepresentation. He knew that was a lie and I couldn't let it pass. 'They are quite capable themselves on that score. In fact I'm the last man to phone... In my condition, I need to take two Viagra a day just to make sure I don't wee on my Hush Puppies'.

Now, more muted cheers than laughter. The jury was right behind me.

He was trying to wind me up of course, hoping my jovial demeanour would slip. The last desperate measures of a drowning man, clutching at straws, 'When you met Shane Martin at Highpoint Prison, you came across a man who was a cheat, a liar and a fraudster on the same level as yourself'.

This was my chance.

'I was on £9 a week, working full time. After tobacco, Rizlas and Mars Bars, I was left with £1.50. Shane Martin was a different matter. He was the most powerful man in the land'.

Everyone was listening now, Judge Hone asked quietly, 'Could you elucidate, Mr. Madani?'.

I continued. 'He was known as the *Ginger Robert Mugabe*. You could thrive or starve on a whim, he was in charge of a large scoop in the canteen. If he liked you, extra mash or sausages would fall on your plate. But he also had weapons of mass destruction'.

A serious gasp went up. The judge and the prosecution were all ears.

'His own-recipe onion bhajis and cauliflower cheese which could cause wicked havoc with your bowel movements', I replied.

A black juror was guffawing loudly, slapping his thigh with delight. Women had tears in their eyes. I'd got the judge, he was away.

'Five minute recess'.

It was the first time in my court appearances that the courtroom hadn't stood up for a judges departure. It was too late, he was gone.

The judge returned shortly after, 'You got me there Mr. Madani. You have a most interesting way of expressing yourself'. I cheekily said he should have taken ten or twenty minutes if he needed it, but he shook his head while pouring himself a glass of water. Was this all a dream? A phantasmagoria? Whatever I tried, came off. The Gods were with me. It would be sacrilege to cock it up at this late stage.

I was still having a ding-dong with Nicholas Hearn, but at least I was holding my own. Popular opinion may have even had me ahead on points. I enquired at one stage where Detective David Sutton was. Hearn loyally covered for him by stating he was away on important police work. I informed the courtroom that this was a shame, because I was worried about him, as I'd had a disturbing revelation which I conveyed to all assembled...

The top of his head had been removed and in the orifice was a note signed by God, 'I owe you one brain'.

The jury loved it. They had known for days that this had been a stitch-up by City of London, but it was one trial they were all glad to be a part of. Hearn wasn't safe himself, so I gave him both barrels, 'You are the unluckiest barrister I have ever met. Your witnesses have included; a bent copper, a drug dealer, a money launderer, a dyscalculic cabbie, and four billy liars. You haven't run over a black cat - you must have run over a basketful'.

He was a good sport. He was nodding thoughtfully.

I followed up with an analogy for him; 'You are not a chef, I'm not a chef, but by the size of our bellies, we both know a good steak. If anyone thinks that the prosecution witnesses are good steaks, then they are very much mistaken. They are worse than me and I would give anybody a month's diarrhoea'.

One last tease wouldn't go amiss. I asked Hearn what CPS stood for. He came back with, 'Crown Prosecution Service'.

I made out that I'd just lost a big bet, and added, 'I was sure it meant *Criminal Protection Society*'.

I'd had my fun it was time to take a back seat, but not before the judge asked me one last question, 'The first witness, Mr. Wafaie mentioned you had been on the board of Manchester United, is that true?'.

As you know from previous chapters, there was a member of the board who had the surname Midani, and if people thought it was me, no problem. 'I can do better than that Your Honour. I bought Manchester United twice'.

The prosecution woke up from their near comatose death. '...But on Play Station for £75'.

They went back to sleep, the jury was with me right to the end. Judge Hone was most excellent. 'I'm sorry Mr. Madani, your time in the box is finished, regretfully, just as we were so intrigued and the jury were enjoying themselves so much'.

I puffed out my cheeks. I'd given it my best shot. I knew it was enough, but it had knocked the stuffing out of me. I could sleep for a month on a greasy clothes line rocked by Hurricane Katrina.

Judge Hone began his summing up and direction for the jury, even though the result looked a formality, he had to go through the motions. He directed a few kind words towards me, 'This was your finest hour. Now retire gracefully and slowly fade into the shadows'.

A lovely tribute which I'll take with me to the other side. He schooled the jury with a little gem, 'This has been a privilege for us all. You may have witnessed the most entertaining case ever heard in this historic building. I for one cannot recall an occasion to better it'.

After he finished his learned advocacy, he instructed that I didn't have to be in court while the verdict was being reached. Another astonishing act of kindness by this great man who, for me, was standing on the shoulders of legal giants.

It never came to fruition of course. The jury was out for less than an hour. They were beaming when they returned and, surprise, surprise, *not guilty* on all charges for Shane and myself, including the ridiculous allegation of paying the drug dealer's fiscal penalty for the proceeds of crime. I gave Shane a hug and a handshake, 'I'm going for a kip'.

He was going for a pint. The courtroom emptied quickly, like it had all never happened.

There were just two people left, 'Come on Sharon, let's go home'. We sprang out of the Old Bailey into London's early evening, fading light. It was raining quite heavily.

Where the bloody hell was Eric, just when you needed him.

*   *   *   *

CHAPTER 20

AFTERGLOW

Old English saying: Good girls are just bad girls that never got caught

Richard Hone retired in February 2017. The man deserves a long and happy retirement. In my eyes he is an immortal and should live forever, truly one of the good guys involved in jurisprudence. I wish the same could be said of detective David Sutton, who apparently has joined the National Crime Agency. I only hope now that the police will back off and leave me be, but they still seem to be sniffing around, looking for something that isn't there. Giles Bark-Jones, a top fraud lawyer, has been looking into my case to see if there are any grounds for harassment, maybe some compensation, but all I want is the same as Greta Garbo. *We want to be alone.* Giles reckons that after what I've been through the police shouldn't come within twenty miles of me... About the same distance that lunatic Field Marshall Douglas Haig and his gallant generals were away from the killing fields of Flanders.

Giles's bite is definitely worse than his Bark. He's fought and won shed-loads of high profile cases, so my advice to the constabulary would be; *Don't mess with the best.* Your standing with the public is at an all-time low, so tackle some real crime, like moped gangs or people traffickers. Cressida if you're listening, don't do a *Duncan Norvelle* and 'Chase me, chase me', sit down and look what's occurring. It would be nice to find a police station that isn't un-manned or shut down completely, or spot any real coppers on the beat, or not wait three days for some uninterested forensic adolescent to come round to one's burgled house. On the credit side, speed detector vans are multiplying like randy rabbits on rhubarb. Not great Miss Dick, bashing the beleaguered motorist. What's that? 'Mind how you go'. I do mostly, at less than thirty mph, slowing down for sleeping policeman, crawling on the motorways and stopping at every bleeding red light. 'Evening all'.

Before we run round the final bend of the last lap. I want to mention two men who have been supporting me directly and indirectly for nearly two decades. Firstly Mike Ashley: a man who has had really unfair and prejudiced reporting from the media. I've only met Mike twice, and he is a shy person by nature. He isn't a man craving publicity like Richard Branson. When I needed a shirt supplier in the new millennium for Auction World TV, he was the man I contacted. I became the largest private buyer of Brazil, England, Manchester United, Liverpool and Chelsea shirts in the country.

Not only did I receive top quality football shirts promptly dispatched, but always highly-discounted, also accompanied with great credit terms. Mike Ashley went out of his way to provide me with a world class service. Sports Direct are simply a great 'more for your money' retail company. There can't be many people who haven't picked up a tidy bargain in their superstores.

Now, see if you can spot the difference. As the football shirts were flying out to all corners of Britain, straight after being sold on the television, we took a call from JD Sports, warning us not to sell any Wigan Athletic shirts on the programme. When I first heard about it, I thought it was a hoax, but it was followed up by the company's official literature. Fuck me, I've never seen anybody in a Wigan shirt, even on the occasions I've been there. We never lost any sleep over the shirt embargo, but if someone wants to win friends and influence people that wasn't the way to go about it.

Dave Whelan comes across as a courteous and altrusitic person, but behind that kindly exterior hides a ruthless business man, exactly the same as Mike Ashley - one doesn't get their money and success by being charitable - both very different, but both winners. They've locked horns and clashed in the past, but that's just the nature of the beast. Which one can get the biggest market share of the sportswear industry. They probably don't like each other, but neither would lose a minute's sleep over it. My own position, I love Mike Ashley, I just wish Dave had given me a chance with his Latic shirts. I bet I could have sold two or three and got on his Christmas card list.

Secondly, more recently I'd like to publicly thank Keith Bishop for his sage advice and his concern for my plight regarding the authorities. It is wonderful to have him in my corner, as he is one of the top public relations men in the country. He is often cited in the press as Mike Ashley's right hand man, but all I know is that he is a very trusted confidant, one of a few in the inner circle. *The Bishop*, as he is known, is a crisis management specialist. He's the man you send for when your company, or the situation you find yourself in, is heading for choppy waters. He has Newcastle United and Rangers (Glasgow, not Stafford) among his many clients. Keith has very strong relationships with a lot of the newspapermen who really matter, as well as massive experience, acumen, and a perceptive insight into what is happening in this country.

So with all that going on in his burgeoning career, just to have him take an active role in my predicament is such a buzz that I am extremely confident everything will turn out for the best.

Thank you again, Keith.

I'd come full circle, now with half a century of experience behind me. Many times I'd been told I had the sense of humour of a 14-year-old boy. Folk walking into a lamp post, someone's new haircut, a mate's dodgy clothes, pedestrians splashed by a car or people tripping over the dog - all these things would make me laugh. It got me thinking, just hypothetically, how cool would it be to stop ageing at that time, not dying as a teen like some sort of weird junior Logan's Run, but to live seventy years in a 14-year-old body. No more worrying about politics, work-related problems, the stress of bad sexual relationships, angst, misery and disharmony. I bet a lot of people would sign up. Well, maybe a few anyhow.

Peter Pan never grew up. Dreamers have been searching for the elixir of eternal life for centuries. It doesn't exist. The ageing process is portrayed as a bad thing, but it's perfectly natural. Money people have tried cryogenics: that's freezing the body or head after dying, with the hope that they would be revived sometime in the future when a cure had been found for their particular cause of death. Even if it did work, what fun would it be coming round in two thousand years time? You wouldn't know a soul apart from Cliff Richard. *Nah, give it the old heave-ho*. There is a rumour about Walt Disney being frozen. Not true: he was in fact cremated in World Cup glory year 1966. He was his own man. A man of the 20th century. Don't meddle with the ticking clock - time will always win... and on its own terms.

When I first entered Copford College at 14, I thought it was the norm to go to public or private boarding schools, but Britain has changed beyond belief in my 50 years, and the education system has lacked direction. Only one child in a hundred now goes to boarding school. And still I have no idea which is the best system. All I do know is that every kid deserves the very best education possible. They are Britain's future, and it's not right for English students to have to pay to go to university. Welsh and Scottish parliaments provide free courses, better by far.

I turned out well-rounded from boarding school. I was initially clueless, but latent ability was eventually teased out of me, and I thank all my old teachers for that. I can class myself somewhere between George MacDonald Fraser's ex-Rugby School anti-hero Harry Flashman, the womanising, cheating, gambling cad who always fell on his feet, and Mick Travis - the English public schoolboy with the rebellious streak. He was let loose in 1968, appearing in Lindsay Anderson's ground-breaking film *If,* brilliantly played by Malcolm McDowell. It changed everyone's perception of public schools. Give it a viewing on DVD, you won't be bored or disappointed.

Half of the Conservative Cabinet went to public or private schools, which dwarfs the 7% for the rest of us plebs. David Cameron, Boris Johnson, Zac Goldsmith and Jacob Rees-Mogg were all Etonians. George Osborne went to St. Paul's, but seemed to have a fair knowledge of the working class psyche, before he quit politics. All these MPs came from wealthy families, but not anyone can commit to university. It's a massive financial burden, but if you are determined, nothing is impossible. You can achieve what you want in this country. I'll tell you this, sit on the sofa every day watching Jeremy Kyle and his dysfunctional guests and nothing good will ever happen in your life. The front door bell won't ring... unless it's a visit from the bailiffs.

You must get out into the world and mastermind your own destiny. Here's a quote from a man who reached the top and stayed there a long time - *Life isn't just about the chances we are given, but more about the chances we create for ourselves.*

Thank you, Herr Sepp Blatter. He went about it the wrong way, but that advice is rock solid to any honest hard-working individual.

I was also mentored to be individualistic - 'There's only one Faisal Madani'. That's got a certain ring. I do hope people think I'm a one-off, as there's a lot to be said about mavericks. Names mean a lot. George Best and Michael Winner had an early head start, up-and-coming rocker Reg Smith went right to the top when his manager changed his name to Marty Wilde. Actress and singer Judy Garland was born Frances Gumm and Tony Curtis was plain old Bernard Schwartz. On the other foot, my pal's mother had a favourite actor; debonair leading man Robert Taylor. His parents had a sense of humour, and he came into the world as *Spangler Arlington Brugh*. A real no-no for Hollywood. So, if you are christened Orsen Carte, get it changed forthwith to *Steed Brougham*.

If you missed that pun, you're two trots behind.

All the greats do it in their own way. They don't conform for anyone. In fact they are so unique, that they are the ones that rewrite the history books. William Webb-Ellis, Shane Warne, Dick Fosbury, Thelonious Monk, Kate Bush, Jimi Hendrix, James Hargreaves, Frank Lloyd Wright, Jack Kerouac, Salvador Dali, Jackson Pollock, Alan Sugar and James Dyson - all total originals. Just a few amongst the many who are confident enough in their own abilities to say to the world; *this is how it's going to be done from now on.* It can be achieved with drive, determination and talent.

When, as a young man, I got back to Dubai after my American adventure, I effortlessly slipped straight back into import and export. My father, his father, and our great grandfather before him, had all been smugglers. 90% of all the world's trade is delivered via the waves, and I'm proud to have canny smugglers' blood coursing through my veins.

It was a natural progression once I was back in Britain to pay homage to the greatest smuggling and piracy country in the history of the world. This fine island, a sea-faring nation, ruled the waves for 300 years by both fair means and foul. Our English Navy was not averse to raiding the Spanish galleons for their gold and treasure, which sailed out, heavily laden, from their South American settlements. Francis Drake, the Elizabethan hero, was regarded by many astute contemporaries as a pirate first and seafarer second. Britain did indeed rule the waves. In the golden age of piracy between 1650 and 1720, all the home countries had famous pirate leaders, all extremely well-known. They were in fact, the top celebrities of their day.

The pride of Scotland was Captain William Kidd. There are conflicting reports on whether he was a real rotter, or a good man who was unjustly executed for piracy. A Welsh legend was Bartholomew Roberts, the most successful pirate of them all. He captured 470 ships and would go down in history as *Black Bart*. Up for England was Edward Teach, the Bristol boy who became *Blackbeard*. He was romanticised for centuries. Contrary to popular belief, he never harmed or killed any of his captives, so he gets my vote as *Top Sea Dog,* because his ship had the best epithet - the superbly named, Queen Anne's Revenge. The Emerald Isle had a woman as tough as any man - Anne Bonny. She was a pirate who could fight hand-to-hand in all types of combat, and she was respected by all the pirates who sailed with her.

The daddy of them all though was, of course, Captain Horatio Pugwash, master of *The Black Pig*. What kid didn't get excited when that sea shanty theme tune cranked in at tea time? Pugwash was ace. With regular quotes, 'Set sail the Black Pig me hearties', 'Stuttering starfish' and 'Blistering barnacles'. His long suffering foe was Cut-throat Jake. He could never put one over the good captain. Urban myth later insinuated that some of the crew members were named *Seaman Staines, Master Bates and Roger the Cabin Boy.* That even Pugwash was an Aussie term for oral sex. All foul and false aspersions that fell on stony ground. There was a crewman called Willy who was never called out, and Pugwash occasionally would refer to a 'Master Mate'. The Guardian newspaper was actually sued successfully in 1991 for insisting this bullshit was factual. How stupid did they feel when they had to pay out? I used to sleep soundly knowing that Captain Pugwash and his crew on the Black Pig were out there sailing the ocean wave protecting me and Mother England.

Smuggling thrived in the 18th and 19th centuries, little ports and landing points were springing up the length and breadth of England. The Isles of Scilly were wholly dependent on smuggling. The government taxed all types of imports to the hilt to raise money for the exchequer. One would think they had learnt their lesson, after losing America to the colonists, but they were greedy bastards. My father and I had many secret landing areas in Iran. The English smugglers had to stay one step ahead of the despised excise gangs. Free trade was a universal concept, which didn't always apply to hard-working Brits.

The legend of the *Moonrakers* originated in Wiltshire, a county heavily involved in smuggling. Whilst not on the coast, Wiltshire was very important strategically for storing contraband before it went off to London and the Midlands. One evening the excise men came upon two locals using large rakes to try and capture the reflection of the full moon in the village pond. On questioning the rakers, they were informed that the two were trying to land the big round cheese out of the pond. The excise men withdrew, laughing at the futility of two stupid yokels. But minutes later, ten barrels of French Cognac were retrieved from the pond from where it had been secreted. Total bollocks of course, but what a great tale! The folklore has thrived for centuries up to the present day. I can't abide criminals who smuggle drugs - they reap what they sow - but for the heavy-handed customs to penalise working class folk for bringing back a couple of sleeves of Superkings, or an extra bottle of Captain Morgan Rum (another top British pirate by the way) - is a disgrace.

The authorities use the excuse that organised crime is always involved. Maybe if they reduced the ruinous duty on tobacco there wouldn't be a problem. So the next time you see a timid, little 85 year-old granny with five extra pouches of Amber Leaf bought in from Tenerife to East Midlands Airport being roughly interrogated by two burly customs men, do step in and inform the bully boot-boys that the woman in question is Ma Dodkins, leader of the *Ashby de la Zouch Blue Rinse Posse.* You've got to shame them into doing real *Homeland Security.* It's not like they haven't let a million illegals slip by is it?

Media-wise, at school, I'd been living a sheltered life, but I put it right between the ages of 20 and 30. I picked up a lot of English vernacular and various traits from three popular, classic soaps on television; Coronation Street from the North, Crossroads from the Midlands, and Eastenders from London.

The elder statesman, Coronation Street, was originally going to be called Florizel Street, until the Granada tea lady said it sounded like a disinfectant. The television critic from the Daily Mirror predicted it wouldn't last a month. It's still going strong after 55 years. I guess he miscalculated slightly. I picked up gems of phrases like; *by gum, by heck* and *chuck.* You wouldn't find those in the Roget's Thesaurus.

Who could ever forget Ena Sharples's milk stout, Hilda Ogden's ducks or Elsie Tanner's umpteenth new bloke? These were strong, opinionated women from *up North.* One simply didn't mess with them! We had nothing like it down South. I was learning something new and profound in every episode.

I wasn't sure about Crossroads though, which was set in a fictional motel in King's Oak on the outskirts of Birmingham. The sets and scenery all moved, and some of the acting was crap, actors forgot their lines, especially Amy Turtle - the kitchen assistant who regularly went blank. Not that I could understand half of what she was saying anyway. It was just like Stafford Prison. I used to watch it just for the cock-ups, it was hilarious. I'd been dubbed Benny at Copford College. I don't know why, I didn't wear a woolly hat. My favourite period was when the motel took on a new chef - wee Shughie McPhee, played by the cracking little actor Angus Lennie. Sadly he has now gone to the great haggis plot in the sky. The previous year, he had been playing the part of Archibald Ives - 'The Mole' - in the classic POW war film *The Great Escape*. It's on every Christmas, you can't miss it. In a good year it might just follow *Von Ryan's Express*.

If you haven't seen it, Sinatra wasn't on board again at the end.

Here's the irony though - he was teamed up with Steve McQueen in the film. They worked effortlessly well with each other. Twelve months later his next acting partner was Ann George who played Amy Turtle. I bet he learnt a lot from her. He went from a Hollywood all-time superstar to a woman who couldn't remember her lines. When he attempted to climb the barbed wire fence at Stalag Luft and was machine-gunned down, it wasn't because the Nazis had discovered his tunnel, it was because he'd just learnt that the Crossroads gig was in the bag. A man can only take so much.

I couldn't comprehend how Crossroads had regular audiences of over 15 million viewers. Noele Gordon and Ronald Allen could act a bit, but what was the attraction? It even pervaded onto the football terraces in the hooligan era. If your team played away at a Midlands ground, and something kicked off, the home fans would chant, 'You're going home like Sandy Richardson'. (He was the wheelchair-bound son of the motel owner). I imagined they were just being thoughtful though, as I could never avail myself of a seat, going home on those bloody crowded inter city trains.

Finally, in 1985, Eastenders landed in our living rooms. A lot of good actors have been cast as characters in that soap; Dirty Den Watts, the follicly-challenged Mitchell Brothers and Alfie Moon. Danny Dyer, the most cockneyesque actor in the world, is the modern Queen Vic landlord. If he played a South African born in Sweden, he'd play him as a cockney. When you need a Londoner send for Danny. He recently tweeted, 'Just watched *Ratatouille* with the littlun - fuck me, I was rooting for that rat'. Only Danny can phrase like that, it's a gift. But the best method actor was *Roly the Standard Poodle*. Every time the pub landlord departed, Roly was cruelly left behind. He must have had four owners. But his performances never suffered. He was on double rations of Pedigree Chum and extra Bonio Biscuits.

What a trouper the lad was!

I learnt a bit more from the other two soaps than Eastenders. I did live in the South I suppose, but I do think there was an awful lot of stereotyping going on, apart from the *no swearing* mystery. In real life, you'd hear more than a few choice words in a London pub or market, but in Walford there wasn't even a *bugger off* under anyone's breath. An hour later Gordon Ramsay would spew out a dozen f-words. It didn't make any sense. All kids don't go to bed at nine, I've never understood the rationale. Mr Ramsay, by the way, reckons he played two games for Glasgow Rangers first team. There's no record of that anywhere, but he's a great chef and good TV food personality, so two out of three ain't bad.

Lying bleeder.

*　*　*　*

The last decade has been great for Britain. Sport in particular - the Olympic Games and Rugby Union World Cup have proved that nobody puts on a tournament better than the Brits. On a sour note, the police haven't given the public any confidence with some of their arrogant behaviour. An ex-Chief Commissioner has stated, 'A good police force is one that catches more criminals than it employs'.

That's truly outrageous, insinuating that a policeman at the top would turn a blind eye to any internal wrong doing, as long as arrests were at an acceptable level. The belated Hillsborough Inquiry revealed the long-running attempted hush up of the real facts. Top down from Chief Superintendent David Duckenfield to 13 other officers now starting to sweat. Cover-ups always come out sometime in the future. Add the *Plebgate* saga - when the police lied again - to the scandals involving the Oxford and Rotherham forces amongst many, who ignored and turned away young problematic girls who were being sexually abused for years.

When the police have their backs to the wall, all you get is psychobabble. A straight answer is usually all that's required. One of my all-time heroes didn't flannel about - Slick Willie Sutton was a legendary American bank robber, a gentleman, he never had bullets in his gun. If there were women or children in the bank, he wouldn't go through with it. A reporter once asked him why he robbed banks. He replied, 'Because that's where the money is'.

Brilliant answer... boys in blue please take note. I know I broke the law, but the man in the street has to expect better than this. There's more to come out yet. I hope they've stopped hacking phones.

The four nations have all had various degrees of glory in the sporting arena; Scotland have probably underperformed, being the only Home Nation football team not to qualify for the recent Euros in France. Why aren't they producing players of the calibre of Jim Baxter and Kenny Dalglish any more? I like the veteran Charlie Adam, he's a throwback, lovely left foot with a trace of malice, nothing wrong with him, but Scotland could do with ten more.

Scotland versus England will always create a ripple of excitement. In 1990 the Scottish rugby team was playing England at Murrayfield. Princess Anne, the official patron of the home side, was being introduced to the players as they lined up before the national anthems. She was accompanied by her 13-year-old son, Peter Phillips, who followed her down the line of players. England's second row were two policemen: 6 ft 8 inch Wade Dooley, who could certainly dish it out, and the more circumspect Paul Ackford. After all the handshakes, Ackford mentioned that Master Phillips was crying, Wade Dooley said, 'Yeah, I noticed the little bastard had a Scotland jersey on under his jacket, so I crushed his fingers'.

Wrong in so many ways, but it still makes me laugh all these years later.

Wales now have a good young football team after decades in the wilderness. Gareth Bale, Aaron Ramsay and Ashley Williams are all top players who have effortlessly stepped up to be international class. The Welsh are frequently stereotyped, but that won't happen on my watch. There is a scientific report just published, that they have just discovered two new uses for sheep - meat and wool. Sorry folks, I couldn't help myself. The reason goes back to the late 60s and 70s.

A plethora of fantastic Welsh Rugby Union players all magically appeared at roughly the same time in the valleys, a strange phenomenon which very rarely happens. The Class of '92 at Manchester United was the football equivalent. There's just no rhyme or reason why it happens. Gareth Edwards, Phil Bennett, JPR Williams, Gerald Davies and Barry John were part of what was simply a great Welsh ensemble. I used to get the right hump though, as England couldn't beat them. They were light years behind. It's levelled out in recent years, but that Welsh team were the *ram's bollocks*.

The most patriotic people in the United Kingdom must be pinching themselves. Northern Ireland punched well over their weight when they qualified for the Euro 2016 finals in France. If there is a football heaven, Danny Blanchflower, Derek Dougan and George Best will all be looking down proudly. For a country of only two million people, it has produced world class sportsmen such as A P McCoy, Joey Dunlop, Alex Higgins and Rory McIlroy, all top men in their respective professions.

A lot of people don't realise that while Northern Ireland and The Republic of Ireland have different football teams, the rugby union side is an *All Ireland* team. It gives hope for their future. The political situation is so much more stable than it was in the past, and there is a distinct possibility it can keep on moving forward.

Terry Mancini was born in Camden Town, he was a proper cockney, not in the Danny Dyer class, but a *pie and mash and jellied eel man,* a right home town geezer. He played centre-half for Arsenal and Queens Park Rangers to an extremely capable degree, and not too many forwards got the better of him. A chance conversation with team mate and QPR forward Don Givens established that Terry could represent the Republic of Ireland through ancestry - his now-deceased father, who was an Irishman.

This was a time when ancestral heritage was very vague in establishing nationality, there were even rumours abounding that if you owned an Irish Setter, that would get you a game for the Emerald Isle. The Irish team had that many English born players in it that they were known as *England's second eleven.*

Terry's big day arrived in 1973. Poland were the opponents. The teams lined up, the band ramped up the first national anthem, Terry turned to Don Givens and said, 'I don't think much of the Polish national anthem'.

Givens replied, 'Shut up you daft cunt, it's ours!'.

What a card - but it's what makes the world go round. It's not like the English cricket team ever plays any South Africans is it? What's good for the goose...

The Rugby Union World Cup was a magical event, and I fancied England to go all the way. But, like the man in the new orthopaedic shoe, I now stand corrected. The Japanese victory over the giants of South Africa in the 2015 Rugby World Cup was a fantastic once in a lifetime upset, but the best team blew all the others away - one of the great All Black squads - and they were the rightful winners.

England have boxing champions, cycling champions and triathlon champions amongst many more, and things look good on the sporting front. The national football team is rapidly improving - a healthy influx of young players are coming through for the first time in years. The man who came from nowhere, Jamie Vardy, is scaring defences to death with his pace and persistence. Albert Steptoe's love child is a shining example to any lower league player with a trace of talent, speed and determination.

Nothing could compare, though, to the London Olympic Games. It's surely going to be nigh on impossible for any country to top this event. Golden memories that will last forever in the minds of the spectators and competitors. We amassed so many medals it could be forgiven that the other countries could accuse us of cheating, but something magical happens when four nations merge to become Great Britain. Twenty-nine gold medals - not bad at all. That Super Saturday, three athletics gold medals in less than an hour. A thousand years will elapse before that happens again. I wasn't happy about finishing third in the medals table behind America and China, but how lucky were they? Just because they have multi-billion dollar economies.

Talking about the economy, maybe we are finally on the mend. There are projections that we could overtake Japan and Germany in the next two decades, even though Brexit might throw a spanner in the works. I might not be about, but it's surely great, positive news for all. I'll probably be forgotten before I'm gone, but that's life boy. Bart, the casino floorwalker at Lake Tahoe in Nevada, told me - and I've never forgotten it - 'What's coming can't be stopped, it ain't waiting on you'.

That advice applies to us all. We can ride the tiger or we can sign on the dole for thirty years, even get invited to the staff party. You know why the poor kids learn a tough lesson each Christmas?

Because Santa Claus loves the rich kids a lot more.

I've come a long way. I've arrived here today, through consciousness, fate and circumstance. A lot has changed: the mining, car manufacturing and ship building all gone, but in its place, lighter industry, technology and enterprise. This is still a country where dreams can come true.

You know, I'm still waiting for that football score:

East Fife: 5 - Forfar: (so far) 4...

But hey, you can't have everything.

* * * *

That pragmatic pacifist, Gandhi, once said, 'If you see two fish fighting underwater, blame the British'. Should we take heed, or listen to Trigger who hit the nail on the head, 'Gandhi - he made one great film and then you never saw him again'.

One of them was talking sense... and he didn't wear a loin cloth.

So, to all you Romans, Anglo Saxons, Vikings, Normans, Plantagenets,

Tudors, Stuarts and Hanoverians - thanks for coming here. We are now what we are: still respected, feared a little, but never ever underestimated.

Faisal Madani has only one thing to say to all you wonderful people...

Rock on Britannia.

* * * *

Postscript # Finale

This journey has taken us to old Camulodunum (The Roman name for Colchester).

I came, I saw, I convalesced.

The odd leaf has fallen off my autumnal tree, but my conkers remain intact. In fact, my mojo is in the ascendancy.

Every day is a boon, but when a great man like David Bowie doesn't fulfil his three score and ten, that's when it really hits hard. God is greedy for genius, I'm glad a mere mortal like myself hasn't had the call.

If you are in the area, pop in for a cup of green tea and some camel and couscous crisps, stroke the cats, and we can have a good old chinwag about football, fracking, or where the fuck has Rick Waller gone? How can a man of that size disappear off the radar. Sharon and I have miles of smiles, we are now so contented. MI5 have finally come good, sorting out some internal problems in our favour. The family have set up a dowry. Even the boys in blue haven't kicked down the front door in ages (touch wood) - the girl on the Wickes hardwood checkout counter is totally bemused. It's still wonderful to head North to watch my beloved United at Old Trafford, but I stay alert in case I bump into Ronnie Pickering in his red Picasso.

I don't mess with men of that calibre. He's dynamite.

We are homing in on the big finish folks! Good job too, as my wrist is killing me. Let's finish with off something profound, 'Now is the winter of our discotheque'.

That was written by Shakespeare's poorer brother, Frank. Experts say that quote was 350 years too early, so remember everything in life is about good timing. My time with you is almost over. Would I now risk everything again on the toss of a coin? You bet I would. But best of three please, the heart couldn't take anything sudden.

Seize the day, let lady luck work for you, fortune always favours the brave man, the meek won't inherit the earth, even if they ask nicely, please go for it and reach for your dreams.

The Madanis love you all.

Bye bye... Would the last one out turn off all the lights please.

End

Michael O'Rourke

LIFE IN THE FAZ LANE

* * * *

Also by Michael O'Rourke:

Black Eyes and Blue Blood - The Amazing Life and Times of Gangster Norman 'Scouse' Johnson.

Arguably the most unusual gangster story ever told... *Black Eyes and Blue Blood* combines violence and humour with an exotic twist of romance. It also offers a fascinating insight into the underworld on both sides of the Atlantic as Johnson mixed with some of the world's best-known gangsters, sportsmen and showbiz personalities....

Mainstream Publishing, 2008.

Printed in Poland
by Amazon Fulfillment
Poland Sp. z o.o., Wrocław